25 Diabolical Adirondack Murders

25 Diabolical Adirondack Murders

The Twisted, Fiendish Deeds of North Country Killers

Lawrence P. Gooley

Bloated Toe Publishing
Peru, New York 12972

Other books by the author:
A History of the Altona Flat Rock
Lyon Mountain: The Tragedy of a Mining Town
Out of the Darkness: In Memory of Lyon Mountain's Iron Men
The Battle of Plattsburgh Question & Answer Book
A History of the Altona Flat Rock – Silver Anniversary Edition
Brendler's Boys: The House That George Built
Oliver's War: An Adirondack Rebel Battles the Rockefeller Fortune
Terror in the Adirondacks: The True Story of Serial Killer Robert F. Garrow
History of Churubusco and the Town of Clinton, Clinton County, New York
Adirondack & North Country Gold: 50+ New & True Stories You're Sure to Love

Bloated Toe Publishing, Peru, NY 12972

© 2012 by Lawrence P. Gooley

All rights reserved. No part of this book may be reproduced without written permission from the publisher, except by a reviewer who may quote brief passages or reproduce illustrations in a review; nor may any part of this book be reproduced, stored in a retrieval system, or transmitted in any form or by any means electronic, mechanical, photocopying, recording, or other, without written permission from the publisher.

Library of Congress Control Number: 2012907639

ISBN-13: 978-0-9836925-3-9
ISBN-10: 0-9836925-3-X

Copies of this title and the titles listed above may be obtained by writing to:
Bloated Toe Enterprises
PO Box 324
Peru, NY 12972

or

Go to Bloated Toe Enterprises website:
URL: www.bloatedtoe.com
email: info@bloatedtoe.com

Covers designed by Jill C. McKee of Bloated Toe Enterprises

Printed and bound by
Versa Press, 1465 Spring Bay Road, East Peoria, IL 61611-9788

Manufactured in the United States of America

Contents

	Preface	vii
1	The Aiken Brothers: Achin' for Trouble	1
2	The Meanest of Teens, and Toxic at Twenty	11
3	The Burning Bed	27
4	Liar, Confessor, Killer: Prolific at All Three	41
5	The Man of Mystery: Coast-to-Coast Crook	59
6	A Family Man Fingers His Killer	71
7	Brutal Execution for $9.03	77
8	Callous Killer Confirmed by a Kid	89
9	A Murder Victim Goes to Court	97
10	A Delayed Murder?	107
11	Decades of Depravity	111
12	Evil Personified: Neighbor in a Trunk	133
13	The Candy Killer	161
14	Passion, Poison, Prison	171
15	Victim of a Historic US Range War	179
16	The Four Accidental Confessions	187
17	Wickedness in Warren County	191
18	Merciless Murder for Meager Money	199
19	Burying the Hatchet	211
20	Scissors to the Sinus	219
21	Pieces of Louise	225
22	Murder in the Mucklands	231
23	A Blade for His Brother	245
24	Dalliance, Deceit, Death, Double-Cross	251
25	Confession Conned from a Convict	257

Preface

Presented within are twenty-five true murder stories from across the Adirondacks and foothills—we who live here call it the North Country. No matter where you're from, you'll enjoy them all, but for reference, there are murder stories here from Clinton, Essex, Franklin, Fulton, Jefferson, Rensselaer, St. Lawrence, Saratoga, Warren, and Washington counties.

The crimes are graphically described, but as so often happens, the real tales lie in the backstories: the twisted, convoluted lives of the criminals and/or their victims, and to what lengths the common man (or woman) will go in order to carry out their intricately planned or impromptu crimes.

The ranks of murderers here include tough men, devious women, older folks, teenagers, family men, and housewives. Their victims' backgrounds are just as varied, as are their methods of killing. Some chapters are short, while others address lengthy criminal careers.

But for all the variety within these pages, there are two common threads: death by violence, and the often unexpected evil that lurks among us in seemingly average folks. Historically, both are subjects of unending fascination.

Note: Throughout the book are actual headlines and images, necessarily lacking in quality due to age and source, but helpful nonetheless in illustrating the text and framing the stories as they once played out in the media.

1

The Aiken Brothers: Achin' for Trouble

Why had they done it, and why in heck did they drive a hundred miles to remote territory to steal $150?

In 1924, a minor story out of Whitehall, New York, evolved into a fascinating, convoluted tale involving bootlegging, robbery, and murder. In the end, it caused an international dispute over crimes committed along the border between the United States and Canada.

Whitehall is located at the southern tip of Lake Champlain, while the lake's northern end lies just inside Canada, one hundred miles away. During Prohibition, the lake's surface and many roads that parallel the shoreline were commonly used by bootleggers. Selling illegal booze in the States was a lucrative business.

Residents living close to New York's border with Canada, especially in rural areas, understand the unique element it brings to life. Prior to the 1980s, except during wartime, locals routinely crossed the border at inspection stations, courtesy of nothing more than a "Where are you headed?" and the wave of a hand (truth be told, it was often just the wave of a hand).

Many more crossings were made daily without inspection stations; it was just neighbors visiting neighbors (I'm speaking from both knowledge and experience). The American-Canadian divide is an unfenced border, but when the occasional dispute arises between the two countries, that invisible line can mean the difference between life and death.

This story began, in part, with a crime that was routine for the times: a car loaded with 250 bottles of bootleg Canadian ale, and a team of local constables in hot pursuit. Whitehall police caught up with the vehicle just south of the village, where the occupants, a woman and an older teenage boy, pulled over and fled on foot. It was a risky move. Several shots were fired by police during the ensuing chase. The woman was captured, but the boy evaded arrest until the following day.

In Albany's federal courthouse, where Volstead (Prohibition) violations were adjudicated, the woman was fined the grand sum of one dollar. Her Hudson car remained confiscated by authorities, and the woman's accomplice (and driver) Francis Aiken, 18, of Whitehall was ordered to pay $1000. That fine set off a chain of unlikely events with more than one tragic result.

Two months later (May 7), about a hundred miles north of Whitehall as the crow flies, a terrible crime was reported near the US-Canada border in Clinton County. Farmer George Benton, 40, of Roxham, Quebec, just a short distance north of the US hamlet of Perry's Mills, was working on daily chores when he was accosted by two masked men, one of whom carried a shotgun. When they demanded money, Benton dropped his lantern and fled.

With his assailants in hot pursuit, Benton attempted to cross a fence, but a blast from the 12-gauge shotgun brought him down. He was robbed, roughed up, and left bleeding on the ground by his assailants, who drove off in a pickup truck. A few minutes later, Goldie Clark, Benton's neighbor across the border in Perry's Mills, came to his aid. A doctor was summoned, and after Benton's injuries (to both legs and one arm) were tied with tourniquets, they rushed him to Physician's Hospital in Plattsburgh, New York, twenty miles south of the border.

During the ride, Benton remained conscious and told both men about the attack. Halfway to Plattsburgh, in the village of Chazy, the doctor noticed a Ford truck matching the description provided by Benton. After arriving at the hospital, they notified the sheriff, and when the pickup rolled into Plattsburgh a short time later, Francis Aiken and his younger brother Charles were taken into custody.

Witnesses had seen their truck near Benton's home, and in the truck was a double-barrel shotgun, with one barrel discharged. The two boys, giving their ages as sixteen and fifteen, denied everything, claiming they had been on a hunting trip to Chazy.

Plattsburgh's sheriff took them to the hospital so Benton could confirm they were his attackers. However, the boys were of similar size and build, and both had worn masks, preventing the victim from positively identifying them. The money found in their pockets was a different story. It was Canadian currency, and obviously the money they had stolen from Benton. After intense questioning by the sheriff, the boys confessed to the crime and admitted that Francis had done the shooting. Additional money was found in their pockets, along with the handkerchiefs used to disguise their identity.

For the local constabulary, this was great news. The victim was being treated for his injuries, the criminals had admitted their guilt, and assorted evidenced confirmed the events as reported by several witnesses. Other than a few loose ends to tie up, it was an open-and-shut case.

The next day, the boys offered a revised version of their story, although the details seemed insignificant. They now gave their ages as eighteen and sixteen, and claimed the gun had gone off accidentally while they were chasing Benton. At least the shooters were in custody, and it could all be sorted out in court.

But one day later, all bets were off. George Benton had died.

Doctors determined he had succumbed to blood poisoning and loss of blood, both of which were attributed to the shooting. This presented some unique problems. The boys had already confessed, and then revised their story, but both admissions of guilt were made with the full expectation that Benton would recover.

Instead of perhaps a short jail term for robbery, the Aikens were now facing something entirely different. Their first confession carried a state-mandated murder charge, and the second likely called for manslaughter. And those were the *easy* issues.

The victim was from Canada, but the perpetrators were US citizens. Which country had jurisdiction? Where would the defendants be prosecuted? Who would prosecute them—the Canadian government, the US government, or New York State? Was extradition likely in light of the claim that one of the accused was less than mentally competent? Were they minors in both countries, or were they adults? The answer to that last question alone could well determine their fate—permanently.

When Benton succumbed, an arrest warrant was issued. The Aiken boys were ordered held without bail until the case could be reviewed by the grand jury. On their behalf, prominent attorney J. W. Davern requested dismissal, a move that was successfully opposed by Clinton County District Attorney Harold Jerry, who represented the interests of the Canadian government. In their view, a Canadian citizen had been murdered on Canadian soil, and the perpetrators should be sent north to face Canadian justice.

Davern promised to vigorously rebut any attempts at extradition, citing the possibility that the crime had actually been committed in the

US. Oddly enough, there were two arguments in support of that view. For one thing, the attack had occurred very close to the border, so it seemed possible it had happened on the US side.

A second distinction was far more important. If the attack took place in Canada, it was an assault that the victim clearly had survived. Benton's death occurred at the hospital in Plattsburgh, muddying the waters as to where the murder took place—where the victim was shot, or where he died. With two countries involved instead of two American states, it wasn't clear whose claims took precedence.

Davern also noted a supposed "trace of hereditary insanity in the [Aiken] family," and promised to use the defense of mental incapacity if the case was tried in Canada. In the meantime, Canadian authorities prepared warrants for the transfer of both boys to their custody.

A full murder investigation was soon under way. Witnesses on both sides of the border were questioned, and accounts by several of Benton's neighbors suggested there was little hope for the Aikens' acquittal should the case go to trial. Evidence was gathered and examined, including blood samples from where Benton had crawled while yelling for help. Official inspection of the site determined that the shooting had, in fact, occurred about a half mile beyond the US side of the line.

It looked more and more like the Aiken boys would soon be heading north for a date in Canadian court.

Amid all the controversial issues surrounding the Aikens' story, one important thing had not been addressed: motive. Why had they done it, and why in heck did they drive a hundred miles to remote territory to steal $150? (When captured, they had $153.62. Benton said he was robbed of about $150.)

A Glens Falls attorney provided a possible explanation for the trip north. Among his clients was the woman arrested earlier with Francis Aiken for smuggling booze. On her behalf, he had negotiated a settlement with Francis to

WHITEHALL BOYS' CASE INVOLVES PECULIAR POINT

Fight Extradition to Canada Because Victim Died in Plattsburg reimburse the woman for the lost vehicle (a Hudson, which the government had kept). According to the attorney, Francis agreed to pay $250 and said, "We'll have the money here for you at 9:00 tomorrow morning." George Benton was attacked that very same night.

The lawyer's story was just another nail in the Aiken boys' coffin.

While Quebec officials worked towards obtaining extradition papers, the British Consul's office (Canada was still ruled by the United Kingdom) pursued the same goal. In the meantime, a very sad funeral service was held. Folks from north and south of the border gathered in Roxham, Quebec, to pay last respects to their lost friend, George Benton.

News arrived in late May 1924 that the boys had been released, but they weren't actually freed. They were discharged by US Commissioner Pattisson, only to be immediately re-arrested by Canadian officials "upon the application of the British Consul at New York." Nothing was firm yet, but an extradition hearing was scheduled.

Even while awaiting court action, it seemed the Aikens couldn't stay out of the news. A Whitehall cohort, twenty-year-old Edward Gordon, confessed to police that he had joined the brothers in October 1923 when they robbed a store in Elizabethtown. The goal was to steal supplies needed to run their own bootlegging operations. Suspicion about several other area robberies was inevitable.

The Aikens' father, Charles, was surely busy operating a store and lumberyard, but people wondered—how was it that two boys, seventeen and fifteen years old at the time, were robbing stores and planning extensive criminal activity? And now, murder?

Sympathy for their current plight was out of the question, and though it hardly seemed possible, news from Plattsburgh only served to solidify public opinion against them. From their cells in the Clinton County jail, they enlisted the aid of a young handicapped boy who sold newspapers in the jail at night, paying him five dollars for hacksaw blades (which he procured for four dollars each). They hoped to saw through the bars and escape, but the plan was foiled when the boy was overheard bragging to a friend about his profits. The Aikens' cells were searched, and the blades were found where Francis had hidden them—beneath his mattress.

The scheme caused three things to happen: the escape attempt infuriated the public; further outrage followed the revelation that the hacksaw blade incident was their *fourth* escape attempt; and officials began investigating how the blades had made their way between the brothers' cells, which were quite far apart. Lots of questions, but no answers.

Soon enough, none of that mattered, thanks to US Secretary of State Charles Evans Hughes. Historically one of America's most

> **QUESTION JURISDICTION IN AIKEN CASE**
>
> Claim Made Because Benton Was Shot in Canada, But Died in United States

noted politicians, Hughes was a native of Glens Falls, just twenty miles down the road from the Aikens' home. Commissioner Pattisson had set a legal precedent in border law by ruling that the suspects could be extradited. In late October, Secretary Hughes supported the court's decision and ordered their surrender to Canadian authorities. When the boys left Plattsburgh for Canada's Bordeaux jail, a reporter wrote:

> … they presented a direct contrast. The elder brother, Francis, was quiet and silent. He held his head down and did not notice any of the guards. He walked out of the jail and never turned his head.
> His brother Charles walked gaily out of jail, said goodbye to the guards, and shook hands with the sheriff and his assistants. He was talkative.

In Canada, the Aikens' defense counsel was John J. Creelman. Luckily for the boys, this was no ordinary "appointed" attorney. Creelman had been a Lieutenant Commander in World War I and was a crusty, outspoken, no-nonsense leader (reminiscent of George Patton in World War II). A famed jurist and a fierce advocate for his clients, Creelman went right to work.

A preliminary hearing was held, for the most part proceeding routinely. Witness testimony was strong for the case against the boys. The sheriff from Plattsburgh admitted he had taken the boys' confession without warning that anything they said would be used against them, but the judge allowed him to continue testifying "under reserve." This was four decades prior to the Miranda ruling, but protection against self-incrimination was still of primary importance.

The hearing was otherwise unremarkable until Creelman dropped a bombshell, moving for dismissal on the grounds that the court lacked jurisdiction in the matter because the victim had died in the United States. At Plattsburgh, Davern had argued similarly during extradition hearings, and lost. But this was a prominent, famously patriotic Canadian barrister, claiming that his own government could not legally pursue the case.

Creelman's motion caused Canadian Justice Lamay to adjourn the hearing. His ruling would establish a legal precedent and could not be made without considerable research.

For the defense, the move was a brilliant tactic, and it almost worked. Revisions and consolidations of Canadian law over the years seemed to confirm Creelman's claim. In the interest of justice, though, Lamay felt that the charges were too serious to dismiss. He cited the old English common law that provided for continuance. The Aiken boys were going to trial.

Excited headlines blared, AIKEN BROTHERS TO BE TRIED IN FRENCH, and TRIAL OF WHITEHALL YOUTHS PROMISES TO BE MOST SENSATIONAL IN BORDER HISTORY. Likely exaggerating, a reporter wrote: "They are haggard, and but living shadows of their former selves." But the boys did have something to worry about. A noose was their fate if they were found guilty of murder.

The language barrier presented a problem. Much of Canada is English-speaking, and the defendants knew only English, but Quebec is largely French. Everyone—the judge, jury, lawyers, court reporter, and the Aiken brothers—needed to be fully engaged in the proceedings. Interpreters were needed, and the boys' prospects would have been dismal without Creelman looking out for their interests. After addressing the language issues successfully, his further attempts to quash the charges failed. The trial was set for summer 1925, with Crown Justice Wilson presiding.

AIKEN BROTHERS TO BE TRIED IN FRENCH

Trial of Whitehall Youths Promises to be Most Sensational in Border History

During testimony, the evidence appeared indisputable. Several people had encountered the boys near Benton's home; many saw the truck they used (their father's Ford); they had the money, gun, and handkerchiefs with them; and they had admitted to the shooting. Accidental or intentional was the only unresolved issue, and basically, the boys offered no defense because they didn't have one. Despite that fact, Creelman raised some doubts, not by calling into question the testimony of eyewitnesses, but by revealing that some folks were not entirely forthcoming with all that they knew.

During the year that had passed since Benton's death, it was the popular belief that a poor farmer had been murdered by strangers. In layman's terms, the general feeling was, "String em' up." During cross-examinations, Creelman tested the judge's patience but scored some points with the jury. His probing questions shed new light on the story and prompted some disturbing revelations.

After covering a bit of bootlegging information that seemingly led nowhere, Creelman elicited some surprising answers from a critical prosecution witness. Addressing events at the hospital shortly after the shooting, the crafty attorney questioned Goldie Clark, Benton's close friend from just across the border in the US.

> Creelman: Did Benton appear to know either of the boys?
> Clark: Yes.
> Creelman: Which one?
> Clark: Francis.
> Creelman: Did you see Benton and Francis shaking hands?
> Clark: I am quite certain I did.

Now that was a shocker. Two men, believed to be strangers to each other—a potential murderer and his badly wounded victim, who had been left to die in a pool of blood—shaking hands as the man lay suffering in a hospital bed? What in the world could explain that?

Clark further admitted that Benton had mentioned the Aiken name a few weeks earlier. The revelations begged another question: If Benton knew the Aikens, why couldn't he identify them as his assailants? The strong impression was that "couldn't" was actually "wouldn't." Further inference suggests Benton was protecting them for a reason.

Creelman's follow-up questions implied that bootlegging was the reason for that protection, and bootlegging was probably the reason why other witnesses weren't offering all that they knew. He couldn't force them to come forward, and since the Aikens offered no defense, Creelman suggested other possibilities. Was Clark's testimony self-serving? Were he and Benton smugglers? Did Clark shoot Benton? Were the other witnesses, including Benton's neighbors, somehow involved?

Creelman didn't necessarily believe any of those were true, but it was an ingenious tactic aimed at raising reasonable doubt among the jurors. What appeared to be a simple case now held many unanswered questions. Yes, Francis shot Benton. But, in the minds of many laymen, shooting a stranger was an unforgivable, egregious act. Shooting a partner in crime was sharply different: a terrible offense nonetheless, but not a crime against an innocent, and an act not likely to be punished by execution.

No one had confirmed that Benton, Clark, or anyone else nearby was a smuggler. But the Aikens were proven smugglers, and it seemed highly unlikely that two teenagers from Whitehall could happen across a remote farm on the Canadian border after driving well over one hundred miles on unfamiliar roads. From that point of reasoning, it wasn't hard to deduce that Francis Aiken's earlier arrest for bootlegging was somehow connected to Benton. But for all the questions that cried out for answers, there were none to be had. The woman's smuggling case had been settled, Francis wasn't talking, and Benton was dead. Any secrets were buried with him.

Within three days, the trial was finished. Defense Attorney Creelman, handicapped by having no defense to offer, had brilliantly turned nothing into something by digging relentlessly for details. A few days earlier, the Aikens were a cinch to be lynched. Creelman's efforts now suggested other possibilities—perhaps a finding of manslaughter.

The judge, however, was having none of it. In charging the jury, Wilson said no elements of manslaughter existed in the case. The verdict should be either guilty of murder, or acquittal. He termed "illogical and absurd" Creelman's intimations that others were involved in the crime. The jury was instructed to stick to the facts.

Inexplicably, the entire Aikens family remained calm throughout the trial. The boys' lives hung in the balance, but they appeared unaffected by the proceedings, even the lively closing arguments. They remained unflinching as well when the verdict was announced—guilty of manslaughter (a victory for Creelman, who won a decision that defied the judge's instructions).

During pre-sentencing, Wilson welcomed any input, and Creelman obliged. He described Francis as "mentally backward," and said Charles "was a mere child, sixteen years and one month at the time of the shooting." He also submitted documentation from Whitehall's school, indicating that Charles' mental age was lower than twelve. Considering their youth, the judge might be influenced by the additional claims of impairment.

Again, Wilson wasn't buying any of it, and he did have his reasons. It appeared that bogus documents were provided to the judge in hopes of provoking sympathy during sentencing deliberations (the penalty could range anywhere from two years to life). In his own words:

> I am not at all satisfied with the birth certificates that have been given me. One, yours, Francis, contains but your family name, and Francis is written in pencil. In the other case, the certificate was made out "William Edward," and the name Charles was written above in pencil.

The source of those documents is unknown. The boys had two sisters and a baby brother (Kenneth), but there was no one named William Edward in the family, or in the town, for that matter. Judge Wilson continued, offering a blunt assessment of the pair:

> You are a danger to society, and as such must be removed by death or imprisonment. ... You look like young men, but you must bear the responsibilities of grown-up ones. ... You will go to the penitentiary for life.

There was no option for parole. As before, neither boy moved or spoke, seemingly unfazed by what constituted a terrible fate even for hardened criminals, let alone a pair of teenagers. Soon they were off to St. Vincent de Paul Penitentiary on the shores of the St. Lawrence River, a pair of unsupervised, dangerous youngsters who never attained free adulthood.

> **AIKEN BROTHERS GET PRISON FOR LIFE**
>
> Whitehall Youths Who Killed Canadian Farmer Took Sentence Without Emotion

2

The Meanest of Teens, and Toxic at Twenty

The sheriff's office is besieged with requests to visit the boldest desperado Fulton County has ever produced.

In 1911, a young fugitive on the loose in the Northville area of Fulton County became the focus of statewide attention. Although he was already deemed a ruthless killer, few of the searchers knew that his string of crimes had begun long ago.

Charles Edward Baker had led a chaotic life, constantly in trouble at school (he attended only through the eighth grade), and a real thorn in the side of the local police. Early on, he established a pattern of committing a crime and then running. As a young teenager in 1906, he robbed an uncle's store and fled north to his sister's home in Montreal. This latest theft was a serious escalation of his bad behavior, netting him a stint in the Rochester State School, generally known as Reform School. Perhaps well intentioned in theory, reform schools were essentially prison for kids.

After his release from Rochester at the end of the year, Charles returned home briefly. In January 1907, still six months shy of his sixteenth birthday, he moved in with an aunt and uncle, Mr. and Mrs. Edward Lofts, who owned a farm at Blue Corners in the town of Charlton, about ten miles north of Schenectady. It was hoped that life on the farm might set him on the straight and narrow, but in mid-February, an incident there stunned locals and sent shocking headlines across the region.

On a February morning, Edward Lofts left for Amsterdam with a load of wood. Shortly before noon, Mrs. Lofts, 63, was writing a letter, closing it with the line, "Eddie is standing by me and smiling." A moment later, Mrs. Lofts was fighting for her life after dear Eddie pumped four bullets into her from a .32-caliber handgun.

From nearly point-blank range, two of the bullets struck Lofts in the forehead. Another penetrated her arm as she sought to fend off the attack, and a fourth struck her in the ear, causing a skull fracture.

Eddie (he was known as Eddie to some and Charlie to others) fled the scene, taking $15 and two handguns, and leaving his aunt to die. Initial news reports mentioned a robbery and shooting by a farmhand, and the fatal injuries suffered by Mrs. Lofts.

Except that Mrs. Lofts wasn't dead after all. Her defensive efforts had paid off. Murder was clearly Eddie's intent, but of the three bullets that struck her forehead, one entered the flesh above the left eye and came out the eyelid, while another grazed the skull. The third slug penetrated the ear and lodged in the skull.

Despite her age and the serious injuries, Lofts managed to get up and walk to the house down the road, where she finally collapsed near the mailbox. The neighbor, Mr. Case, found her in dire straits. After taking her inside and administering remedial first aid, Case saddled up and rode for help. Before reaching Amsterdam, about eight miles south, he caught up with Mr. Lofts, who quickly reversed direction to aid his wife while Case rode on to find a doctor.

The Montgomery County sheriff was also notified, and soon all parties converged on the Lofts farm, which, as it turned out, was just inside Saratoga County, preventing the sheriff from acting. The delay may not have mattered much. While Mrs. Lofts was taken to the hospital, it was clear that her nephew was already long gone.

The Baker family once lived about twenty miles east of Syracuse, but had recently moved to Gloversville, where Charles' father, Emmitt, worked as a carpenter, and his mother, Anna, worked at home for the glove company.

Based on one of his earlier crimes, it was assumed that Baker had fled north through Gloversville and continued towards Canada. That route became the focus of the investigation. Thanks to a remarkably resilient victim, police knew the perpetrator, and they knew he was armed and dangerous.

It was about ten hours after the shooting that Mrs. Lofts arrived at the hospital. She remained conscious, but refused to say anything about the incident other than that her nephew was a "poor,

AGED WOMAN SHOT BY NEPHEW

Four Bullets Fired at Mrs. Edward Lofts.

CRIME NEAR BLUE CORS.

Charles Edward Baker, Described by His Victim as "Poor Foolish Boy," Seeks to Murder Aunt, Who is Living Only by Reason of Youth's Bad Marksmanship, Although Four Pellets of Lead Lodged in Her Head.

foolish boy." One bullet was removed from her skull, and her condition was assessed as critical.

The search continued for Charles Baker, and if he proved to be anywhere near as tough as his elderly aunt, authorities had reason to worry. Despite four bullet wounds, walking to the neighbors, waiting hours for help, and reaching the hospital nearly a half day after the shooting, Mrs. Lofts not only survived, but rallied. About ten days after surgery, she was pronounced well on her way to recovery.

In the meantime, the search for Charles Baker had intensified, but no solid leads were found. Circulars featuring his photograph and a full description of Baker were dispersed across the region. Though obviously capable of killing, he came across as not much more than a child: 16 years old (he was actually 15 years, 7 months); 5 feet 3 inches tall; 135 pounds; grayish-blue eyes; light-brown hair; teeth white and even; and a small, round face with pink cheeks. It was hard to believe that such an innocent-sounding youth could be considered armed and dangerous.

Mrs. Lofts' recovery continued to amaze doctors and just about everyone else. It hardly seemed possible, but exactly two weeks after the assault, she was back home on the farm with her husband. Baker, meanwhile, was nowhere to be found. The search in all directions had come up empty.

Then, nearly two months after the shooting, the mystery was solved. Since shooting his aunt, Charles Baker had been a very busy boy. Fleeing the state, he had made his way south (he may have boarded a ship from Portland, Maine, to Norfolk, Virginia). At Norfolk, he assumed the name George Hunter and shipped on the schooner *Alice T. Turner*, sailing under Captain Bonsai. While they were docked at Sharptown, Baker broke into the captain's quarters on March 20 and stole a gold watch, a watch chain, and a revolver. The total value was estimated at $65 ($1500 in 2012). He then hired a liveryman and left the area.

When the captain discovered the break-in, he successfully tracked Baker's movements and arrested him, finding all the stolen material on his person. Bonsai wasn't fooling around—by April 1, an indictment was issued, and three days later, Baker was sentenced to three years in the Maryland Penitentiary.

During the investigation, George Hunter had stated that he was actually Charles Baker from New York State. Maryland authorities contacted the Saratoga County sheriff's office, and when it was learned the story was true, Baker was offered to the New York lawmen just as soon as he completed his sentence in Maryland.

True to their word, Baker was turned over to Saratoga authorities in November 1909 after serving two years and seven months. Without delay, he was arraigned on a charge of first-degree assault for the shooting of his aunt, and opted to plead guilty to a lesser charge of second-degree assault. When Baker's sanity was questioned, a commission was appointed to examine him. Within a few days he was described as "sane, but a dangerous person to be at large."

On November 24, Judge Rockwood at Ballston Spa sent him to Dannemora for a term of two years and two months. Within a short time, Charles Edward Baker, a seasoned criminal at the age of eighteen, was working as a weaver behind prison walls.

Nearly two years later, around the end of September 1911, he was released. Returning to his family in Gloversville, Baker had apparently learned nothing from reform school or serving prison time in Maryland and New York. Almost immediately, he resumed his illegal activities.

On October 10, he was arrested for robbing a noted glove manufacturer, Charles H. Dye, and was held on $1000 bail, an amount that was unfortunately supplied by his mother. He was released pending action by the grand jury.

Two weeks later, the body of thirty-year-old Norman Briggs was found along the roadside about three miles south of Northville. He had been shot in the back of the head, but the damage was such that authorities surmised the rifle butt was used to subsequently crush the top of the victim's skull.

Briggs was a livery driver (taxi service) utilizing horse-drawn vehicles (in 1911, a car was still a novelty item in the region). Early in the investigation, it was discovered that Charles Baker had hired Briggs to take him north into the Adirondacks, where he planned to hunt for several weeks. That information, along with Baker's deplorable past, immediately made him the prime suspect.

It was surmised that on the trip

Norman Briggs

north, at a point near Sweet's Corners on the road to Mayfield, Baker had murdered Briggs, stolen $80 from his pockets, and dragged the body away from the road to hide it from passersby. He then took the rig and continued on his way.

A posse was organized, consisting of sheriff's deputies, police, and a number of outraged citizens. The heavily armed group headed north in pursuit of Baker, whose whereabouts were as yet unknown. Initial suspicions were that he was headed for Canada.

In the meantime, Baker was on the move. After killing Briggs, he took the livery wagon and headed north about five miles to the Adirondack Homestead, a hotel owned by William Cole, where he spent the night. After procuring supplies in the morning, Baker asked Mrs. Cole to mail two letters he had prepared, one for his mother and the second for his brother, Hiram.

Before departing, he told the Coles that while driving his father's wagon, a hard bounce on the roadway had left him with a bloody nose. The cover story was concocted to prevent any suspicion by the Coles regarding ownership of the fine team of horses he was driving and the blood that was splattered on the wagon. (As it turned out, they hadn't noticed the blood, although the stains were plentiful.)

Baker then headed north, ostensibly to hunt deep in the forest near Hope Center, about seven miles beyond Northville. Later in the morning, the Coles had other visitors. A group of lawmen, led by Sheriff Thomas Vill, was hurriedly trailing Baker. After learning of his supposed hunting plans, they headed north in hot pursuit.

Baker, meanwhile, had meandered along, stopping just two miles down the road at Sanborn's Blacksmith Shop. Around noon, he traveled another two miles north, deciding at that point to ditch the wagon. Taking one of the horses, he grabbed his weapons, reversed direction, and headed south on horseback, occasionally leaving the main highway to avoid detection.

But the story of Briggs' murder had circulated by then, and the lone horseman seen riding south was reported to authorities. To confirm the sighting, two men waited innocently by the roadside, and as the fugitive approached, one of the men stepped into the road and asked him for a match. Baker quickly replied he didn't have one and then raced away, with the two men in pursuit. Upon reaching Northville, they telephoned ahead that Baker was heading south.

Two cars were immediately dispatched to intercept him. In the meantime, after finding Briggs' rig and one horse hidden in the woods several miles north, Sheriff Vill had followed Baker's trail south.

Coincidentally, all three would soon converge near the place where Briggs' body had been found. Traveling through the woods had slowed Baker's pace considerably, and Sheriff Vill had passed him. When Vill encountered the two automobiles of searchers, he prepared an ambush. The cars were positioned farther down the road, while Vill and two other men, including Deputy Sheriff Stoddard of Mayfield, hid behind trees, completing the trap as dusk enveloped the area.

When Baker came along, it was clear he was prepared for trouble. A rifle was at the ready, strapped against the saddle, and a pistol was in his hand. Passing the sheriff's men without noticing them, he had fallen into the trap. Suddenly, he saw the lights of the cars parked in waiting, and then heard the men in the road behind him. Without hesitation, Baker stopped, turned, and fired. Vill and his companions were nothing but lucky that they were unhurt. As they ran for cover, Baker, in what seemed like an odd move, tied his horse to a telephone pole. He then climbed a fence and ran off into a nearby field.

The two cars advanced and joined the sheriff about two hundred feet from where Baker's horse was tied. They agreed that under cover of darkness, their quarry was more dangerous than ever, and it was best not to attempt pursuit. While discussing their options, the noise of galloping hooves reached their ears. Baker had taken the horse and escaped!

The men rushed into the two cars and gave chase, but after traveling a few miles, they realized Baker had fooled them once again by hiding off the road until they had passed. To cover all possibilities, one car continued towards Northville, while Vill and company doubled back. After encountering a man who had seen Baker, they once again sped south in pursuit.

At the village of Mayfield, Vill spied Baker and opened fire from the moving vehicle. Other officers on horseback joined him, and as the car stopped on the roadside, Baker returned fire. With that, a full-fledged gun battle erupted, during which an estimated twenty-five shots were fired.

Early in the exchange, one of Baker's slugs struck Deputy Sheriff Edward Stoddard of Mayfield in the left hand, almost completely severing his second finger, which dangled by a few sinews. Another shot hit Gloversville Police Officer John Pollock, who was on horseback. Pollock's right thigh was badly injured, the femur shattered amidst heavy blood loss.

With two men down, the posse stopped firing so they could tend to the wounded. Baker took advantage of the opportunity to seek cover in the woods. Both victims were loaded into the cars and rushed to the hospital in Gloversville. Doctors had no choice but to amputate Stoddard's finger, but he was otherwise going to be okay. Pollock, though, had lost a lot of blood. His condition was listed as critical.

Baker was still on the loose, but his riderless horse was soon captured while running through the streets of Mayfield. Authorities now knew he was on foot and much less mobile. A report came in later that Archie Snyder had been fired upon near Hammond's Hotel, leaving officials confident that Baker was still somewhere between Mayfield and Gloversville. They would later learn he had set up a campsite and spent the night, holding his position while deciding what to do next.

The attempt to capture Baker had been a catastrophe. While he had escaped uninjured, two officers were now lying in the hospital. Sheriff Vill met with other authorities to assess the situation, and the decision was made to call in the National Guard. Company G, Second Regiment was quickly dispatched to the scene, where they formed a picket line across the road north of Gloversville and stood watch the entire night.

In the morning, the soldiers began a methodical search of every house and outbuilding as they slowly made their way north. Much to their surprise, when they were past the area where Baker was believed to be, they still had found nothing. Somehow, he had eluded the soldiers, plus searchers using thirty cars, and a posse of more than fifty men, including police, sheriff's deputies, and local citizens.

Sheriff Vill then called Utica for reinforcements, this time in the form of bloodhounds. For hours, searchers and dogs slogged through thick mud and dense underbrush, all to no avail.

Finally, a credible lead surfaced. A farmhouse near Riceville had been broken into. The burglar had stayed long enough to fry and eat about a half-dozen eggs. Baker was the obvious suspect, but after a thorough search of the farm, he was nowhere to be found.

A short time later, not far from the farmhouse, a lone man carrying a gun was sighted by a pair of searchers who were scouring the countryside. Calling for the man to halt, they suddenly found themselves targeted by the man's rifle. Whether or not he realized they were unarmed, the man lowered the gun and headed off into the woods.

The sighting was reported to other searchers, and soon a number of men, including Sheriff Vill, converged on the site about two miles north of Gloversville. There began a hurried pursuit of Baker, who was on the run. As they closed in on him at the Washburn farm, he was almost completely surrounded. Sheriff Vill shouted out an order for him to surrender. Baker, true to form, answered with lead. Vill replied in kind, shooting at Baker and ordering his men to open fire.

A hail of bullets was sent towards the fugitive, who fought back as he ran. Finally, he went down, but even injured, there was still some fight left in him. Supporting himself on one elbow, Baker fired three more times at the approaching posse.

Finally, exhausted and disabled, he was captured. Despite considerable blood loss, Baker was shackled where he lay, ensuring that the manhunt was over. He was taken to the Nathan Littauer Hospital in Gloversville, where his two victims from the previous night's gun battle were still undergoing treatment.

While receiving medical care for two bullet wounds to the thigh, Baker was questioned by police. He admitted killing Briggs, claiming they had been drunk while traveling together on the highway. An argument between the two men erupted into a fight, and during the battle, Briggs

MILITIA IN MAN HUNT WITH FIFTY SHERIFFS

Charles Baker, Wanted for Murder, Wounds Two Pursuers in Adirondack Chase.

TWICE SHOT, BUT WILL LIVE

Desperado Fires Upon Posse While Lying on the Ground, Wounded—Bloodhounds on His Trail.

was shot and killed.

Baker was also suspected of another crime, the recent murder of Matilda Martin, 56, of Johnstown. She had been visiting relatives in Gloversville, but after leaving to return home in the evening, Martin's body was found the next day in a stream on the outskirts of the city. She had been robbed and strangled, and her head was immersed in the water.

Police at first could not identify the victim, and an appeal had gone out to the public. During the next few days, hundreds filed by to view the corpse. Among their number was her brother, who confirmed it was Matilda. The murder occurred a week before the killing of Briggs by Baker, and less than two weeks after his release from Dannemora. For suspicion to fall on Baker was natural. After all, the only time he wasn't committing crimes against the public was when he was under lock and key.

Early on Friday morning, November 27, only a half day after the shootout, Gloversville Police Officer John Pollock died from his wounds. Baker now had two murders to his credit, and remained a suspect in the Matilda Martin case.

Authorities at first withheld the information on Pollock's death, fearing repercussions from the public. In the early 1900s, it was still not uncommon for an outraged citizenry to storm a jailhouse, remove a prisoner who was known to be guilty, and lynch him. The folks around Gloversville were already enraged over the killing of Briggs. Pollock's death was certain to up the ante.

And it sure did. When the news finally leaked out, people began to gather around the hospital. Some simply wanted to make their feelings known, but many others wished to get rid of Baker once and for all. Officers worked quickly to disperse the crowd, but as soon as they did, more groups gathered. By noon, it was feared the mob would surge into the hospital and deliver Baker to their own version of the gates of hell.

The police held on throughout the day, managing to avoid disaster, and by evening, Baker had been moved to the Fulton County Jail at Johnstown. The broken bone is his leg had been set, and the healing process, guided

Officer John Henry Pollock

by a set of weights attached to the leg, required a bed for Baker instead of the standard cot. To aid his rehab, he was assigned a trusty prisoner, Edward "Sausage" Remington, who acted as nurse and attendant.

Baker maintained his stoic, nonchalant demeanor until two days after his arrival at

> **OUTLAW KILLS A PURSUER**
>
> STORY THAT READS LIKE A JESSE JAMES TALE.
>
> Dropped With Two Bullet Holes in His Thigh, Young Desperado Raises Himself on Elbow and Fires Rifle Three Times at Officers.

the jail. Then, reporters couldn't resist writing blaring headlines describing the young, hardened criminal's tearful breakdown when visited by his parents. It made great press, but ignored the fact that this was the same young man who, four years earlier, had shot his aunt four times at point-blank range, and had been on a nonstop, escalating crime binge since he was a young boy.

Like most repentant criminals who cry, he was doing so because he had finally been caught, and this time there was a big price to pay. The focus of the news stories was on how Baker and his mother cried in each other's arms. No reporters mentioned that when Baker killed Briggs, he was out on bail for committing a robbery less than two weeks after completing a two-year term at Dannemora. Worse, they failed to note that bail (which allowed him to murder Briggs) had been provided by the mother on whose shoulder he was now crying.

While Baker was recovering, evidence was gathered for the pending court case. The wagon stained with Briggs' blood was recovered, and Baker's tent and campsite had been located (where he spent the night after the shootout that sent two men to the hospital). Supplies at the tent site indicated Baker had intended to be there for a while, but had suddenly departed, perhaps when searchers came too close for comfort. It was also discovered that Officer Pollock's gun was in his pocket, suggesting that when he was fatally wounded, he was carrying his flashlight. It had previously been believed he was firing at Baker when he was felled.

On the same day that Baker and his mother cried and commiserated in his jail cell, far more tears were being shed in Gloversville, where Officer Pollock, known to all and friend of many, was laid to rest. Thousands attended the largest funeral in the city's history, lining the streets for nearly two miles. They gathered early, and a great number of them lingered after the ceremony to vent their grief.

In the days to follow, several fundraisers were held for the families of Baker's victims. By November 3, the Pollock fund was at about $1000 ($24,000 in 2012) and the Briggs fund was at $500 (about $12,000 in 2012).

In December, word leaked out that Baker was not so comfortable in jail any longer and had taken a real dislike to confinement. Some rumors even said he had escaped, and as often happens with stories of that type, the reports were based on elements of truth.

In January, some of the facts were revealed by a jail attendant, Stephen Heart, who had spent twenty-four days in the same cell with Baker. Heart's job was to care for the prisoner until he could move about on crutches, and in such close quarters, Baker perceived an opportunity.

After spending three weeks gaining Heart's confidence, Baker reached out on a personal level, discussing the problems he had faced and the probability that he would be executed for his crimes. Since Heart was now his friend, Baker worked the sympathy angle, assuring his attendant that he knew Heart didn't want him to die.

The prisoner, scheduled to appear before the grand jury within a week, knew he had little time. Building on the confidence he felt had been established, Baker eventually asked Heart to bring him a saw and axe so he could escape. Two days later, the stress was too much for Heart. Fearing for his own safety, if not his life, he resigned his position.

After Heart revealed his story, constant observation ensured that escape was not an option. That may have actually worked out in Baker's favor. Rumors frequently surfaced that local citizens planned to forcibly remove him from jail and administer justice in their own way.

The intense outrage against Baker had hardly subsided after several months, and it played a role in the upcoming trial. The atmosphere in Gloversville suggested it wasn't possible for the defendant to receive a fair trial, so a change of venue was sought and granted. The case was scheduled for March 12 in Schenectady.

When the trial began, Baker's attorney entered an amended plea of insanity in place of the original claim of not guilty. During jury selection, Baker's family attended each court session. While the prisoner appeared detached from the proceedings, defense attorneys consulted his father, Emmett, several times during the selection process.

Among the early witnesses called was Hiram Baker, Charles' older brother by four years. The intent of his testimony was to add credence to the insanity claim. Hiram said that just prior to the shooting of Briggs, he and Charles shared an extended conversation during which his brother was acting strangely, had "a wild look in his eye," and "seemed moody for half an hour."

Other members of the family offered supporting testimony, sometimes in rather frank manner. A frequently retold story was of Charles being struck on the head by a plate when he was two years old, "… which made him stupid for a long time."

His mother claimed that as a young child, Charles "often liked the sight of blood so much that he smelled it." To reinforce his supposed mental instability, she also noted that shortly before the murder of Briggs, her son had threatened to commit suicide. Emmett Baker swore that his son was peculiar even as a young child.

One seemingly insignificant act by Baker did much to seal his fate. On the morning after he killed Briggs, Charles was leaving Cole's Adirondack Homestead. Before departing, he asked Mrs. Cole to mail two letters for him. The one sent to Hiram provided damning evidence during the trial.

> Dear Hime:
> I have done it at last. I shot and I think killed that fellow last night. I mean the driver. He was drinking all the way up from there. We got to quarreling and then to fighting. We rolled out of the carriage. I got away from him, grabbed my gun and he started to run, and I nailed him behind the left ear. Will you please keep this from mother as long as you can?
> Am writing to you as if I was dying, as I will before I let them take me. I was drunk when I did it, but oh, if I could turn the time back and start fresh yesterday morning, nothing like that would have happened.
> Will you come up and see me and bring two or three boxes of .32 specials up? Will you do this for me? It is the only thing I shall ever ask you, and you will never regret doing it.
> I live at the same place where he was. I am sending $2 to you. You can buy what you want with it, and I will give you more when you come here with which to pay for the gun and your expenses in coming up.
> I am your brother,
> Eddie

After the third day of testimony, Baker's fate was placed in the hands of the jury. The defense summation claimed there was no motive and no premeditation, and that the proper finding was for clemency because Charles was insane. The prosecution felt the evidence was overwhelmingly in favor of conviction. There was an excellent chance Baker would receive a death sentence.

After only two hours, the jury came back with the verdict. Baker stood stoically, seemingly unmoved as he learned his fate: guilty of second-degree murder. A jurist later explained that Baker's killing of Briggs lacked the motivation and premeditation necessary for a first-degree murder conviction. The insanity plea had nothing to do with their findings.

Although his mother was not in court, Charles' father, sister, and brother were present and were positively elated with the outcome. Baker would remain alive, which was more than they dared hope for—and they were pretty much alone in their thinking. Most others were hoping for a death sentence. For his part, Baker expressed relief at the outcome and admitted he expected the chair.

Justice Henry T. Kellogg immediately sentenced him to a minimum of twenty years in Dannemora Prison. Nearly a week passed before he was transferred from the Fulton County Jail, and during that time, Baker swore revenge on his captors and prosecutors, promising to extract retribution no matter how long he was in prison.

County officials noted that there was still the matter of bringing charges against him for killing Officer Pollock. For now, though, Baker's next destination was maximum security at Dannemora.

Since childhood, Charles had proven himself to be a dedicated criminal and completely untrustworthy. There was no reason to expect him to change, and he didn't. For years, his record at Dannemora was deplorable. Just six months after incarceration, he was found to have been working for some time on an escape plan. Tools had been secreted in his living quarters, and parts of his cell had been altered.

And that was only the beginning.

Among the several violations to follow were: using a screwdriver in an attack on another inmate; joining other inmates in a strike; smoking in his cell; insolence; and insubordination. His record revealed a total of 1310 punishment days for those and other infractions. He was considered an incorrigible—nothing the institution or the law could impose would change his ways. He was apparently destined to be a criminal for life, whether within prison walls or on the outside.

In January 1921, Charles was transferred to Auburn Prison, but after a month in the discipline company, he was returned to Dannemora. Five years later, he was again moved to Auburn, and from that point forward, there was an unexpected change in Baker's behavior.

Suddenly, he was no longer building up demerits on a prodigious scale. In fact, he was not getting any at all. Charles worked for a time as a weaver, a job he had held as an eighteen-year-old convict in an earlier stint at Dannemora.

During the series of riots in New York's prisons in 1929, Baker's story was one of the real surprises. Despite his abominable record of years past, he sided with the guards during the rebellion. Surprisingly, one of New York's most notorious convicts seemed to finally be turning over a new leaf. Maybe the fact that more than half of his thirty-eight years had been spent behind prison walls had something to do with it.

Whatever the case, Baker worked in the State Shop at Auburn, and then became a clerk in the main keeper's office, perhaps hoping to prove his trustworthiness. His sentence was twenty years to life, and as the twenty-year mark approached, he began seeking release from prison.

In late 1930, his application for executive clemency was turned down, after which he began applying for parole. His fourth effort, in 1932, garnered much attention. Representatives from Fulton County and the cities of Johnstown and Gloversville pressured the state parole board to keep him behind bars. Letters from many prominent officials were used to bolster their claims that Baker was a menace to society and did not deserve to see the light of day.

It was also noted that if he was released, the DA's office would likely pursue charges against Baker for the killing of Officer Pollock, a crime that had not yet been addressed. However, there was one very important problem regarding the Pollock case: most of the witnesses had since died.

Baker's plea for parole in 1932, his fourth such effort, was denied, but in 1933, when he had served the minimum required sentence of twenty years, he tried again. Once more, vigorous opposition was offered, but a nightmarish scenario soon played out. Although Fulton County's twenty-year-old case (for the death of Pollock) had weakened considerably over time, the parole board followed an unusual line of reasoning. They would free Baker, who would then face trial for Pollock's death, and would almost certainly be returned to prison for the rest of his days.

> # Fate Mocks Convict Who Served 21 Years With Murder Charge
>
> Freedom for Baker Only a Travesty as Gloversville Sheriff Waits at Gate to Arrest Him, and He Will Now Be Tried for Slaying Policeman 22 Years Ago During His Reign of Terror In Fulton County

Despite vociferous protests against his release, and the threat of a new trial, Baker's request was granted. A murderer was going free.

Well, not just yet. Released at the beginning of June, Baker was immediately re-arrested on charges of first-degree murder. Even with the passage of two decades, feelings were still strong against him. The public wanted him to pay for all of his crimes—not just the murder of Briggs.

Fully aware that for the second time in his life he faced the possibility of the chair at Sing Sing, Baker still welcomed release from confinement. He left Auburn Prison with a smile on his face, joining sheriff's deputies for the trip to his next home, one he was more than familiar with—the Fulton County jail at Johnstown.

Despite the well-intentioned decision by the parole board, county officials soon realized that a terrible mistake had been made. Proving second-degree murder charges would be extremely difficult with the additional obstacles they faced. The crime was now twenty-two years past; all the posse members who pursued Baker were now dead or moved away; Officer Stoddard and the policeman who accompanied Pollock when he was shot were now deceased; both the prosecutor and the presiding judge in the Briggs case had died; and the bullets that were said to have come from Baker's rifle were nowhere to be found. The only living witness was sixty-year-old ex-Sheriff Thomas Vill, hardly enough to ensure a conviction.

Everyone knew Baker had killed Pollock, a crime that devastated the community and nearly drove calm, rational people to the point of lynching the suspect. It now appeared that crime would go unpunished.

> **SECOND TRIAL FOR BRIGGS' MURDERER MAY FIZZLE OUT**
>
> Evidence That Charles Edward Baker Also Took Life of Gloversville Policeman Suffers From Lapse of Time and Death of Some of the Prominent Witnesses.

Supreme Court Justice Ellsworth Lawrence was saddled with a thankless task, and the Fulton County DA was forced to admit there were no prospects for a conviction under the circumstances. Baker, now forty-two-years old, was described as "gray-haired and sober-faced" as he faced Ellsworth to hear his fate. Citing insufficient evidence and the high cost of a trial (in the depths of the Great Depression), the judge, the DA, and Baker's attorney concurred that Baker should be set free. It was over.

The justice granted a request to visit his relatives for one last good-bye, to be supervised by the DA. Charles Baker was then banned from Fulton County for the remainder of his life. Still on good behavior, he bid his keepers adieu and was soon on his way to Buffalo, where the parole board had arranged for him to begin life anew as a barber.

Perhaps with a mix of irony and slight amusement, it was an interesting choice of careers: placing deadly straight razors in the hands of a murderer and lifetime criminal and releasing him to civilian life.

3

The Burning Bed

If the deceased victim exonerated her husband of all blame before she died, could a coroner's inquest find otherwise?

Fort Covington, New York, is a small, village in northernmost Franklin County. Lying along the US-Canada border, it is generally a quiet, rural place. The prevailing calm has sometimes been disturbed, but never more so than on the early morning hours of February 4, 1925.

Living in the apartment above Cappiello's Garage at Fort Covington was the Barney family, who had moved there from nearby Bombay five months earlier. On the night of February 3, the father, twenty-nine-year-old Edward Barney, slept in one room with the two oldest children, ages six and four. His wife, twenty-eight-year-old Hazel (formerly Hazel Hollenbeck), slept in another room with their sixteen-month-old daughter, Betty Jean.

At about 6:30 AM, Edward Barney was in the kitchen when he heard a loud noise, followed by his wife's screams. Rushing to her side, he found the bed ablaze. In the chaos that followed, Barney shouted for help as he attempted to stifle the flames and save his family. Neighbors and passersby came to his aid, followed later by firemen.

The two older children were safely removed, but both Hazel and little Betty Jean suffered serious burns. A physician arrived and did his best to care for them. Hazel, still conscious, spoke with the doctor while he tended to her injuries, but she was clearly slipping into shock.

Edward, meanwhile, cursed his bad fortune, explaining to firefighters that an oil lamp had exploded, setting the bedclothes ablaze. He and a neighbor had tried to douse the flames during those frantic first moments, splashing water on Mrs. Barney and smothering the burning blankets.

Despite the attempt, the news was dreadful. By noon, baby Betty Jean had succumbed to her injuries, and several hours later, Hazel was lost as well. Fort Covington was a village in mourning, stunned by the results of the tragic fire.

At first glance, it was a terrible tragedy requiring the community to unite in support of the grieving family. A wife, mother, sister, and daughter had been taken away, a tragic loss almost too great to bear.

At second glance, though, Edward Barney seemed to be bearing up unusually well. Investigators became suspicious of his behavior, and holes began to appear everywhere in his story of how the calamity had occurred.

As word spread of the possibility of foul play, the outpouring of sympathy turned into rage and disbelief. Could Edward Barney actually have played a role in the death of his wife and his tiny, innocent daughter? What kind of man could do such a thing?

Come to think of it, no one in Fort Covington knew what kind of many Edward Barney really was. The family had moved there only five months previous to the fire. Little was known about them, but that would soon change as investigators probed Edward's background.

It didn't take much detective work to determine that Barney's story of the fire was suspicious. A few key pieces of information were particularly telling. The exploded lamp that caused the fire? It was seen intact in the bedroom by a neighbor, the first person to come to Barney's aid. No other witnesses reported any broken glass or signs of an explosion.

Then there was the fire damage, which was confined to the bed—yet somehow, the combined efforts of Mr. and Mrs. Barney were not enough to save her life or the baby's. And despite his heroic attempt to quench the flames, Edward Barney was somehow completely free of injuries.

His behavior after the fire gained him no sympathy either. Barney remained calm and never seemed appropriately distraught on the heels of such a catastrophic loss. Soon growing weary of all the questions from investigators, he left town to avoid further scrutiny.

But the little sojourn didn't last long. On Friday, two days after the fire, officers from Troop B in Malone arrested Barney at his parents' house in Bombay. The warrant contained no specific charges, instead naming him as a material witness in the investigation. Aware of the suspicious circumstances surrounding the fire, District Attorney Harold W. Main had issued the warrant to ensure Barney didn't leave the area.

He was taken to Fort Covington, but feelings ran so strongly against him, it was feared locals might storm the jail and save the county the cost of a trial. The next day, for his own protection, Barney was taken to the county jail at Malone.

Saturday morning brought a packed house to St. Mary's Church in Fort Covington for the victims' funeral services, but there would be no burial ceremony. DA Main ordered that the bodies be held in a vault until many unanswered questions had been addressed.

Just a few hours after the funeral, County Coroner W. N. MacArtney began an inquest to determine if criminal charges were justified. During the next several days, damning evidence from several sources pointed the finger of blame directly at Edward Barney.

During the first session of the inquest, five witnesses told their stories. Neighbor Paul Prudhomme, son-in-law of building owner William Cappiello, was the first to respond when he heard loud noises and Barney's cries for help.

> CORONER: What was the noise you heard?
> PRUDHOMME: He (Barney) opened the door and I heard glass smashing up, and he hollered like a fool. Barney was yelling. I went in with two pails of water. Barney took one pail from me and went into the kitchen. I went into the parlor as Mrs. Barney came out of the bedroom.
> CORONER: What did you notice about Mrs. Barney? Was her clothing on fire?
> PRUDHOMME: Yes, and then I noticed all the blood coming down her face, and she was screeching, too. I threw a pail of water on her. She held on to the wall with her hand, and then took a chair in the sitting room. She said when he came into the room, "Ed why did you strike me? You struck me hard enough to kill me. What did you strike me like that for?" Then Barney screamed, and I went out to ring the fire alarm.

Despite the frantic first moments after he arrived, Prudhomme also noticed the oil lamp standing by the bedside. The glass chimney was missing, and there was still some oil in the lamp. That observation contradicted Barney's claim that the lamp had exploded.

But there was more. Although the lamp was present *during* the fire, it was missing *after* the fire—and Barney had been observed behind the Cappiello building. When Prudhomme poked around there the day after the fire, he found the lamp, intact but empty, buried in the snow bank. It was turned over to the coroner's office as evidence.

'You Struck Me Hard Enough to Kill Me'--Woman's Words May Send Barney to Chair

Hazel Barney's sister, Olive Hollenbeck, testified

that Hazel and Edward often fought over family matters. When asked why they argued so often, Olive replied, "He was a man who did not like to work. My sister was not that kind, and that was mostly their quarrels."

On the morning of the fire, Olive rushed from Bombay to Fort Covington and encountered her brother-in-law as she entered the home. The DA asked for any comment Edward might have made. Her answer: "He said, 'Isn't it a terrible thing? Neither one can live.' He told me the lamp exploded."

She then hurried to her sister's side and asked what had happened. According to Olive's testimony, "The first she knew of the fire, Ed hit her with a towel and yelled, 'Get up. Your bed is afire!' "

John Derochia, on his way to work when the fire broke out, also appeared at the inquest. When he entered the building, he found the two older children and led them to the home of a neighbor, Mabel Allen. Returning to the apartment, he found Hazel Barney "sitting at a table, crying and groaning. The infant was sobbing and growing weaker." He took Betty Jean to Mrs. Allen's home and returned to the apartment for a third time, removing the burned mattress and bedclothes to the yard, where they posed no further danger.

Under oath, Mabel Allen said that, after the fire, she spoke with Hazel Barney while Edward Barney and Mrs. Cappiello were present. Hazel reportedly said she tasted kerosene in her mouth when she was jarred awake by her husband. Allen's testimony was supported by Mrs. Cappiello. It was Mabel Allen who, late in the afternoon, had seen Edward Barney behind the building. In his hands was an oil lamp.

The building's owner, William Cappiello, also offered testimony. When he asked Mrs. Barney how the fire had happened, she said, "God knows how it was done." Hazel asked if he thought she would die, and William noted that she only talked openly until Edward Barney entered the room. According to Cappiello:

> I asked her more questions, but Barney was in back of me, and she never spoke. Barney then told me to go down to my store and get a bottle of olive oil to cool her down.

The only other role Cappiello played was to remove the bed to the back yard and cover it with snow.

Comments by the physicians who treated Mrs. Barney suggested Edward's culpability. Hazel told them she smelled oil in the room and tasted it in her mouth. Both doctors described injuries that included terrible burns and at least two notable bruises, one above her eye and one on top of her head. The wounds appeared to have been inflicted recently, probably the morning of the fire. It was surmised that neither was a killing blow, but the effects might have rendered her unconscious, accounting for the extent of her burns.

All things considered, the weight of the evidence heavily favored an indictment for murder, but there was one exception, and it bore huge implications. Shortly before her death, Hazel Barney told the coroner there had been no problems between her and Edward.

If the deceased victim exonerated her husband of all blame before she died, could a coroner's inquest find otherwise?

The short answer is, "Yes."

In the mind of the coroner, Mrs. Barney may have been intimidated by her husband into covering for him, and at the time, she didn't know she was going to die. There was also the comment attributed to Hazel by more than one witness, a statement that played well in the headlines: "You struck me hard enough to kill me."

Six days after the fatal fire, Ed Barney sat unflinchingly in Fort Covington court as he was formally charged with first-degree murder. He remained stoic as well on the eighteen-mile return trip to Malone. Upon arriving at the jail, Edward was informed that no visitors would be allowed except for legal officers.

From the results of the inquest and some investigative reporting, much more of Barney's past had been uncovered. The son of William and Christie Barney, he was born in the town of Bombay and worked on the family farm until the age of twenty.

In 1917, at the age of twenty-one, he married Hazel Hollenbeck in Bombay. They soon embarked on what is best described as a nomadic lifestyle, moving at least ten times in the next seven years. Beginning in Bombay, they moved to Watertown; to his brother-in-law's home; to Bombay with his parents; to a separate location in Bombay; to Syracuse (in 1920); back to Watertown; back to Bombay with his father-in-law; to Massena; to Bombay; and finally, to Fort Covington.

The frequent moves took a toll on both their marriage and the growing Barney family. Their time at Massena was particularly fraught with problems. While working for Alcoa, Edward was arrested for stealing tools from his employer, earning him thirty days in the county jail. Shortly after, without consulting Hazel, he enlisted in the army. Upon learning that he had left his wife and children, Edward's sister became upset with him and notified the military of the situation.

Within twenty days he returned home, claiming rejection by the military because of flat feet, but the real reason was because he had deserted his family. Edward confessed that he had enlisted after losing his job. He feared telling Hazel about the employment loss because his inability to support the family had long been an issue between them.

One other item surfaced from Barney's past, revealed by his family as a possible explanation for criminal behavior if he had, in fact, played a role in his wife's death. Edward was said to have been ill with influenza in 1918, a disease that killed millions around the world. Some described his sickness as pneumonia, but regardless of what it was, the results were important. According to the family, the flu had left him badly disabled.

After recovering and returning to work, Edward had again become extremely ill within a few days. His mind was deeply affected, prompting such a violent reaction in the hospital that a straightjacket was required. Even that wouldn't hold him, and when Edward broke free, he was tied to the bed. The family claimed that since the illness in 1918, he was never the same physically or mentally.

While held in the county jail at Malone, Edward was placed in solitary confinement (he was the lone prisoner on the top floor). In his first attempt at contacting the family since being arrested a week earlier, Barney wrote to his mother. He asked about his two young daughters (who were living with his parents), and professed the loneliness he felt in jail.

But soon enough, Barney found himself with plenty of company. Besides frequent meetings with his attorney, doctors arrived to perform court-ordered assessments of Edward's sanity and overall mental state.

When all testing was completed, the doctors declared Barney sane, and on Monday, March 9, the grand jury returned an indictment, charging him with first-degree murder. Police believed the case against the defendant was strong. The investigation suggested that the deaths of his wife and daughter were well planned, except for one critical slip-up that Barney could not adequately explain: the exploded lamp that he blamed for the fire was later found intact in a snowbank.

Attorney E. W. Scripter, appointed earlier by Judge John C. Crapser, had acted as Barney's counsel. For the trial (set for March 30), Scripter was joined by Andrew B. Cooney, retained by Barney for his reputation as one of the North Country's top criminal lawyers. Perhaps his efforts could spare Edward a trip to the chair.

Jury selection lasted only two days, after which Barney sat silently during opening statements. The prosecution described his shortcomings as a father and husband, habitually roaming from job to job, and frequently seeking help from various family members. Beyond being a poor provider, he had engaged in criminal activity and served time in jail.

Finally sinking to the depths of murder, Edward had struck his wife with a stick, knocking her unconscious, and then set the bed on fire, killing both her and their youngest child. He then told conflicting stories of what had happened, punctuated by outright lies. There was the unexploded lamp, the comments his wife made about being struck, and the questionable effort he made to save Hazel and the baby. Edward Barney sat calmly through it all, despite the dark picture it painted of his future.

Among the witnesses called to support those claims was Frank Hollenbeck, Hazel's father, who recounted a recent instance where his daughter asked for help after Edward slapped her during an argument. Hazel's friend, Mary Cadore, told of another fight during which Edward had thrown a hand mirror at his wife.

Those who appeared earlier at the inquest repeated their testimony during the trial, building a solid case against Barney. But it was three doctors who provided the most compelling details, suggesting the fire was far from accidental. The two autopsy doctors, Dalphin and Blackett, described four wounds on Hazel's head, injuries that they said might have rendered her unconscious, and may have contributed directly to her death.

Dr. William MacArtney, the coroner, knew the Barneys, and he was at the crime scene, tending to Hazel and Betty Jean. When he arrived, Hazel was sitting in a chair, her upper torso badly burned. She had no clothing above the waist, and her hair and other clothes had been burned. While examining her, he noted three head wounds. Besides injuries near the eye and ear, there was an open, bleeding wound on top of her head. MacArtney said all the damage was recent, having been inflicted around the time of the fire. He ascribed her death to serious burns and the attendant shock. He also treated Betty Jean, whose death was assigned the same causes.

Aside from the medical facts, Dr. MacArtney also identified the now infamous lamp that was said to have exploded, claiming it was intact when he saw it at the scene of the fire. Adding to the story was the building owner's son, Andrew Cappiello, who told of seeing Edward Barney burying something behind the garage. That something turned out to be the lamp.

Late in the trial's third day, the prosecution rested. Defense attorney Cooney moved for dismissal of the indictment, citing the prosecution's failure to show any intent on the defendant's part to commit a crime.

> **BARNEY ON TRIAL FOR DEATH OF HIS WIFE AND CHILD**
>
> Fort Covington Man Faces Jury Today In Franklin County for Killing

Judge Crapser denied the motion, and the defense began its journey, hoping to prove that there had been no quarrel between husband and wife, that the fire had been accidental, and that Edward had made every effort to rescue his wife and child.

On day four of the trial, the courtroom was crammed to capacity in anticipation that Edward Carney might take the stand on his own behalf. Early in the morning, other defense witnesses were called, but the effectiveness of their testimony was minimal.

The most powerful piece of evidence on Barney's behalf was then offered—the statement Hazel Barney had made to Coroner MacArtney hours before she died, relieving Edward of any responsibility for her death. DA Main rose in objection, citing grounds that the document was "irrelevant, hearsay, and no proper foundation has been laid for it as a dying declaration." The court agreed, and Hazel's statement was excluded, dealing a potentially fatal blow to the defense.

At that point, all seemed lost. In the majority of cases, defense attorneys refrain from putting their clients on the witness stand. Cooney, a man of great experience, knew it was his last, best, and perhaps only, hope. Edward Barney would take the stand before a packed house of anxious spectators. The media was fairly salivating with anticipatory glee.

Contrary to reports he and Hazel had quarreled the night before the fire, Carney testified that he was with the family all evening and played checkers with his wife. In the morning, he rose shortly after 6:00 and took care of a few duties, including lighting the oil stove in the kitchen.

> I then heard a sizzling noise and heard my wife scream and the baby cry. (Here the witness paused for a moment, apparently overcome with emotion). I rushed to the bedroom, saw my wife trying to get out of bed, and I tried to put out the fire with a towel. She fell and tried to get up. She ran toward the kitchen. I threw a curtain around her and put out the fire.

> My wife said: "For god's sake, save the baby." I got the child out and gave it to John Derochia. My wife was screaming and rushing about the bedroom at first. She first fell in the bedroom, and later near the kitchen door. I yelled "Fire!" at first.
>
> Paul Prudhomme was the first to come in, about eight minutes after the fire had started. Prudhomme had two pails of water. I grabbed one pail and put water on Mrs. Barney. Prudhomme went away to ring the fire bell.
>
> He came back in half an hour. Mrs. Barney was then in the sitting room. I did not hear my wife say to Prudhomme, "Ed, why did you hit me so hard, you hit me hard enough to kill me." I was in her presence and she did not make the statement sworn to by Prudhomme.
>
> I filled the lamp … at about midnight; the oil was low in the lamp. I lit it in the kitchen and brought it back into the bedroom and put it on the trunk.

On day five of the trial, Edward returned to tell more of his story. But in the coming hours, he would face questions from an unfriendly prosecutor during cross-examination. Any inconsistencies in his retelling of the story could negatively affect the outcome. It would be a difficult day for Edward Barney on the witness stand.

> This lamp was the only one in use in the house. The lamp was lighted every night and kept in the bedroom. There was no stand in the bedroom that night. My wife had weaned the baby and the baby would cry for milk.
>
> When I opened the bedroom door, the bed was in flames and my wife's clothing in flames. She was getting out of bed. I threw water on the floor and bed. The lamp was blazing on the floor on the east side of the bedroom. I did not see the lamp chimney. The burner was not on the lamp. It was a foot from the lamp. I think the lamp was blazing.
>
> After the fire was out, I picked up the lamp and put the burner on top of it. I think I screwed the burner on tight when I filled the lamp. I filled the lamp nearly full.
>
> My wife's clothing in bed was a knit suit of cotton underwear and an outing nightgown. I put my shoes and stockings on after she was moved into the sitting room. I did not have my stockings on when Prudhomme came in.

> I told Edith Barber when I took the lamp that the lamp had done trouble enough. I threw it out into the snow. I took the lamp out about 7:00 PM.
>
> Before that, I took out the clothing my wife had worn, took them out in the yard and burned them up. I took out other articles of partly burned clothing. I took out the stick of wood which had been in the kitchen. It was used for two purposes—to keep the door partly open, and was placed behind the door to keep the door from hitting the oil stove.
>
> When the doctor was dressing her wounds, I saw blood on my wife. I went into the bedroom after the fire and picked the lamp up. I saw a mark on the door and a blood spot on the casing of the doors. The blood spots were on the floor, from the foot of the bed leading to the kitchen table. I don't recall if there was blood on the kitchen table. Dr. MacArtney called my attention to the blood spots. I saw MacArtney examine the trunk and open it, and examine the lamp. There was clothing on the trunk. I heard conversation between Dr. MacArtney and my wife about the fire ...

Edward was subtly revising his story in hopes of explaining some of the facts that were of particular interest to the prosecution. At the beginning of his testimony a day earlier, he described first using a towel to suppress the flames on his wife's clothing. Now he claimed to have initially thrown water on the bed and floor. He also described opening the door to find the bed ablaze, but earlier said the stove was lit and the bedroom doors open to allow the heat in. To help explain the fresh bruises on his wife's body, he described how she ran about the house, falling down and bumping into things.

In the version of his story told on the second day, Edward seemed to have spent an inordinate amount of time in the bedroom while his wife was elsewhere in the house, badly in need of care. His concern seemed focused on the evil lamp and the stick of wood. (Shortly after the inquest, a stick of wood with apparent bloodstains on it was recovered near where the lamp had been found. It, too, was passed on to the sheriff as possible evidence.)

A St. Lawrence University chemistry professor, appearing as an expert witness, offered the opinion that an accidentally toppled lamp may have caused the fire, and Hazel's flammable clothing may have ignited. But it wasn't enough. Just as Hazel and Betty Jean had burned, Edward Barney was grilled by Main, the prosecuting attorney. One reporter described it as "a long, grueling examination under the direct fire of machine-gun questions." During the intense session, new information was elicited.

Barney admitted that on the day of the fire, he had taken the rubbish out, seemingly an odd thing to do when his child and wife were critically injured. He also discarded the lamp, the lamp's chimney, and the stick of wood (referred to as a "club"), but offered no explanation as to why the lamp and club had been submerged in the deep snow rather than deposited on the pile of rubbish.

It was further determined that nearly six minutes had passed before the neighbor, Prudhomme, heard Edward's cries for help and arrived with the pails of water. This was very significant. No more than a half-pail of water (if any at all) had been used by Barney while waiting, despite the fact that a full barrel of water was kept in the kitchen.

He was also pressed on certain choices made during the crisis. Why would he rescue the two older children from a room untouched by the fire, even while his sixteen-month-old daughter lay in the burning bed? Why would he go through the kitchen and down a hall to tear down the curtain he used to help put out the fire when there were curtains hanging in the burning bedroom? Why did he have no injuries to his hands or feet, even though, with bare hands and admittedly no shoes and socks on, he had battled the flames?

Main was relentless and very effective, but when the prosecution was ready to rest its case, he made a truly unorthodox legal move. Citing his duty as district attorney to pursue justice and determine the truth, Main told Judge Crapser he wished to withdraw his earlier objection to admitting Mrs. Barney's statement. He would allow Barney's most important defense information to be used.

What followed was a highly unusual court event—a victim speaking from beyond the grave. Hazel Barney's statement, read into the court record, is here paraphrased:

> I don't know how the fire started. The room was all afire when I awoke. When I rose from the bed, I fell against the apartment door. My husband tried to put out the fire, and I told him to save the baby. We had no trouble of any kind, and my husband helped me all he could during the fire.

Hazel's words may have been heartfelt, but taking into consideration the testimony already heard in court, her statement certainly had a suspicious ring. It was made by a woman who likely feared her husband, and also believed she was going to survive, which meant further consequences if she directed blame towards Edward. And it clearly sounded like a coached statement, addressing several specific issues facing a husband who had already said he believed Hazel would die from her burns.

Reversing his earlier objection may have been a risky move by Main, but it was now a done deal. All that remained were the closing statements, which featured two eloquent speakers at their very best.

For a man who acted nonchalant in the face of such serious charges, Edward became acutely emotional several times during Cooney's plea on his behalf. The re-reading of his wife's final statement elicited tears from Barney, as did Cooney's closing lines:

> I can see the poor old mother in Bombay, waiting for the verdict, quivering with suspense to know whether her son will be consigned to a felon's grave, or returned to comfort her in the few remaining years of her life. I can see two little girls, happy if their papa is returned to them at your hands. Are you going to make them orphans when they are now motherless? Deprive them of a father on such flimsy evidence as is produced here?

A different range of emotions surfaced as he listened to the DA's counterstatement. When Main offered a dramatic display, taking the sturdy club and swinging it violently to indicate how Hazel had suffered her injuries, Barney smirked and was said to have "laughed derisively."

Main stressed the points about the lamp, the fire itself, and Edward's past, closing with this:

> Barney entered her room for some reason that I do not know. Only he and his wife can tell, and her lips are closed forever. I do know he had previously deserted her. I do know he stated he'd be glad when her mouth was closed forever. Would not he do the other to this frail little woman, hit her over the head with this club, and then pour oil and set fire to complete the dastardly job he started? I want you, gentlemen, to return a verdict of first-degree murder. Mr. Cooney has spoken of the old mother

and two children anxiously awaiting the verdict. I tell you, gentlemen, when crime is committed, the innocent always suffer more than the guilty. Thousands in this country are also anxiously awaiting your verdict in this case.

When the jury departed, the courtroom remained packed. Every nook and cranny was filled with humanity, and the same was true outside in the street, where anxious residents sought bits of information from those lucky enough to be inside. Deliberations lasted just under three hours, and during that time, no one, inside or out, surrendered their positions.

They soon learned that the jury had not bought into any of the defendant's feeble explanations. Just two months after the fatal fire, Edward Barney was found guilty of second-degree murder. He reacted only slightly to the verdict, and stood silently as Judge Crapser pronounced what is known as an indeterminate sentence—a minimum twenty years in Dannemora, and a maximum of life. Factoring in the possibility of time off for good behavior, he was expected to serve about seventeen years before becoming eligible for parole.

Jury members later revealed a shared unanimity from the start regarding Barney's guilt. The only decision to parse was whether the charge would be first-degree or second-degree murder. For Edward Barney, it was literally the difference between life and death. All findings of first-degree murder mandated execution.

After the jury's declaration of guilt, defense attorney Cooney made the standard motion to set the verdict aside, a request that was denied by Crapser. Finally, it was over.

Barney was returned to jail for the weekend, allowing relatives, including his two surviving children, to visit and say their last good-byes.

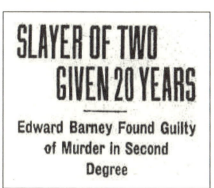

On Monday, April 6, 1925, a taxi arrived in Malone for the trip to Dannemora. Prior to departure, Barney's behavior was anything but normal for a man facing perhaps two decades in a maximum security prison. Reporters noted he was alternately singing and chatting, seeming much more like a man in celebration.

The deputies who accompanied him on the long ride said Edward laughed and joked about his situation. It was almost as if he were trying to support an insanity defense, although at one sober point, he did say, "I'm an innocent man, but I'll serve my sentence."

Barney's time at Dannemora was largely routine, but not uneventful. Sheriffs and deputies often made trips to deliver convicted criminals to state prisons. In doing so, they routinely inquired about the behavior and status of others they had delivered in the past. Less than two years after he was incarcerated, reports came back that Barney had been in trouble and had paid the price. Some said he was a snitch, and others said he frequently brawled with other prisoners. Whether or not prison officials allowed such behavior was irrelevant. The prison barber had administered inmate justice, slashing Barney from below his right eye down to his mouth, and across to his left jawbone.

Not long after that incident, Barney was transferred to Auburn Prison, and there were no further reports of trouble. In October 1928, he was escorted to Bombay to visit his mother, who was near death. She passed away two days later. In 1935, he was allowed the same courtesy for his ailing father, who died on the day of his visit.

In 1937, popular Franklin County judge (and former lawyer) Andrew Cooney died. Noted among his accomplishments as an attorney was saving Edward Barney from an almost certain date with the electric chair.

Barney was released in 1939 on the earliest possible parole date, but there were extenuating circumstances: he had been seriously ill with tuberculosis for two years. Despite winning freedom, Edward was forced to return to Dannemora's prison hospital when he again became gravely ill. His demise came on May 6, 1941.

He and Hazel died sixteen years apart, one from disease and one from burns. By some odd coincidence, both passings were officially attributed to shock (hers was circulatory and his was peptic).

4

Liar, Confessor, Killer: Prolific at All Three

> He is a bad man. Hypocrisy and deceit seem to have been born in him.

In the northern Adirondacks, on the shores of the Raquette River, lies the village of South Colton, about fifteen miles southeast of Potsdam. The river once flowed unhindered through the area, providing spectacular scenic views at nearby Rainbow Falls in what was referred to as Gain Twist country, one of the most dangerous river rapids in the north. Much of the Raquette has since been drowned or subdued by a series of power dams built in the 1950s.

In 1878, about two miles northeast of South Colton, where the waters of Dead Creek joined the Raquette River, lived a reclusive man by the name of Michael Daulter (his preferred moniker was the ever-common "Mick").

Daulter kept to himself, and little is known of his past. He was of Irish stock, evidenced by a thick brogue, and had lived in New York City and Potsdam before coming to the South Colton area around 1874. For nearly two months, he lived in Armstrong's Hotel, where he mostly kept to himself, preferring to wander the countryside alone.

Daulter eventually purchased a piece of land near Dead Creek, and it was there that he made his home, albeit an unusual one by common standards. Within about fifteen feet of the road, Mick had begun digging a well, but after considerable effort, decided that the hole he had opened would serve better as a home.

With no one to please but himself, he went to work widening the excavation to suitable dimensions for daily living. This "dugout" home consisted of three rooms, each lined with logs, and with holes cut through to access each section. A windowless, 8 x 10 room with no flooring served as the kitchen and main living quarters. The middle room served as sleeping quarters, lined with boughs and straw for comfort and warmth. The third room was the largest and most comfortable of all, more than adequate for its sole tenant—Daulter's cow.

The entire structure was about 10 x 25 feet, and was described by one visitor as "the most cheerless, filthy, and unlivable place imaginable."

But for Mick Daulter, it was home. Over time, he cleared and fenced about six acres, planted a garden, wandered the nearby forest and fields, and generally lived in solitude. Locals knew him as an odd, eccentric character, both for his unusual homestead and his general behavior. He was friendly to area children and welcoming to visitors, but avoided the sit-down chats that country folk engaged in—to Mick's way of thinking, passing acquaintances were preferable to close friends. To earn cash for some of life's necessities, he hired out to local farmers. Most people perceived him as peculiar, but harmless.

On the morning of Tuesday, April 30, 1878, nearby resident Sydney Morgan passed Daulter's home and saw Mick outside, seated on a stool, cutting potatoes. A few hours later, Morgan's two sons, George, 13, and Frank, 11, traveled the same section of road. Frank noticed someone inside the cabin and mentioned it to George, who glanced at the cabin, only to see the door closing quickly.

When the boys arrived home, young Frank told his mother that "Uncle Mick" had company, referring to the man he had seen in the doorway when they passed by his home.

The following day, the two boys were again on the road. While returning home, they noticed that Daulter's door was open slightly, and that his cow, wandering the yard, had not been milked, a chore he normally asked neighbors to cover when he was away. The boys informed their father, who was concerned enough to search Daulter's property. He found no sign of Mick, but there was blood on both an axe and pail in front of his home.

On Thursday, Morgan returned with several men to look around, but Daulter's absence remained a mystery. They agreed to join forces for a systematic search of the area near his home on Friday, and in the meantime would begin an informal investigation. Evidence at the scene suggested foul play was involved, and all discussions aimed at finding the perpetrator settled on one strong possibility: Peter Bresnahan.

On Friday, several men accompanied Constable William Horton to Peter Bresnahan's home about five miles southeast of the village. As they approached, Peter went inside, but the group followed, uninvited, and began questioning him. Bresnahan claimed that a lame back left him unable to join the community search for Daulter, whom he had never met.

Constable Horton informed Bresnahan that he was under suspicion and should accompany them to town. Peter said he couldn't walk because of his injured back, but Horton said they would outfit a litter and carry him. Bresnahan finally agreed to go with them.

The citizens of South Colton, meanwhile, were not sitting idle. Mention of the bearded stranger seen a few days earlier at Mick's place led to fears that a terrible crime might have been committed. More than a hundred people showed up by 8:00 AM to help with the search for Daulter.

Many more joined the effort in the ensuing hours, combing the roadside for any type of evidence. Finally, in the early afternoon, an old and empty moneybag was found about a hundred yards into the woods. Scattered in a nearby pool of water were several papers, including two IOU notes payable to Daulter, plus some receipts. It was evident that Mick had been robbed, and searchers were convinced that they were now hunting for Daulter's corpse.

Among the search teams was neighbor Sydney Morgan (his sons had first reported Mick's absence), and a friend, Benjamin Adams, whose dog had suddenly became animated. Following the canine's lead, the two men noticed blood on the leaves. A few hundred feet from the road, they found poor Mick lying on his side, dead. He was surrounded by dried blood, and in his clenched hands were leaves and mud, suggesting he had fought for his life after having been struck down and dragged into the woods.

His clothing and pockets were open, indicating the body had been searched. Nearby lay his hat with three holes in it, matching three holes in Daulter's head. A buckshot pellet (about one-third inch in diameter) was embedded in his scalp; a second lay against his skull; and a third had penetrated the skin, ricocheted off the skull, and exited the body. Daulter also had what appeared to be an axe wound to the top of the head (his hat bore a corresponding slice). Above his left eye was a severe injury, caused by a large, bloody rock that was found hidden beneath a nearby log. The body was loaded into a wagon and taken to town.

Meanwhile, as the constable's men (with Bresnahan in tow) made their way back to the village, they learned that Daulter had been found dead, the victim of axe blows and gunshot wounds. Upon hearing the news, Bresnahan showed no emotion.

Their arrival at South Colton coincided with the arrival of Daulter's corpse. With hundreds of people lining the street, Bresnahan was shown the body, a gruesome sight that caused him to wince and look away. To some, his reaction suggested guilt, but the condition of Daulter's battered form was no easy sight to gaze upon, even for those of stout constitution. The constable mentioned that the red stains on Peter's clothing appeared to be blood, but Bresnahan said they were from strawberry juice.

Justice of the Peace Morell Beckwith issued an order detaining the suspect until an inquest could be held and further investigation could be completed.

Although it wouldn't be politically correct today (and perhaps not legal), newspapers of earlier times often professed critical opinions of a deeply personal nature. The following assessment of Bresnahan was among those published while he was held on suspicion of murder:

> Bresnahan came to South Colton last October. He has a wife and child, a daughter ten or twelve years old. He is a very poor man and evidently has seen times when he had not the necessities of life. ... he is not what might be called an industrious man, on the contrary rather shiftless, and fond of laying around in stores, etc., at South Colton. So much so that to some, his presence had become irksome. He was moneyless, poverty stricken, ragged, his personal appearance was uninviting, and his manners and conduct were such as to gain no friends.

While in the custody of Constable Horton, the prisoner was monitored around the clock. He was allowed to speak to a reporter, who noted Bresnahan's tattered clothing, unkempt appearance (including plenty of face stubble), and that he looked nearly fifty years old, but claimed to be only thirty-five to forty (Peter wasn't certain of his actual birth year).

In describing his life, Bresnahan was forthcoming. Of Irish descent, he was the oldest of ten children born in Packingham, Quebec, Canada, about thirty miles from Ottawa. He married in 1855, and his twelve-year-old daughter and wife both still lived with him. Peter left Canada in 1870, living and working in Redwood (Jefferson County), Hammond, and Macomb (for six years) before moving to South Colton in October 1877.

Bresnahan admitted to being functionally illiterate, which was not uncommon in those days: he could write his name and read at a low level, and had always been poor. In response to questions about his recently altered facial hair (from a full beard to merely stubble), Peter told an unusual story. Two days earlier, while keeping a close watch on a fire in front of his house, much of his beard was burned away when a gust of wind blew embers into it. To make his facial hair appear uniform, he then trimmed it closely. (The suspicion was that he changed his appearance because the Morgan youth had seen a bearded man in Daulter's cabin.)

Answering direct questions about his supposed involvement in the murder, he said he never knew Mick, but while playing cards recently with a group of men, some of them mentioned knocking Daulter off to get his money for gambling. Bresnahan finished by saying there was no reason to suspect him more than anyone else.

He provided details of his movements on the day of the killing, entirely excusing him from culpability. Unfortunately for Peter, the elaborate explanation of his whereabouts that day had been shot full of holes as the investigation grew. On the official record of the coroner's inquest, several people he claimed to have interacted with said the stories had been fabricated.

The specifics of Daulter's injuries were reviewed at the hearing, including the axe wound that had caused a fracture of the skull. A smaller fracture occurred on his forehead above the left eye, where he was struck heavily with a rock. The brain remained intact, but heavy bleeding and clotting between the brain and its protective membranes compressed the organ itself, causing severe damage to the delicate tissues, resulting in death (in modern terms, a subdural hematoma).

The testimony of several witnesses, combined with an analysis of Daulter's injuries, led authorities to a theoretical scenario. Bresnahan had taken aim on an unsuspecting Daulter, who was bent over on the stool, washing potatoes. The bullet struck Mick on top of the head, wounding him, but somehow he began running down the road toward the nearest neighbor. Bresnahan, realizing the shot had lacked the desired effect, pursued Daulter, grabbing the axe as he passed the yard. About a quarter-mile down the road, he caught Mick, struck him over the head, and then dragged his limp form into the woods. After searching his clothes for money and finding almost nothing, Bresnahan went to Daulter's hovel and did the same, dropping the bloodied axe in the yard and washing the blood off his hands in the pail of water where Mick had been preparing potatoes.

Returning to the crime scene, he found Daulter was still alive, and so used the rock to deliver the final blow to the forehead. There was a bit of uncertainty regarding that portion of the theory. Daulter was found almost exactly three days after he was killed. Since the body had hardly decomposed, some authorities suggested that Mick might have survived his initial injuries for a day or more, and that Bresnahan returned at some point to check on his handiwork. Finding Daulter alive, he used the rock to dispatch him.

Comfortable in that assessment of the crime, the coroner declared Bresnahan responsible for Daulter's death. Peter immediately denied it and demanded an examination of the facts. Beginning on Monday night, the case was reviewed, including the entire testimony from the coroner's inquest. Represented by Potsdam's William Faulkner of Swift & Faulkner, Bresnahan pleaded not guilty, but when the hearing ended at 8:00 AM, he was ordered held for grand jury action.

On June 3, 1878, barely a month after Daulter's murder, the trial of Peter Bresnahan on charges of first-degree murder began. Theodore Swift joined Faulkner at the defense table, opposed by District Attorney John Brinckerhoff and Assistant DA Horace Ellsworth. The prosecution's opening statement revealed that their case was largely woven around circumstantial evidence, some of it quite compelling, supported by the testimony of nearly two dozen citizens. Many had seen Bresnahan walking the road that day with a gun over his shoulder, and several others swore they had no interaction with Peter on the day of the murder, contradicting his earlier claims.

Even the young Morgan boys were called to the stand. George recounted the events of that fateful morning, but when his brother had alerted him, he caught barely a glimpse of the man in Mick's cabin. Eleven-year-old Frank described what he saw, but was unable to swear that the man at Daulter's door that day was Bresnahan. By cutting his hair and shaving his beard, Peter had drastically altered his appearance, making it impossible for the boy to verify his identity.

One witness testified to loaning a gun to Bresnahan. A local man, William Love, reported giving powder to him, purportedly for shooting hen-hawks. It was noted that Peter purchased only enough powder for one or two shots, hardly enough for shooting hawks.

Constable Horton testified that Bresnahan claimed the small amount of powder was for medicinal purposes. Calling his bluff, Horton had asked if he needed more. When Peter said yes, a quantity was procured, and Bresnahan, to prove his point, ate a teaspoon of it as the constable watched.

Another witness heard a gunshot from the direction of Daulter's home on the day of the murder. Several more testified to facts that differed from the alibi offered by Bresnahan when he explained his whereabouts on the days surrounding the crime.

It was a damning case, to say the least, supported by the testimony of several doctors proficient in the use of microscopes, the cutting-edge technology of the day. Close examination of Peter's clothing, the axe, and the rock revealed multiple bloodstains. Each doctor swore they found blood, but because the blood of some animals was nearly indistinguishable from that of humans, none could state with complete certainty its identity, an issue that the defense lawyers seized upon as a component of reasonable doubt.

Cross-examining the prosecution witnesses did little for the cause of Bresnahan, and when the defense case was presented, there was meager evidence on his behalf. Swift and Faulkner could only hope to raise a reasonable doubt by focusing on the blood issue. Other points of information were trivial at best. Two men who were present when Bresnahan viewed Daulter's corpse said that Peter hadn't shuddered at the sight, which was contrary to the constable's claims. True or not, it hardly seemed enough to challenge the overwhelming evidence against Peter.

Closing arguments were presented on the trial's fourth day. At 7:00 PM, after only ninety minutes of deliberation, the jury returned a unanimous verdict of guilty. When Judge Judson Landon asked if he had anything to say, Bresnahan replied, "All I have got to say is that there is nobody knows but me and another, and that is God, that I am innocent."

The judge cited extensive evidence that left no doubt as to the defendant's guilt, at which point Bresnahan interrupted with, "Well, there is only one other and myself that knows I am innocent, and that is the Lord." Landon ignored him, calling the murder "an appalling and a cruel act," and ending with the ultimate finality:

> The sentence of the court is that you be taken hence to the county jail of this county, and there be confined until the 26th day of July, 1878, and on that day between the hours of 10 o'clock in the forenoon and 2 o'clock in the afternoon, you will be taken thence and be hanged by the neck until you shall be dead, and may God have mercy on your soul.

The courtroom, which had been filled to capacity for days, was soon empty, and Peter Bresnahan was returned to his jail cell.

About a week after his conviction, a letter of remarkable content arrived in St. Lawrence County from Pembroke, Quebec.

> At the sittings of the court of quarterly sessions, held here on the 13th day of December, 1866, Peter Bresnahan was arraigned on the charge of robbery with intent to do grievous bodily harm to the person of one James Batfield. Bresnahan at first pleaded Not Guilty, but as the case proceeded and the evidence against him accumulated, he withdrew the plea and pleaded guilty, and threw himself on the mercy of the court. He was found guilty and sentenced to four years confinement in the penitentiary.
>
> The attack on Batfield was wholly unprovoked and most wantonly wicked. The victim was an old man, and at the time of the attack was in a totally helpless condition through the excessive use of liquor. Bresnahan struck him with an axe handle, then robbed him of his watch and chain, and while insensible and to all appearance dead, dragged the body to the river and hid it in a pile of slabs.

But Batfield was not so dead as Bresnahan thought, for the victim afterwards appeared at the trial and gave important evidence against Bresnahan. A second letter provided additional details of the crime:

> Peter ... always bore the name of being a lazy, worthless man, and was always noted for his untruthfulness. About seventeen years ago, he broke into a store in Eganville, and in order to escape punishment had to clear out of the place.
>
> He next turned up in Arnprior in the same county, where he worked in the saw mills. He ... attempted to murder a man named James Bothfield [Batfield], a fellow workman, the deed being committed for the sake of a watch and a few dollars of money the unfortunate man, Bothfield, had on his person.
>
> Bresnahan, after having, as he thought, killed the man, and robbed him, threw his body into a ditch. Bothfield was not killed, and being discovered in time, afterwards recovered. Bresnahan was arrested, tried, and sent to the penitentiary at Kingston.
>
> Since writing the above, I was shown your issue containing Bresnahan's likeness, which removes all doubt

as to his identity. It is Peter Bresnahan, and no mistake. He shows his old character for telling falsehoods. ... Peter Bresnahan is a bad man. Hypocrisy and deceit seem to have been born in him.

One reason for the second letter was to clear up the confusion surrounding the recent murder of a man named Moore in Torbolton, Quebec. It was later deduced that the killer was Peter Bresnahan's uncle.

The two letters, which appeared in St. Lawrence County newspapers, set off an incredible series of events. Trial, conviction, and sentencing were already completed, but to a twisted mind like Bresnahan's, it wasn't over yet. For more than a month after the trial ended, he maintained his innocence.

Then, in July, just two weeks before his execution date, Bresnahan experienced an epiphany of sorts. He admitted to his spiritual advisor, Reverend John Pearce, that he had in fact shot Daulter, but it was an accident that occurred when he mistook the victim for a deer.

Pearce sensed the story wasn't true, but recognized the significance of Bresnahan's first admission. Following up, he pushed and prodded until Peter confirmed it had not been an accident after all. Two days later, he came forth with a full confession. The details of his story closely matched the testimony of the trial witnesses, with one important exception. He

Peter Bresnahan

admitted to walking on the road and stopping at Daulter's, where the two men engaged in conversation. When the subject turned to religion and the possibility of a resurgence of the Fenian movement, they began to argue. In the heat of the confrontation, he had shot Daulter.

According to Peter's account, Daulter regained consciousness about ten minutes later, rose to his feet, and began stumbling down the road in the direction of the Morgan farm. About an hour later, while walking in the same direction, he found Mick lying in the roadway, whereupon he used a rock to deliver the killing blow. He insisted no axe was involved in any part of the attack. He hid the body after searching it thoroughly for money. It was noticed that Peter's version of events once again aligned nicely with testimony given in court. The ending of his statement reaffirmed his guilt:

> I sacredly declare that murder was not in my heart when I left home Tuesday morning, April 30. I did not go for the purpose of killing Michael Daulter. I had no intention of taking his life, and I should not have shot and killed him if he had not talked so about the Protestants.
>
> My motive in killing him was not money, but because he angered me. I had heard many people say Daulter was a miser, a hermit, and a peculiar man, but I did not kill him for his money. I don't know what possessed me to take his money after I killed him.
>
> But I committed the deed and it has proved the fatal act of my life. I am sorry to the bottom of my heart, and I hope, trust, and pray that God will forgive me for having done the deed. No other person had anything to do with the killing of Daulter but myself.
>
> My lawyers, Swift and Faulkner, are entitled to the highest praise. They did for me everything possible before and during my trial. I have nothing to pay them. They worked without hope of reward. I thank them from the bottom of my heart for all they have done for me.
>
> Peter Bresnahan

Along with the confession, he offered a complete retelling of his life story. The details were not unusual for the 1830s and 1840s: he was the oldest child, with four brothers and five sisters; he went to school for only a few years, and attended Sunday school until about age fifteen; he was sickly, but learned to be a carpenter and worked in sawmills; and his marriage had resulted in three children.

Peter claimed that in his early twenties, he broke into a store and stole fifty cents ($15 in 2012), but paid it back the next day, offering the excuse that he had stolen it while drunk for the only time in his entire life.

He also described an incident from 1866:

> I gave James Botsfield a severe pounding, such as I had given persons before and since. There were two or three around. Two days after, I was arrested for it. During the fight, Botsfield lost his watch on the ground, which I picked up the next morning, and my wife had it on when I was arrested.

For that crime, he was sentenced to four years in prison at Kingston. He ended the interview session with one simple line:

> I solemnly declare that I never committed any crimes in my life except those I have given you.

The statement was sworn to before a notary public, with St. Lawrence County Sheriff Orson Wheeler once again observing. With the specter of death nearly at hand, it appeared Bresnahan had finally bared his soul in preparation for the afterlife. But appearances aren't everything.

Instead of relief and acceptance by the public, the confession (his second, coming after the deer-hunting story) prompted a firestorm of criticism. Although it was carefully crafted, the public saw it for what it was: an admission of guilt that confirmed the prosecution's theories, but redefined the most critical part of the crime—Daulter's final moments.

Bresnahan hoped that his "honest" description of the murderous assault would be deemed credible. At first glance, it seemed to ensure his guilt and support his sentence of death. Closer examination revealed the payoff. The crime, as now admitted to by Peter, fit the description of manslaughter rather than first-degree murder, making the commutation of his sentence to life in prison a distinct possibility.

Among the unrestrained critics of his story was the *St. Lawrence County Republican*:

> … He is an unmitigated liar. He premeditated the murder days and weeks before he committed it. … a

> confession ... made in hopes of saving a worthless neck. If he has any regard for the hereafter, be will amend this confession.

Another letter arrived from Renfrew County in Quebec, claiming that Peter's story was filled with lies and deceptions:

> I have read the confession of Peter Bresnahan, and was much shocked to see that the unfortunate man should, in the awful position in which he now stands, give such a very untruthful history of his early life. ... I made some enquiries respecting him ...
>
> Peter was not brought up, as he says, to attend Sunday school regularly, for the simple reason that there was no Sunday School in his time in the settlement. When Peter was residing in Eganville, he broke into a store and took about $2 in cash, and some goods. He did not settle it the next day, as he says, but the next day, on finding out that it could be proved that he committed the robbery, he fled out of the place.
>
> The next heard of him was his marriage. The next, his attempt at murder and robbery of James Bothfield. His statements in his confession, respecting his attack on Bothfield, are purely imaginary. It was a cold-blooded, willful, deliberate attempt at murder, committed after dark, in a lonely place, and when Bothfield, who was a weakly old man and a hard drinker, was very much under the influence of liquor.
>
> His statement as to his learning the trade of a carpenter is also false. The man never learnt the trade unless he learnt it in the penitentiary; and the only time he ever spent in Pembroke was while he lay in the jail there awaiting his trial for the attempt on Bothfield's life.
>
> ... The fact of his making such unnecessary false statements at such a solemn time shows the character of the man, and must throw a doubt on the reasons he gives in his confession for committing the murder of Daulter.

Bresnahan apparently read the newspapers. In short order, he come up with a third confession in which he modified the Daulter story to satisfy certain evidence, but added horrific details of his earlier life in Canada.

During the trial, reference had been made to a pail of water in front of Mick's home. Peter now stated that the blood and hairs in the pail were the result of Daulter washing himself after being shot. He also said that after hitting Mick in the head with the axe, he left the axe at the cabin. Later, when he returned to the crime scene in the woods, he struck Mick with the rock. Since the change in story did nothing to further his own cause, authorities suspected it was the truth.

Far more shocking, though, was the additional information provided by Peter about his earlier criminal exploits, an effort to bare his soul within days of his execution date. At the urging of his one true friend in life, John Richardson, and with a reporter present, Bresnahan began:

> The following circumstances and history of my life, including the murder of Michael Daulter as I am about to relate to John Richardson, my truest friend living, are as follows: These facts, which I now tell for the first time, as far as they relate to the crime for which I am soon to suffer death, agree in the main with the evidence as produced on my trial. And I now, having lost all hope of having my sentence changed, have no reason, disposition or motive in having things appear any different from the real truth. There is no one whom I care enough for, to tell it to, except John Richardson, and in his presence, to H. G. Reynolds of the *Gouverneur Herald*, I tell it for the first time, as follows:
>
> The scrape in which I was first engaged, and which resulted in my first crime, was the killing of an Indian when I was about seventeen years old. ... It was back in the wild woods ... I had my little bark canoe, and was mainly trapping for beaver, otter, and mink, and hunting deer. The wilderness all about the lake was divided off into hunting grounds, and different Indians claimed the exclusive right to them. I had been trapping there a few days when, one morning, I was going into camp with two beavers, and came upon an Indian who was on the lake in his canoe. He paddled up to me and asked where I got the beavers. I pointed out the place and he said, "It is my hunting ground and I will take the game." As he said this, he paddled close up to my canoe, when we were a number of rods out from the shore, and as he reached for the game, I struck him on the head with my paddle. He dropped forward, and upsetting his canoe at that instant, caught hold of the side of my canoe. I instantly drew up my gun and shot him through the head, and he sunk to the

bottom. I never saw nor heard of him after that.

… My second murder and next crime was in the following fall, I think in the year 1851 [the year he reached the age of twenty]. I had then left Pembroke and gone to the Big Opeongo Lake, about two hundred miles north of Pembroke. Duncan McCrimmon went from Pembroke with me. He was Scotch, and about twenty-five. We went for the purpose of hunting, and buying furs from the Indians. It was in November, the last of canoeing, that we went up. We had not far from $150 each with us. I got my money from my father. We remained there all winter and got ready to start for home about the last of March. We started for our camps, six miles away, by different routes so as to pick up all the furs we could from the Indians. I was three days getting to camp, and McCrimmon got there a day earlier and had assorted out some of the choicest of the furs for himself, and left the poorer ones for me. I was not satisfied with this division. The next forenoon, we started out to buy more furs. We had our guns with us. We crossed a small bay on the ice of Opeongo Lake to go to some Indian camps. The matter of the division of furs came up as we were crossing the lake. He told me to hold my tongue or he would leave me there for good. We got into a dispute, and I hauled my gun up and fired, the bullet taking effect in his shoulder. I rifled his pockets of the money; he had a few dollars only, and dropped him into an air hole, gun and all. I returned to the camp and packed his furs and my furs together and started for home by way of the Mattawasca River. I got home in April, after two weeks journey. I told his cousin, John McCrimmon, his only relative at Pembroke, that Duncan went off trading with the Indians and never returned. I gave him some few of the poorest furs.

My next crime was committed about seventeen years ago, before I was married. This was on Shaw Lake and near Boneshore Point. The name of the man was Michael Crowley. I saw Crowley first at the tavern of James Conroy on Boneshore Point. He was in the tavern, and in the course of the conversation, spoke of the large sum of money he was worth. The second time I saw him, he was at Birches Creek, some four miles from this tavern. There was eleven other men with us. They heard of his having some money. We were in canoes, going across Shaw Lake to peel cabin bark. Crowley was fishing from a rock on the shore. We went across and peeled the bark. We were all lumbermen, or getting out timber. We all talked it over, and decided to have his money before we started to return, if we found him there. One man, Joe Lamarsh, peeled off a long strip of slippery elm bark before we started back, to hang him up with. We found him in the same place when we came back. We rowed up to him and rifled his pockets but found only $1. Incensed at not doing better, and fearing he would tell of the deed if he escaped, we tied the bark to his neck and then suspended him from a tree, where we left him. The $1 we spent at Conroy's tavern for whiskey. We finished binding the cribs of square timber together, and in about three days started down the Grand River for Quebec, and arrived there about two weeks afterwards. When we arrived there, we heard of the murder of Crowley, it having been published in the papers. I first heard last week, the day I made my former confessions, that Crowley was originally from the States and had friends in St. Lawrence County.

My trouble at Arnprior in 1866, as stated in my former confession, was partially true. For that offense, I was sentenced to four years in the penitentiary at Kingston, Canada. My wife did not have the [victim's] watch on when I was last arrested, as was stated in the former confession.

Since coming to the States, I have had it constantly in my mind that I would commit some deed of violence or murder, with a view of adding to my scanty means. I have suffered for food and my family has been quite destitute. I had resolved on resorting to some means to get money. While in Macomb, I contemplated the murder of Billy Patterson, a farmer who lived in hermit-like seclusion. I went to his house in June 1876, about ten or eleven o'clock in the forenoon for that purpose, and was intent on taking his life. He was not there, and I returned and gave up the idea, but set my plans on another man, one John Lockie. Lockie lives in the Scotch settlement of Rossie. He is a man of reputed wealth. I lived at the time about two miles from him, in the house rented of Robert Flemming. About ten o'clock at night in June, 1877, I left home and went up to Lockie's. I secured a heavy club and large-sized rock and walked up to his door. His light was dimly burning. I looked into the window and saw him and a woman. When I started to go there, I supposed he was living alone. I rapped at the door, and he came and invited me in. I asked him to come out, as my horses were there and would not stand. He seemed to mistrust me, and went back and got his revolver and gun and told me he would shoot me if I didn't go away instantly. I ran from the house.

The facts and circumstances of the killing of Michael Daulter are as I am about to relate them to John Richardson. I had fully resolved to kill and rob Daulter, and my only motive was to get his money, of which I believed he had several hundred dollars. [Bresnahan then described again the same sequence of events surrounding Michael Daulter's death as told earlier, finishing with the following avowal]:

The above is the only full and true confession I have ever made of my life, history, and bloody crimes. To Rev. Pearce I have confided part of the foregoing, but now declare solemnly and unreservedly that every statement herein made is the solemn truth. Any and all previous admissions conflicting with this, I do positively declare to be untruthful, and were either given by me freely, or extorted from me by hopes of benefit to myself. I owe alike to Sheriff Wheeler and Deputy Sheriff Tanner my deepest and profoundest thanks for all their acts of kindness, and now reassert the truth of the foregoing in their presence.

Peter A. Bresnahan

Sworn and subscribed before me this 16th day of July A. D. 1878. Wm. E. Tanner, Notary Public.

There appeared to be nothing in Bresnahan's story that might save his hide, lest he hoped to be put on trial in Canada for the offenses he admitted to. Whatever the case, he wasn't finished just yet. A fourth confession was soon revealed, this time in the presence of Sheriff Wheeler and a reporter from the *Watertown Times*. In this latest story, just days before his scheduled execution, a new twist was introduced—Bresnahan had indeed

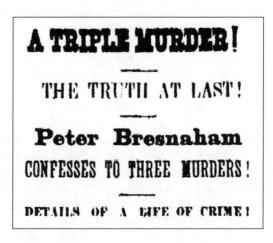

killed Daulter, but it was a murder for hire.

His explanation was simple. The Bresnahan family moved to South Colton in October 1877, and in the early months of 1878, Peter purchased a farm from William Tupper. With meager resources at his disposal, it would be a long time before the farm was paid off. Tupper wanted to purchase other property, and so he came up with a scheme whereby Peter could quickly obtain the full amount owed on the farm: kill Mick Daulter, who was rumored to have substantial cash hidden away.

> Some time after this, Bill Tupper, the man of whom I purchased the farm ... suggested a plan to me, which he thought, if I carried it out, I could find a ready means for paying for the property.
>
> He first contrived the plot for the murder of Daulter. I did not, at the time the plot was first proposed to me, consent to it; but the plot having been once suggested, and knowing the hermit life the old man was living, my mind reverted to it from time to time, and I finally yielded to the temptation of perpetrating the act. Then, to avoid suspicion resting on me, Tupper said I could go to Canada for a time and return, and say that I had been to my father's and borrowed or obtained the money. I state this fact not for the purpose of incriminating another, particularly in the bloody work I did, but chiefly to show how the thought of murdering Daulter first found birth in my heart.
>
> ... on Tuesday, the 30th of April last, when the fearful deed was committed, I solemnly declare that the thought of murder was rankling in my heart when I left my home, between 6 and 7 o'clock AM; that with the fixed purpose to commit the crime I set out; that the obtaining of what money I could find was the sole motive actuating me to take the life of the old man.
>
> Peter A. Bresnahan (23 July 1878)

According to Peter, he and Tupper discussed the murder plan on several occasions. He was, in fact, carrying Tupper's own gun when he set out to kill Daulter on that fateful April day. Before reaching Mick's home, he discovered the weapon to be malfunctioning, so Bresnahan borrowed a gun from a local man to complete the deed. Tupper's known criminal history caused some to wonder about his possible involvement—he had twice been arrested in the past (once for rape), but had eluded punishment.

There would be no fifth confession. The last few days of Peter Bresnahan's life were spent with Reverend Pearce, reading the Bible and preparing spiritually for his imminent end.

At 11:00 AM, July 26, 1878, Peter ascended the gallows and stood beneath the noose, where he made his final comments:

> Well, I have only a few remarks to make. I feel thankful to the sheriff and his family, and deputy Tanner, for their many kindnesses to me. Also to my spiritual advisers for their kindness and attention. May the Lord have mercy on my soul.

Twenty-two minutes passed, absorbed by readings from two reverends. With the black hood in place and the noose applied, the mechanism was triggered. Two doctors monitored his vital signs as life slowly drained away. Fifteen minutes later, Bresnahan's body was lowered and placed in a coffin, ending the saga of an admitted four-time killer.

PETER BRESNAHAN HANGED AT CANTON

5

The Man of Mystery: Coast-to-Coast Crook

With several aliases, the Man of Mystery had an arrest record dating back to when he was just nine years old.

In early June 1904, Emily Burns, 69, wife of Patrick Burns of Croghan (in Lewis County), died at the Watertown home of her son, Thomas. She had moved there after more than fifty years on the family farm situated on Beech Ridge, about twenty miles east of Watertown and five miles southeast of Carthage village.

Of three surviving daughters and four sons, only twenty-six-year-old William lived with his father on Beech Ridge. Patrick, 74, of strong build and a hard worker, had farmed in Croghan all his life. He carried on for several more years after his wife's death, but by the time he reached 80, the farm was used for little more than the sale of standing hay, although he and William continued living there.

In July 1912, William, by then 32, was appointed to a state forest ranger position in Lewis County, requiring him to be away from home often. His father's rheumatism had worsened to the point where he needed crutches to walk. On a trip to Carthage in late August to pick up some supplies, the elderly Patrick met a young man named Roy Farrington, who had just lost his job working on the state dam and was seeking other employment. Farrington was hired to assist Patrick in managing the home when William was away.

After a week had passed, the Burns men came to know Farrington a little better, discovering one particularly unusual fact. Despite his youth (he was just 22), Roy had been very successful as a magician and escape artist, having performed with a traveling troupe across thirty-five states. The Burns didn't have to take his word for it. He gladly demonstrated remarkable sleight-of-hand skills and other trickery for them. Both men were very impressed.

On Friday, September 6, the morning after that impromptu

performance, the relationship among the three men quickly deteriorated.

While preparing to mail a letter, William discovered that a dollar's worth of stamps ($25 in 2012) was missing. Farrington at first denied having been in the room, but later changed his story. William was convinced something was amiss, and during the ensuing argument, he threatened to have Farrington arrested.

The elder Burns admonished Farrington for lying, but when the confrontation continued to escalate, Patrick fired him. The hired man seemed to ignore the order, instead going outside to split firewood. The old man followed him and made it clear he was to leave the property.

Farrington was still owed seventy cents in pay, and while emptying his pockets in search of change, Patrick pulled out a roll of bills. William had only twenty-five cents, which he gave as partial payment. His father promised to meet the hired man in Carthage later in the day to pay him the remainder due. With that, Farrington packed his belongings and left.

William spent the day working on his new job, returning home around 7:00 PM. Entering the house and turning on the kitchen light, he could see through the doorway into the living room. There was his father, seated awkwardly in a chair, his head and clothing a mass of blood. The old man had obviously met a terrible end.

William immediately called the neighbors for help and summoned the authorities. The police chief, sheriff, coroner, and three doctors were on the scene by 10:00 PM. They found the Burns home a bloody mess, with large pools on the kitchen floor, and fingerprints and smeared blood in almost every room throughout the two-story house.

While the three doctors conducted an autopsy, the coroner began taking statements in the kitchen. Several neighbors testified, but it was William who spoke at length, detailing the recent hiring and firing of Roy Farrington, who was instantly the prime suspect. He was assumed to be heavily armed. It appeared that Patrick had several bullet holes in the skull, possibly from a handgun, and William noted that a Winchester .38 caliber rifle was

OLD MAN IS BRUTALLY MURDERED NEAR CARTHAGE

Struck Down with Hammer from Behind—
About $80 Taken from House
By Murderer

PATRICK BURNS, THE VICTIM

missing, along with a full box of cartridges. In the rifle's stock was secreted William Burns' hunting license.

The autopsy had all three physicians puzzled. There were skull fractures associated with three of the dozen or so holes in Patrick's head, but the source of those holes was in question until Sheriff Stoddard found a hammer beneath a set of stairs. The hammer's head had both a blunt and a pointed end, and stuck to the hammer were blood, hair, and pieces of tissue. William recognized the tool as one they used for breaking cakes of maple sugar. Repeated blows with the pointed head of the hammer had severed an artery and caused multiple punctures in the victim's skull. Torn ligaments in his left arm and wrist suggested that Patrick, although struck severely, attempted to block the blows rained upon him by Farrington.

The coroner's immediate finding was murder in the first degree. The roll of bills was missing from Patrick's pocket, indicating that the motive was a combination of robbery and revenge. Lawmen across northern New York were alerted, and a search of the immediate area began.

A trail of bloody footprints and fingerprints detailed the killer's movements. After going through the old man's pockets, Farrington searched the home, grabbed the rifle, and headed for the nearby woods. Questioning of neighbors revealed that his route led towards Castorland, about three and a half miles south. Someone was seen using a boat to cross the Black River, and near the village, a rifle was found between the railroad tracks on Saturday morning. The stock was checked, and sure enough, William Burns' hunting license was found, verifying it was the rifle missing from the crime scene. The gun held fourteen cartridges. It was surmised that Farrington either dropped it accidentally or disposed of it as he jumped a train under cover of darkness. The Castorland rail agent reporting that no one matching Farrington's description had recently purchased a ticket.

It was later learned that a slim young man had been spotted trying to ride the bumpers between the train cars, causing the operators to stop the train. He then paid his fare and rode in one of the coaches. Authorities were only able to track him as far as Utica.

Later on Saturday, a freight train crashed at Fort Plain, about thirty-eight miles east of Utica. Three men were killed, and for some time their bodies remained unidentified. It was at first suspected that among them was Farrington, but this later proved to be untrue.

Investigators managed to determine the approximate time of Patrick Burns' death, which was originally believed to have happened in the early morning. A neighbor had reported seeing Burns at about 12:30 PM that day, and the lone boatman on the Black River was seen around 1:30. Since the killing occurred at about 1:00 PM, Farrington had about an eighteen-hour head start on his pursuers.

Ten days after the murder of the old man (although newspapers gave his age as 91 or 92, records indicate he was 84), there were still no leads. Police had collared two suspects, one in Rome and one in Carthage, but they were only held briefly, and only because they bore a resemblance to the description of Roy Farrington—about 21 years old; slightly built; 5 feet 7 inches tall; approximately 165 pounds; dark complexion, dark hair, dark eyes; and a face covered with pimples. His nose was flattened on the end, and his eyes were said to droop.

Lewis County offered a $500 reward, but with no results. The public was urged to pay close attention to the detailed description of the suspect. From the lack of information on his whereabouts, police suspected that Roy Farrington may have been an alias.

Two months after the murder, not one iota of information on the killer's whereabouts had been gathered. For all intents and purposes, the case had gone cold. And, in a great bit of literal irony, cold proved to be Roy Farrington's undoing.

In late November, with winter weather looming, William Burns was on the farm, working in the woodpile. While cutting firewood, he made a remarkable discovery. There, secreted in the pile, were the missing stamps that had led to Farrington's dismissal. And that's not all. With the stamps was a piece of paper, damaged by the weather, but fortunately still intact.

William was at once flabbergasted and elated when he read the contents. It was a letter from Farrington to a friend in Holyoke, Massachusetts. Among other things, Roy expressed his strong feelings for a young lady there. Seemingly from out of nowhere, a solid lead! If Farrington felt strongly about the girl, as the letter suggested, there was a good chance he might be found in Holyoke.

William notified local authorities, who contacted their counterparts in Holyoke. It was decided to mail the letter and track it to its destination. The man who received it denied knowing Farrington, but finally admitted that Roy Farrington was the alias of Rene Ouimette of Holyoke.

Police located the room rented by Ouimette, staked it out, and arrested him when he showed up. As it turned out, Ouimette was no stranger to them after all. Better known as Rene Brodeur, he had an extensive arrest record dating back to when he was just nine years old.

His was an impressive rap sheet. After being hauled in for several petty offenses as a boy, he was convicted of larceny in late 1904 at the age of fourteen and sent to Reform School. Brodeur proved incorrigible, and was again arrested on the same charge in summer 1906 and fall 1907. He also did time as an inmate in the State Insane Asylum at Northampton, and always seemed to be in some sort of trouble. His last recorded crime in Holyoke was breaking into and robbing a poolroom in the fall of 1911.

Brodeur was so well known to Holyoke police that, when he was brought to the station for the Burns case, one officer said, "Well, Rene, what are you in for now?" When questioned about the New York case, Brodeur said he knew nothing about it and had never been to Croghan.

The charges he now faced were much more serious than past transgressions, but verification of his aliases was needed in order to hold him for New York State authorities. On Sunday, December 1, William Burns arrived in Holyoke and verified that Brodeur was the same Roy Farrington who had worked for his father at Croghan. At long last, justice might now be served. The reward money offered by William remained in his possession, for it was he who had cracked the case.

Five days after his capture, and within hours of his arrival in Lowville, Brodeur found himself standing before Judge Edward Merrill in Lewis County Supreme Court, where he entered a plea of not guilty to murder in the first degree. The trial was set to begin three months later. Reporters noted that Brodeur seemed comfortable in the court setting, which was not at all surprising considering his lengthy criminal history.

Before Christmas, one hundred juror notices were disseminated, and on the morning of February 4, 1913, jury selection began in the highly anticipated trial of Rene Brodeur for first-degree murder. But within moments, it was all over.

Attorney Frank Bowman stepped forward on behalf of the defendant, informing the court that he would agree to plead guilty to a lesser charge. A brief conference was held with District Attorney Perry Williams, who accepted the offer in view of Rene's "mental deficiency," and the fact that he had been placed in an insane asylum at various times over a three-year period. The revised plea (guilty of second-degree murder) avoided the likelihood of the young man's death in the electric chair.

Brodeur asked to be sentenced immediately, and Judge Merrill obliged, imposing a term of life behind bars, with the possibility of release after twenty years if he maintained good behavior. Smoking a cigar and smiling, Brodeur left the courtroom, apparently a very happy man.

Five months after the murder, three days after his trial began, and two months before his twenty-third birthday, Rene Brodeur was delivered to Auburn Prison.

> **BRODEUR SMILES AT 20-YEAR TERM**
>
> ---
>
> **Self-Confessed Murderer Will Be Taken to Auburn This Week.**

During his incarceration, Rene became known for some unusual capabilities. Just as he had demonstrated for William and Patrick Burns the night before the murder, Brodeur was adept at sleight-of-hand and escape artistry. Those skills may have seemed of little use in a maximum security prison, but on occasion, they served him quite well.

The Mutual Welfare League of Auburn Prison worked closely with the inmates on all sorts of endeavors. One that fostered good public relations was an annual show featuring dozens of prisoners talented in the field of entertainment. Singers, dancers, acrobats, musicians, and comedians, many of whom toured professionally before falling wayward of the law, put on a show each year that sometimes drew more than two thousand attendees.

In 1919, the show was highly lauded, playing two consecutive nights to a packed house, as crowds of disappointed fans were turned away at the door. Among the acts were legitimate vaudeville stars, impressionists, cabaret performers, and singers.

A unique performance earned plenty of attention, as described here by an *Auburn Citizen* reporter who took part in a dress rehearsal:

> One of the amazing features of the whole performance is the series of marvelous tricks done by Rene Brodeur, the Man of Mystery. Brodeur puts on the act that, only a short time ago, he was doing on one of the highest class vaudeville circuits of the country. He does the packing-box trick and the milk-can stunt that is bound to give rise to some of the tallest guessing on the part of the audience.

The Man of Mystery: Coast-to-Coast Crook

This *Citizen* reporter was asked to assist in locking Brodeur in the heavy galvanized metal can last night, and he thoroughly examined the can in order to discover its hidden secret. The can was filled with water and Brodeur got into it in full sight of everybody, then ducked his head under the water while the heavy cover was put on and the six padlocks clamped through the hasps. Brodeur was out of it in just fifty seconds, and this reporter assisted in unlocking the cover and removing it, when nothing was disclosed but the water.

Another marvelous trick was that of extricating himself from the prison restraining sheet [straightjacket] in full view of the audience. This sheet is the last thought in contrivances for keeping an insane man from inflicting harm on himself or others. The arms are thrust down into a deep sleeve on the inside of the sheet, which is one piece, and then it laces up the back with heavy rope. He should be absolutely helpless, as he has not the slightest use of his hands. Yet he got out of this, unaided, in five and one-half minutes.

Following the performance before thousands, Rene's act was reviewed in the same newspaper:

… and then comes one of the acts that alone is declared to be worth the price of a ticket and then some more:

A Handcuff King

Rene Brodeur was pulling down $1000 a week as an all-round wizard and mystery artist before a slip in the cogs put him to work in Auburn Prison at forty-five cents a month. He can work himself out of any bonds that may be put on him, and he astounded his fellow inmates and the guards at a rehearsal the other night by working himself out of a prison straightjacket (that had been fitted to him by experts) in just thirty-five seconds.

His two biggest stunts are getting out of a trunk that is securely locked, and which is bound up by ropes tied by volunteers in the audience. The Welfare League has had a heavy galvanized iron can made, with heavy hasps to clamp down the cover, and Brodeur is placed in this, and the can filled to the brim with water. There is no question about his being in there, and then the public is invited to bring to the show its own padlocks, and come on the stage and lock down the hasps.

Brodeur then gets out of the can with no outside help. He is the originator of this stunt that has been seen before on the stage, but the mystery remains yet unsolved. Besides these marvelous stunts, he performs many other tricks of legerdemain. ... From his demonstration of getting through and out of everything, it would appear as if he is a voluntary prisoner.

In other years, when the show focused on musical performances, Brodeur played the tuba in the Mutual Welfare League Orchestra, a group that received rave reviews.

On January 16, 1928, Rene was released on parole, having earned a five-year, good-behavior reduction of the minimum sentence. His pre-Auburn life had been one of disruption and crime since a very young age. It was hoped that Rene's post-Auburn life would serve as commentary on the institution's ability to reform troubled individuals.

But Brodeur's actions as a free man were anything but a ringing endorsement of New York's prison system. His mastery as an escape artist translated into everyday life, and this was one parolee who proved difficult to track. He was soon wanted for crimes committed in Buffalo, but unbeknownst to police, Rene had moved on to other venues. At some point, he married and fathered two children.

Besides police, Auburn officials sought him as well for violating the terms of his release. On November 6, 1931, a warrant was issued by the parole board for Rene's arrest. If returned to their custody, he would remain locked up for life.

Just a day after the warrant was issued, Brodeur and a partner robbed the palatial residence of Mrs. Winthrop Scarritt in the Hutton Park section of West Orange, New Jersey. As Mrs. Winthrop slept, the pair spent the entire night in her home, tying up four victims and making off with jewels and securities valued at approximately $10,000 ($140,000 in 2012). It was strongly suspected that the pair had robbed the same residence during a card game several months earlier, and were involved in other area robberies. New Jersey police issued a bulletin with Brodeur's image, but they were no luckier than the Buffalo police had been in locating him.

And for good reason. The next time he was heard from, Rene's name surfaced in headlines on the West Coast. As slick and elusive as he was, and considering that Lewis County authorities had found him by tracking a letter sent to his Massachusetts hometown, Brodeur remained remarkably oblivious to the sheer lunacy of openly using the US postal service. On December 21, 1931, he mailed a Christmas package from Portland, Oregon, to his wife on the East Coast. The receipt of that package alerted New Jersey police to his new location, but as they would soon learn, much more had recently been added to Brodeur's criminal file.

Besides New York and New Jersey, Rene was already wanted in Oregon for two serious offenses. Posing as a police officer, he had abducted a nine-year-old Portland girl who was playing in the street with her brother. Forcing her to ride with him on a streetcar, Brodeur took her to his apartment, raped her, and then released her.

The young girl was remarkably observant. After reporting the story to police, she identified her assailant from a group of photos and then led officers to his apartment. His clothing and personal effects were still there, but Rene was nowhere to be found. Detectives staked out the site, but after a few days of waiting, it was concluded that he had left the city.

> **GIRL ATTACKER SOUGHT**
> Police Believe Man Rene Brodeur Wanted in New Jersey.

Lawmen across the Northwest, already alerted to Rene's crimes, were warned that he appeared once again be on the move. In February 1932, Seattle police were notified by Portland authorities that Brodeur was believed headed for their city, but four days after the rape, a robbery in Portland convinced authorities that he was still in town after all.

During the crime, a houseboy was handcuffed and then tied with wire. The victim's description of his attacker strongly resembled Brodeur, and the noted droopiness in one of the robber's eyes provided an easily identified feature.

Portland police worked feverishly in trying to locate Rene, fearing he may rape, rob, or kill someone else. Amidst stakeouts, searches, and investigations, it was an observant young girl who came to the rescue.

Nine-year-old Betty Woodhouse was doing nothing more than paying a visit to the apartment of a young friend. Like many other girls in the city, she had been alerted to the recent rape and shown a photograph of Rene Brodeur as a man to avoid.

Arriving at her destination, Betty knocked repeatedly on the door, but on one answered. Finally, a nearby door opened, and the tenant informed her that no one was home in that apartment. Betty departed the building with a strong sense of fear and recognition—by remarkable coincidence, she felt certain she had just seen the face of Rene Brodeur.

Betty ran home and told her parents, who immediately called police. The stakeout team, posted several blocks away at Brodeur's previous residence, rushed to the scene, but Rene had once again vanished. Trusting the girl's story, patrolmen J. L. Crawford and E. D. Officer—that's right, Officer Officer—hid in the building and awaited his return.

At around 10:00 PM, their patience was rewarded when Rene was seen entering his apartment. Knowing Brodeur was considered dangerous, they approached cautiously and knocked on the door. It soon opened, but just as quickly was slammed shut. Brodeur was on the run!

Both officers rushed into the room and Crawford opened fire, striking Rene in the back. The bullet passed through his abdomen, but he kept running. Officer Officer began firing as Brodeur fled the building and raced down the street. Two detectives joined the pursuit, with the four men

The men who finally shot and captured Rene Brodeur. Left, Officer Crawford; Right, Officer Officer.

firing a total of fifteen shots. Rene was struck a second time, in the right leg, but he continued running for several more blocks.

Police headquarters, informed of the shootout, quickly dispatched a large detail of men to aid in the search. Though twice wounded, it appeared the one-time escape artist had successfully pulled off another remarkable disappearing act.

While scouring the streets, Officer Crawford recalled that Brodeur had never returned to his original apartment after the rape. Acting on a hunch, he went to the building to hide and wait, but that didn't prove necessary. When he reached the top of the stairs, Crawford heard a key in the street-level door, and as it opened, in staggered Brodeur. Seeing the policeman, he instantly turned and ran.

Crawford rushed down the stairs in hot pursuit, but as he turned a corner down the street, Brodeur was already half a block away and running hard. Fearing he would escape once more, Crawford stopped, aimed, and fired. With no place to hide, Rene had two choices: surrender or die. He stopped running, raised his hands in the air, and shouted, "I give up! I give up!" No further shots were fired, and he was finally taken into custody.

A search of his clothing revealed no weapons, but police did find a pair of handcuffs, which Rene admitted had been used in a robbery earlier that day. As police suspected, it was Brodeur who had burglarized a home and tied up the houseboy. A large amount of jewelry from that theft was later found in his apartment, along with a gun and three pairs of handcuffs.

Rene Brodeur, the Man of Mystery, a coast-to-coast crook with many aliases

Rene had been armed at the start of the chase through Portland's streets, but told police he had flung his pistol into a hedge at 20th and Hoyt, where they later found it. At the hospital, Brodeur told detectives that he had not fired a single shot during the chase, and in fact hadn't fired a gun in two decades (which may have been true, since he spent most of that time in Auburn Prison). He claimed that his stint in prison resulted from an argument during which he struck a man in the head with a hammer more than twenty years ago. He failed to mention that the victim had died, and was a defenseless, elderly gentleman.

Rene's injuries were considered critical, but successful surgery led to the hospital's assessment that he should fully recover. Plans were in the works to return him to Auburn Prison, depending on whether the district attorney in Portland chose to pursue him on charges of raping the nine-year-old girl. New Jersey lawmen would have to wait in line to get their hands on Brodeur, who, no matter which path was followed, would never again see the light of day.

Although he had escaped tightly sealed boxes, chained cans of water, and legal authorities for much of his life, Rene's future in prison now seemed unavoidable. But in one final escape, he fooled them all.

Exactly a week after his capture, and presumed on the road to recovery, Rene Brodeur, the Man of Mystery, died from his injuries. Nine days later, on February 24, 1932, he was buried in Portland's Lone Fir Cemetery.

It was assumed the nailed lid of the pine box was enough to hold him.

6

A Family Man Fingers His Killer

The perpetrator's identity was provided by a dead man.

In the early 1900s, Edward Lucia of West Chazy (in northern Clinton County) operated the Adirondack Hotel to support his family of eight children, the youngest of whom was barely a year old. Like most people in the area, he also maintained a small farm to supply many of life's necessities. Morning and evening chores were a routine part of the process.

In the early evening hours of December 4, 1919, while Edward, 49, was in the barn milking the cows, the family was inside the house, preparing for supper. At about 6:30, the door suddenly opened and Lucia staggered inside. Unable to speak, he fell hard to the kitchen floor, unconscious.

Rushing to his side, the family found him bleeding heavily from a head injury. Their best guess was that he had somehow fallen, or had been kicked by a cow, which can inflict fatal wounds with one blow. A call was placed, and Dr. Frederick Swift of Chazy was soon on the scene.

The Lucias were surprised by Swift's assessment that Edward's injuries resulted from being struck by a heavy object, but not a cow's hoof. Why would someone attack Lucia, known widely as a salt-of-the-earth family man, a guy who got along with everyone? It didn't make sense, but there was little time to dwell on it at the moment.

Dr. Swift, realizing that Edward was in danger of dying, called for help. Arriving in short order was Dr. Robert MacDonald, a surgeon from Plattsburgh. Together they worked on Lucia to keep him alive and prepare him for the thirteen-mile trip to Plattsburgh's hospital.

Sheriff John Fiske and Deputy Sheriff George Brunell began investigating by visiting the Lucia home and interviewing the family. They learned that Edward usually had plenty of cash on his person, and on that particular evening, it was believed he had as much as $300 in his wallet ($4000 in 2012). They further determined that Lucia's wallet was missing, suggesting robbery was the motive for the attack.

Other than that, they had nothing of substance. No one had seen the assault, and the victim was unconscious. They continued probing for clues and questioning locals, but it became a waiting game, hoping that Edward's condition would improve and he could tell them what had happened.

> **BRUTAL ASSAULT AND ROBBERY OF CHAZY MAN**
>
> Edward Lucia of West Chazy Victim of Mysterious Crime—In Critical Condition.

There soon developed a change in Lucia's medical status that seemed promising at first. Doctors and nurses described rambling vocalizations, but despite the fact that he spoke from time to time, Edward's utterings remained incoherent. No leads developed that would help solve the crime.

Several days after the attack, it was decided to move forward with John Doe proceedings, a legal process frequently shrouded in mystery. In this case, it was strongly believed that a crime had been committed, but there was no perpetrator or victim to speak to the issues. The John Doe proceeding brought eighteen witnesses to court, testifying to the known facts surrounding the case.

No results were publicized, but the district attorney's office had its suspicions. A parade of witnesses and suspects came in for further questioning. Although several leads were developed, investigators visiting Whitehall, Albany, and Massena returned frustrated.

Since the night he was injured, Edward's condition had fluctuated, but after lingering for nine days, his body could take no more. On Saturday, December 13, the Lucia assault case became the Lucia murder case.

Edward had been a community stalwart, prompting the media's use of cowardly, dastardly, and cold-blooded in describing the crime and its effect on his friends across the county. For the Lucia family, the impact was devastating: a widow and eight children were left without a husband, father, and breadwinner.

The *Plattsburgh Sentinel* noted the outpouring of sympathy:

> The funeral of Edward Lucia Monday was one of the most largely attended ever held in West Chazy. ...The church was filled to the doors with sorrowing friends of the man. ... Over fifty rigs and automobiles followed the remains to the little cemetery in West Chazy, where they were laid to rest.

Following the burial, the county board of supervisors voted to offer a $500 reward ($6000 in 2012) for information leading to the arrest and conviction of the killer.

Thirteen days after the funeral, and nearly a month after Lucia was attacked, a suspect was arrested in, of all places, Louisville, Kentucky. What's more, a confession was obtained, including a full accounting of the events leading up to the murder. The perpetrator was Ross E. Clark, 21, of West Chazy, and his identity was provided by a dead man.

His accuser? None other than Edward Lucia. In a moment of clarity while lying injured in the hospital, he had named Clark as his assailant. Keeping that information quiet, investigators had attempted to locate the elusive Clark on December 21, but were repeatedly frustrated by such a convoluted trail.

Once he was in custody, Clark told of having served in the navy for more than two years, after which he worked at the silk mills in Whitehall, New York, before returning home to West Chazy. It wasn't long before he was looking for trouble.

On the day of the killing, he had missed a meeting with a friend, and whether the assault was planned or by happenstance, Clark later ended up at the Lucia farm. Finding Edward alone, milking the cows, he secured a club and struck Lucia from behind. Although Clark didn't say he delivered multiple blows, that appeared to be the case. During Lucia's hospitalization, Dr. MacDonald had performed surgeries on two skull fractures, one on the back and one on the left side.

After robbing the victim of $145, Clark escaped by train to Rouses Point, eighteen miles northeast of West Chazy. From there, he entered Canada and reached Montreal, forty miles north, before backtracking to the United States and heading south to Albany. Next, he was off to Akron, Ohio, where he found work with the Goodyear Rubber Company.

He then moved on to Louisville, where he registered under a false name at a hotel, but used hotel stationery to write a letter (which was later an important piece of physical evidence) to his mother. A telegrammed reply from his brother, Rodger, offered train fare to come home, but the message was never received because Ross had left once again for Akron. At that point, investigators were on the trail, but while they pursued him at Akron, Clark had returned to Kentucky.

A description of Clark had been provided to officials at Camp Zachary Taylor in Louisville, a training facility for World War I soldiers. It was suspected that he might surface there, which Clark did in order to visit friends. He was recognized by guards and detained until the military police arrived. Investigators in Clinton County, New York, were notified that the fugitive had been captured and had confessed.

According to military authorities, Clark wept while telling them he "was a good boy before he went into the navy, and would rather go to the penitentiary than back into the navy," where he had been corrupted by some of the characters he had met. Ross had entered the service by the time he was sixteen, and had been recently discharged in July. The murder, which he said was motivated by robbery and was committed with a policeman's club, happened just over four months later. He also claimed no previous knowledge of Edward's death. He had only intended to knock Lucia out, and assumed the victim had survived the assault.

> **SAILOR ACCUSED OF WEST CHAZY MURDER**
>
> **Clark Arrested as Slayer of Hotel Keeper Found Dead Dec. 4.**

Detectives took custody of Clark and transported him north to Plattsburgh, arriving there on January 2. During the next few weeks, battles were fought in court over the admissibility of confessions that Clark had offered freely to the military officers who arrested him, and to the detectives who returned him to Plattsburgh. Because he had been advised of his rights and openly volunteered the information, it was ultimately ruled that the confessions would be admitted as evidence.

A plea of not guilty to first-degree murder was entered, and in early May, the trial began before Justice Whitmyer. District Attorney Harold Jerry prosecuted, while Clark's defense was presented by attorney John Judge and former justice John Collins.

Compelling and painfully poignant testimony was provided by Mrs. Lucia, who, before a packed but silent courtroom, described her husband's collapse in a bloody heap before the entire family. As reporters documented the scene, Mrs. Lucia sobbed uncontrollably much of the time, speaking only when she managed to gain momentary control. The defense wisely opted to forego submitting her to cross-examination.

Although the confessions were not read aloud in court, detectives and military police were allowed to recount them in detail, further strengthening the prosecution's case. In rebuttal, the defense called Ross

Clark to the stand. He acknowledged having made the confessions, but was under great duress at the time, and had also made self-incriminating statements in order to protect other members of his own family. Clark said that, under intense interrogation, he believed investigators' claims that his brother had been charged with the murder, so he did the noble thing and assumed the blame.

In an effort to invoke patriotic sympathy for Clark, he was asked about his military service at such a young age (he was sixteen when he enlisted). Those present learned that Clark was a seaman on the battleship *Oklahoma* when it served as a protective escort for ships carrying troops to the war in Europe.

After final arguments, the jury deliberated for four hours, returning at midnight to a still-packed courtroom. Clark was deemed guilty of second-degree murder, escaping the more serious charge due to uncertainty regarding intent. It was not clear to jurors that premeditation was involved.

Pronouncement of sentence the following day left the defendant visibly shaken for the first time since the trial began. At the words, "… not less than twenty years, and not more than life," Clark's mother collapsed in a faint, and other relatives began to cry. Affected deeply by the scene, the defendant himself began to teeter, finding momentary steadiness in the hand of his attorney, but finally collapsing as he was removed from the courtroom.

A few hours later, he was delivered to Clinton Correctional Facility at Dannemora. With the potential of time off for good behavior, and credit for time already spent in jail, Clark was destined for potential release in January 1935.

In May 1931, after serving eleven years in prison, he was the beneficiary of a commutation of sentence by Governor Franklin Roosevelt, granted on the recommendation of Judge Whitmyer. It was assumed that Clark's difficult family background, young age, and

> **CLARK, LUCIA MURDERER TO BE RETURNED**
>
> Paroled Convict Who Killed West Chazy Man in 1919 Being Extradited

military service were mitigating factors in the decision.

Twelve years later, and nearly a quarter century after the death of Edward Lucia, Ross Clark was arrested in California. The New York State Parole board investigated the case and reviewed Clark's past record, including the terms imposed by Justice Whitmyer. Finding him in violation of parole, the board initiated extradition for his return to New York, where he would serve the remainder of his sentence at Dannemora.

7

Brutal Execution for $9.03

"Just a bad boy?" said Mr. Russell. "That's about the size of it," said the doctor.

On the night of September 27, 1908, fifty-nine-year-old Hiram Combs of Fine, New York, was awakened by the sound of gunshots shortly before midnight. Rising from bed to investigate, he entered the living room just as the front door flew open. Hiram's son Leslie walked in, threw a rifle on the floor, handed a watch and some money to his stunned father, and said, "I've shot a man named Peabody."

Leslie cried as he told his father the details of robbing and shooting a man and leaving him for dead in the woods. Instead of running, he had decided to give himself up to the law. After asking his parents to check on the victim and perhaps tend to the man's wounds, Leslie was accompanied by Hiram to the home of the local constable, Charles Locke, where the boy related his story and turned over the evidence.

Within an hour or so, the victim's body was found, and the young man from Fine was in a heap of trouble. It wouldn't be the first time.

* * *

James Leslie Combs was born in the town of Macomb in July 1889 to Hiram and Annis Denora (Nora) Combs. By the family's own account, his was a troubled and troublesome childhood. His brother Vilas, five years his senior, said Leslie was prone to seizures for the first several years of his life, and often awakened, screaming, from terrible nightmares.

Nora Comb's description of her younger son was darker yet. He was only three pounds at birth; didn't walk until he was three years old; was delayed in speaking; had convulsions until age six; experienced night terrors for years; and fell hard at age four, cutting his head, resulting in an ear discharge that lasted for some time. He was said to have had headaches frequently and did poorly in school. By the age of five, he began running away from home, and continued to do so into his teens.

Vilas said that Leslie often fought with him, once trying to hit him with a shovel. He also stole from his older brother and others regularly. At around nine years of age, Leslie worked for local farmers, who reported him to be more than a handful. A Combs neighbor said the young boy once cut a hole in the farm's watering trough, and on another occasion added Paris green to the trough from which the farm animals drank daily. (Paris green is an insecticide that was used as rat poison, and was once a common suicide agent.)

Others farmers said he stole often, killed their chickens with stones and sticks, and broke windows. When he was reprimanded, the behavior continued unabated, and when asked by one farmer why he acted so, the answer was, "Just cause." In the farmer's opinion, "Why, he didn't know nothing. He was simple-minded."

For his part, Hiram Combs said he whipped Leslie frequently and severely, but it never seemed to do any good.

In December 1901, the family moved to the hamlet of Fine in the town of the same name, located in the northern Adirondacks (in southern St. Lawrence County). Leslie quickly gained the same reputation he had established at Macomb, and in July 1904, shortly after turning fifteen, he was brought before Justice of the Peace Lyndon Harris on charges of petty larceny. Mr. and Mrs. Combs admitted to Harris their frustration at being "unable to do anything with him."

The accumulated effect of troublesome behavior and running away as often as once a week had finally led to extreme measures. In an effort to turn Leslie's life around, Judge Harris committed him to the Rochester Industrial School, otherwise known as Reform School, which was viewed by many as prison for children.

For Leslie, it made little difference. He was placed on the school's farm unit, but ran away at the first opportunity. After being recaptured, he was sent to the city facility. Under stricter supervision and a stringent point system that monitored work habits, educational improvement, military drills, and general behavior, he was eventually paroled.

Shortly after returning home, Leslie was arrested for burglarizing the Chase & Stevens grocery store in Fine. After smashing the rear window, he entered the store and stole $17, a rifle, some knives, and cigars. Leaving some of the booty at home, Leslie told his parents he was going to work in the woods. Instead, he took the train to Harrisville, returning on the next day—and was immediately arrested by Constable Locke.

There was little Combs could do to claim innocence—on his person were the knives, the rifle, and five dollars. He pleaded not guilty before Judge Harris and was taken to Canton to await grand jury action.

In February, facing indictment for second-degree grand larceny and third-degree burglary, Leslie, just seventeen years old, agreed to plead guilty in exchange for a good-behavior promise. His attorney, George Bowers, noted extenuating circumstances: "There was insanity in the family, and I believe the boy is not quite in his right mind."

In light of that statement, the judge allowed a suspended sentence. Leslie could go home with his parents, but would return to court in June. If he stayed out of trouble until that time, leniency would be employed at sentencing.

On February 18, 1907, under those generous terms, Combs walked out of the courtroom a free man. Only 90 days of good behavior were required of him, but just 33 days later, Leslie was arrested again. Within days, he stood once more in a courtroom, this time before Judge Ledyard Hale. The charges were stealing $20 from his own father, Hiram, and burglarizing at least one local home. Combs, branded a degenerate in the media, was sentenced to eighteen months in Dannemora Prison—and was still several months shy of his eighteenth birthday.

Hard time in the state's most notorious prison did little more than expand Leslie's criminal activity. Authorities later denied that he had been housed in solitary confinement, but admitted to his placement in what they referred to as "the cooler," after which he was assigned to the D-Grade, which was the prison's disciplinary classification.

Leslie's principal violations were against the no-smoking rule and engaging in an act of sodomy with another convict. The second charge was considered serious, and he was punished severely for it, as well as for masturbation, a practice he said began at the Rochester Industrial School when he was fourteen years old. When Leslie was in prison, many highly placed professionals, including psychiatrists, psychologists, and lawmen, considered both behaviors (sodomy and masturbation) to be indicative of perversion and a criminal mind.

But those weren't his only transgressions. Combs was also introduced to morphine while behind prison walls. It would play an important role in his future.

While at Dannemora, he wrote letters to his parents, missives that were adjudged poorly composed, which was no surprise, considering his lack of education. The prison doctor, Theodore Townsend, treated Leslie ten times during his incarceration. In Townsend's judgment, Combs was an insane imbecile, a popular category in the growing field of criminal psychology, but not necessarily indicative of criminal leanings.

But a criminally inclined person diagnosed as an insane imbecile was potentially a very dangerous individual. The combination provided a convenient excuse for committing crimes without facing responsibility.

Dr. Walter Thayer, assistant physician at Clinton Prison, treated Leslie for tuberculosis while he was an inmate and told the young boy he might die from the disease within five years. Thayer also conducted Leslie's final examination on the day of his release, September 25, 1908.

Finally free again, Leslie was escorted to Plattsburgh, where he was left on his own to return home. He immediately went to a bar and began drinking, and also bought a bottle of laudanum. A popular recreational drug of the era, laudanum contained opium, morphine, and codeine, and was used routinely to treat a wide range of maladies, including tuberculosis.

At some point, when the bottle was broken, Combs put the powder in an envelope and sewed it into his vest for easy access.

After drinking at Plattsburgh, he took the train north to Rouses Point, further imbibing at local bars before heading west to Gouverneur, where he did the same. By mid-afternoon on Saturday, he met his father at the train station in Edwards, and together they went home.

Leslie spent a miserable, sleepless night on Saturday, his first taste of freedom in eighteen months. On Sunday, he shot target practice for a while, and in the afternoon went to the woods with Hiram to help fight the forest fires plaguing much of the Adirondacks in one of the worst fire years ever to hit the region.

They returned home late in the day, and after an evening meal, the entire Combs family was in bed by around 9:00 PM. But Leslie, red-eyed and wrung out, complained to his brother Vilas that it was too hot to sleep. He stepped outside and began to walk. Unbeknownst to the family, he had taken a rifle with him. He had been out of prison barely thirty hours.

Young Combs soon reached the home of Justice of the Peace Lyndon Harris, about a mile outside the village of Fine (going west on present-day State Route 3). It was Harris who had sent him to reform school, and it was also Harris who later sent Leslie's burglary case to Canton (which led to the Dannemora sentence).

Considering that he left home at night, carried a rifle, walked over a mile to the judge's home, and that Harris had twice in the past sent him to places of misery, it appears Leslie intended to kill the justice in an act of revenge. But as Combs stood in front of the home, the family dog raised a ruckus. Harris heard the dog barking aggressively, but thought little of it at the time. Leslie hid by the roadside, waiting for the dog to settle down.

Soon after, he noticed a light coming down the roadway. It was a bicycle, carrying Harry Hosmer home after a long day. Hosmer, 21, the son of a local farmer, had spent the day in the woods fighting forest fires, and had stopped on the way home to visit a young lady, Hattie Randall. He left the Randall house at 9:20 and began pedaling for the Hosmer farm, about a mile from the Harris home and two miles from the village.

As he was about to pass the judge's house, Harry was accosted by Combs. The two had known each other since they were children, and there had never been problems between them, but Leslie apparently didn't recognize Harry, believing the person on the bicycle was a man by the name of Peabody. He stopped the cyclist at gunpoint and ordered him to empty his pockets.

Hosmer obliged, handing over his watch and his pocketbook, which contained $9.03. Combs wanted more, but Harry said that was all he had.

Whether Leslie didn't actually believe him, or was just plain bent on violence, is unknown. On the spur of the moment, he decided on a plan. Directing Harry down the highway with his rifle, they continued toward the Hosmer farm. On the outskirts of the property, he directed Harry onto a side road into the family sugarbush, the site of many community gatherings in the past for springtime maple-sugaring parties.

According to Leslie, he attempted to search Harry for more money, but when Hosmer resisted, Combs struck him with the rifle's butt, knocking him to the ground, and then kicked him. As Harry lay there disabled, Leslie bound his hands and feet with rope. He was now totally helpless and entirely at the mercy of his captor.

Except that there was no mercy. Hosmer begged not to be left tied in the woods, but Combs ignored his pleas. Instead, he aimed the rifle at Harry's chest, and at point-blank range, fired.

Hosmer cried out in shock and pain. Mortally wounded, he struggled for words. To ensure no one would hear his victim's moans, Leslie tied a knot in a handkerchief, stuffed the knot into Harry's mouth, and tied the ends of the cloth tightly behind his head.

While doing so, Combs decided on an alibi of sorts—that during the robbery, Harry had pulled a knife and attacked him. To support that claim, Leslie used a knife to slice Hosmer's coat sleeve. Searching Hosmer's pockets, he found nothing further to steal, at which point Leslie stood up, walked away, and left Harry there to die.

Turning his attention to the pocketbook, he discovered that it held less than ten dollars (just as his victim had claimed), hardly enough for him to leave the country, an idea that had crossed his mind. Realizing that his recent release from prison would point the law in his direction once the body was found, Combs decided to go home.

Returning to the village, Leslie's thoughts once again turned towards revenge. He stopped at the home of Mr. Seaman, a local merchant who had once reported him for theft. Combs called Seaman out, but the man refused to leave his home, a decision that may have saved his life. Leslie then continued towards home, firing four shots, including one at the home of Fred Stevens, part owner of the Chase & Stevens store that Leslie had once robbed. Although the house was struck, no one inside was injured.

Finally arriving at home, Combs entered the house to find his father in the living room, having risen from bed to find the source of the gunshots that had awakened him.

*   *   *

After Leslie's confession to Constable Locke and the discovery of Hosmer's body, a neighbor broke the terrible news to the Hosmer family. Others summoned the sheriff and coroner from Canton. Early on Monday, word spread of Leslie's terrible deed, and folks from across the township began gathering at Fine village. Vigilante justice was common in those days, and it was feared the citizens would forcibly remove Combs from jail and administer immediate punishment. There was plenty of sentiment to do just that.

County Sheriff Nylie Hyland arrived on Monday afternoon, taking charge of the prisoner. With the constable and a few residents of Fine, they held him in protective custody while the coroner examined the death scene. Locals had stood guard over the victim's body through the night to ensure nothing was disturbed.

A sad, silent, depressing sight awaited the coroner. Near the Hosmer sugarhouse lay poor Harry, flat on his back and soaked with blood. He had not an enemy in the world, but had died a brutal death. The tight

> **COLD-BLOODED MURDER IN TOWN OF FINE**
>
> Harry Hosmer Led Off Into the Woods by Armed Man Who Shot Him Down---Leslie Combs, Ex-Convict, Surrenders Himself.

handkerchief left bruises on his neck, and the thick knot still filled his mouth. Powder burns amid the bloodstains indicated that he had been shot with the muzzle nearly against his chest. From the moment of impact, there had been no hope for survival—a single bullet had penetrated his heart and one lung. One coat sleeve was neatly sliced, and one pocket remained inside out.

After documentation of the crime scene using photographs and measurements, the questioning of Combs continued. Several residents had already spoken with him, and Leslie openly told the story of what he had done, expressing hope that the young man would survive for twenty-four hours. If a homicide victim lasted that long, the law required a charge of second-degree murder, which carried a maximum sentence of life in prison. The penalty for first-degree murder was death.

Threats against the prisoner escalated throughout the day, and at nightfall, the sheriff resorted to a tactic he had used previously to prevent a lynching—handcuffing himself to the prisoner when they slept. On the following day, their reception at the train station in Canton provided some tense moments, with further fears of vigilante justice. The chaotic scene had been expected, and to ensure his safety, Combs was rushed away immediately upon arrival.

In the days following, Leslie was vilified in the media for what was portrayed as one of the worst, most cold-blooded crimes in northern New York history. Fully two weeks after the murder, local media were still commenting on the difficulty in dealing with Combs' crime:

> All, no doubt, have heard, of the terrible death of Harry Hosmer. It has spread a feeling of gloom over the whole community. He was a good young man, respected and liked by his comrades and neighbors.
>
> He was 21 years old, just at the age when everything looks promising, and both boys and girls are starting out into a broader field of action. He leaves a father, mother, two sisters, Leta and Ivy, and one brother, Floyd. The popular funeral was held at the M. E. church, Rev. J. W. Nesbitt officiating. He was buried at Harrisville.

The grand jury indicted Combs on a charge of murder in the first degree. Since he and his parents lacked the means to hire an attorney, the court appointed representation in the person of Lawrence Russell, a lawyer who had already been consulting with the family.

During jury selection (on January 4, 1909), questioning focused on views of insanity, imbecility, and the death penalty. There was little doubt that an insanity plea would be invoked.

Although Leslie's parents were in the courtroom, he sat by himself most of the time, appearing indifferent to the goings-on. By day's end, a jury was in place. Testimony began the next morning.

The prosecution, handled by District Attorney John Crapser and his assistant, James Dolan, began by detailing the brutal crime scene and describing the events of Harry Hosmer's last day of life. Various legal officials then told their stories, and each piece of Harry's bloody clothing was introduced as evidence.

On the witness stand, Hiram Combs described his interaction with Leslie from the time his son arrived home from Dannemora on Saturday, to that fateful Sunday night when he confessed to Constable Locke. Several others testified as well, leaving no doubt as to who killed Harry.

The defense case was based on insanity, supported by the claim that mental illness was in the Combs family and was hereditary. Former schoolmates, friends, neighbors, and several doctors took the stand to address the issue, describing the defendant's past behavior that might in some way relate to mental instability.

Mr. and Mrs. Combs and Vilas talked about Leslie's difficult childhood, his head trauma, the nightmares, and his general bad behavior. Neighboring farmers from the family's time in Macomb recounted the troubles he had caused as a young boy, which continued even after he was reprimanded repeatedly.

Doctors and attendants from the Rochester Industrial School, the St. Lawrence State Hospital, and the hospital at Clinton Prison in Dannemora were questioned extensively on their work with insane and imbecilic patients, and their interactions with Leslie. There was plenty of discussion centering on "alcoholic confusion" and related topics in an attempt to determine the causes of the boy's behavior. Masturbation, the hearing of voices, and feeling bugs crawling on the skin were discussed as symptoms Leslie had displayed. His letters from Dannemora were introduced as evidence of Leslie's low-functioning brain.

During cross-examination of Dr. Elbert Sommers of St. Lawrence Hospital, a telling exchange occurred when he called Leslie "morally but not mentally defective." Anxious to dismiss the claims of insanity, alcoholic confusion, and other extenuating circumstances, Attorney Russell said, "Just a bad boy?" To which the doctor replied, "That's about the size of it."

Great effort was expended delving into the family's history of bizarre and erratic behavior. Several of the examples—great-uncles and half-siblings—came off as little more than eccentrics or odd ducks.

Leslie's grandmother, Pamelia (Hiram's mother) was a different story. Two of Pamelia's nephews described once seeing her in bed, twitching, jerking, mumbling, and frothing at the mouth. Other testimony related the stories she had told of talking to her deceased parents, and of receiving a visit from the Lord, who she said was wearing a corduroy suit and had come from a nearby limekiln. Pamelia was later seen going to the limekiln and throwing thorn apples into it. When asked why, she said it was to feed the Lord.

The stories left no doubt that she exhibited bizarre behavior. It was effective stuff, but no more so than the testimony of Harry's sister, Leta. On the night of September 27, she was sitting on the steps of the family home with a friend, Merton Perry. Together they had noticed the light on Harry's bicycle as it slowly crept towards home, a trip that ended in tragedy. Aaron Hosmer, Harry's father, also testified to great effect, relating the conversation he had with his son's murderer on the following day. Leslie said he only meant to rob Harry, but shot him when he resisted.

Shortly before noon on Thursday, after two and a half days of testimony, the case was handed to the jurors. Justice Charles C. Van Kirk made his charge clear—the killing was "practically undisputed, so you must decide insanity." They also had the option of finding for second-degree murder.

In less than two hours (with time for lunch included), the verdict was announced: guilty of murder in the first degree. The judge, noting, "This is not an occasion that calls for extended remarks," sentenced Leslie to death by electrocution during the week of February 15. Young Combs had one month left to live.

An appeal was expected, and in nearly every case, it served as an automatic stay of execution, prolonging the defendant's life. But to the surprise of all involved, Leslie decided against it. The matter was discussed with Lawrence Russell and Mr. and Mrs. Combs. Attorney Russell gave them his honest opinion—that the trial had been fair; that an appeal had little chance of changing things; and that to fight further would do nothing more than cost the county money. Leslie fully concurred.

Unlike the long, drawn-out trials we've become accustomed to in the twenty-first century, little time was wasted. Jury selection had begun on Monday morning; testimony ended on Wednesday; summations were completed by noon Thursday; the verdict was announced within two hours; and by 7:00 PM Thursday evening, the convicted killer was on his way to prison.

> **SENTENCED TO DEATH**
>
> Leslie Combs Found Guilty of Murder, 1st Degree.
>
> **PRISONER HEARS FATE CALMLY**

He almost didn't make it. A crowd had gathered at the rail station to watch Combs depart, and passengers who boarded the train noticed that the prisoner, handcuffed to the sheriff, seemed a bit disoriented and sleepy.

He was taken down the line to Norwood, where they would spend the night at the American House before completing their journey the next day. While disembarking at the Norwood depot, Leslie began to stagger and appeared ill. By the time they secured a room at the hotel, it became clear that Combs was very sick.

A doctor was called in to treat him, and while doing so, a packet of morphine was found secreted in the prisoner's clothing. The doctor administered emergency measures, but by 2 AM, Leslie's condition was critical. It was feared he would die before morning.

Within the hour, though, he began to improve, and by early afternoon, the trip to Dannemora had resumed. At the time, Leslie refused to reveal the source of the poison that nearly killed him, but it was the very same laudanum he had purchased in Plattsburgh the day of his release from prison three months earlier. He later admitted that even while sitting in the courtroom during the trial, he had covertly dipped his finger into the envelope on occasion for a small hit of the opiate, which he subtly placed on his tongue.

Sheriff Hyland recalled that on the opening day of the trial, he

> **COMBS HAD POISON**
>
> Condemned Murderer Tries Suicide on Way to Prison.
>
> **IN CHARGE OF THE SHERIFF**

had asked for Leslie's clothes to have them pressed. Before handing them over, Combs had removed a packet of letters. Unknown to the sheriff at the time, one of the envelopes contained the morphine.

Leslie had preserved the bulk of the powder for the verdict announcement, and for good reason. If found guilty of first-degree murder, he planned to commit suicide. If the jury found him guilty of a lesser charge, he would otherwise face his fate and go to prison.

After the trial, while waiting in his Canton jail cell for the sheriff to escort him to Dannemora, he ingested the rest of the laudanum. When a fellow prisoner asked what he was doing, Leslie said it was cough medicine that the doctor had given him.

The failed suicide attempt gained more headlines for Combs, but no sympathy. Subsequent newspaper editorials reviewed his case, ending with the same sentiment: Combs must die.

A group of his friends circulated a petition, asking Governor Charles Evans Hughes (a Glens Falls native) to commute the sentence to life, based on Leslie's age: while on Death Row, he was still a half-year shy of his twentieth birthday.

Lawrence Russell, Combs' attorney, joined the plea, an effort that upset many in St. Lawrence County who demanded justice. They declared that Combs had long been a menace to society, and any sentence short of death would lead to similar crimes if he were ever released.

One editorial phrased the sentiment in convincing fashion:

> The idea of the death penalty is not to punish the criminal, but to protect society: punishment is but incidental.

Leslie's own case supported that claim. After frequent criminal activity led to reform school, jail, and prison, Combs had murdered an innocent victim just two days after being released from Dannemora.

In prison awaiting execution, Leslie underwent a quick conversion to the Catholic faith. Less than four weeks after sentencing, he was baptized, and in the ensuing week made his first communion.

Just five days later, on the morning of February 16, 1909, Leslie Combs mumbled prayers and clutched a crucifix as he walked from his death cell to the electric chair. With the prison priest, Father Hellinger, standing by his side, Leslie sat in the chair and helped the officers properly adjust the straps.

Ten minutes later, after five jolts of current had been applied, he was pronounced dead. An autopsy revealed that Leslie had an enlarged heart (which seemed rather ironic, considering his heartless crime), and was in the early stages of tuberculosis.

His parents had parted, and neither could afford to ship the body home to Fine, so he was buried in the prison cemetery—five months before what would have been his twentieth birthday.

> **COMBS GOES CALMLY TO THE DEATH CHAIR.**
> With Crucifix in His Hand and Prayer on His Lips the Youthful Murderer Pays the Penalty.

8

Callous Killer Confirmed by a Kid

"George was in the house and hit mama on the head with a stick, and then got out through the window."

On the evening of September 27, 1920, four-year-old Ralphie Pelaccia drifted off into dreamland in his first-floor bedroom of the family home, a two-tenement house on University Street in Schuylerville, New York. His father, Sandy (Sante), worked the graveyard shift, 11:00 PM to 7:00 AM, at the United Box Board Company in Thomson, about two miles north of the village. Ralphie, awakened by his father's departure for work, climbed the stairs and nestled in at the foot of his mother's bed. His younger brother, Michael, was already lying beside their mom, 26-year-old Mary Pelaccia, both of them fast asleep. The dim light of a single kerosene lamp flickered across the room as little Ralphie dozed off once again.

At about 2:00 AM, he was awakened by noises in the room. The shadowy figure of a man stood near the head of the bed, beside his mother. A club was in the man's raised hand, and Ralphie watched in horror as it was repeatedly slammed with great force upon Mary's head. The young boy's great fear turned to hysteria, and as he watched the intruder depart through the bedroom window, Ralphie fainted dead away.

At about 7:15 AM, Sandy Pelaccia returned home from work, noticing right away that something seemed amiss. Both the front door and kitchen door were locked, forcing him to climb through a rear window to gain access to the house.

In the bedroom, the kerosene lamp was dark, but the light of morning revealed a horrifying, unimaginable scene. Mary Pelaccia lay nude upon the bed, her head apparently beaten to a bloody pulp with the club lying near her body. Protruding sideways near the club's end was a nail, intended to amplify the terrible damage from multiple blows. Blood and hair clung to the instrument of death.

Beside Mary, mercifully still asleep, was two-year-old Michael. Seated at the foot of the bed, wide-eyed and paralyzed with fear, was Ralphie.

When he was finally able to speak, the young boy told in one simple phrase what he had witnessed:

> George was in the house and hit mama on the head with a stick, and then got out through the window.

Authorities were summoned to analyze the scene and investigate the crime, but Sandy Pelaccia was confident that he already knew what had transpired. Having long been acquainted with the "George" his son had mentioned, he was certain of the killer's identity.

Boarding with families of the same nationality was a common practice among immigrants, and the Pelaccias had taken in two such boarders, Andrew Tomassi (Americanized to Tomason), 31, and George Constanzo (Americanized to Constance), 37, both of whom were co-workers of Sandy's at the mill in Thomson.

Little Ralphie's mention of George referred to Constanzo, who had caused problems in the Pelaccia household by pursuing Mary amorously on several occasions. At one point, Sandy evicted Constanzo, but eventually allowed him to return. When it happened again, including physical molestation, George was sent packing for good. They remained acquaintances, if for no other reason than they worked together. Immigrants often had few housing options, and George was allowed to room at the house of Mary's parents, about a mile away.

About two months after he was kicked out, Constanzo attended a local party welcoming a neighbor's wife on her arrival from Italy. The Pelaccias and several other Italians were also present. By 10:30 PM, several of the men left for their night-shift jobs at the Thomson mill. Sandy Pellacia went home to change his clothes for work, but heard Constanzo say, "I can't go to work tonight. I have some other business on my mind."

Nine hours later, Mary Pelaccia was found murdered, and George had disappeared from Schuylerville. It wasn't hard to put two and two together. But it *was* hard to locate Constanzo. He was nowhere to be found in the Schuylerville area. A complete description of the fugitive was circulated to surrounding cities

> **SCHUYLERVILLE WOMAN MURDERED IN HER OWN HOME**
>
> Husband Returns From Work to Find Wife Lying Dead Near Blood-Stained Club.

and towns, but Constanzo had done a good job of making himself scarce. It was also discovered that just prior to the murder, George had withdrawn from the bank his entire savings account, $100 ($1000 in 2012).

For Sandy Pelaccia, life would never be the same. The family dynamic, so important among Italian immigrants, was destroyed, leaving him unable to care for the children while maintaining employment. The two boys moved in with their grandparents (Mary's parents, Mr. and Mrs. Joseph DeFabio of Schuylerville), where they could be raised in a family atmosphere. In the years to follow, tragedy again struck when young Michael accidentally drowned in the barge canal.

Eventually, Sandy went to New York City, seeking work and perhaps a new lease on life. Time passed, and fall 1930 marked the tenth anniversary of Mary Pelaccia's murder. By then, Ralph had grown into a young man of fifteen, still living with his grandparents, and Sandy remained in New York City, managing to survive the first year of what would become known as the Great Depression.

On November 9, ten years and six weeks after his wife's death, Sandy Pelaccia was silently perusing the offerings in a city shoe store, when a casual glance at another customer froze him in his tracks. The man bore a strong resemblance to an unforgettable figure from his past. Could it be that in a huge city of more than seven million residents, George Constanzo was shopping in the very same store?

Impossible, sure, but he couldn't shake the feeling. As the man left the store, Sandy followed him into the street and called out George's name. There was no response, but at that point, it no longer mattered. Pelaccia broke into action, running Constanzo down and attempting to wrestle him to the ground. A nearby police officer rushed towards the commotion.

While struggling to restrain his captive, Sandy told the officer that Constanzo was wanted for an upstate murder. George claimed to have no idea who Pelaccia was, and in response to further questions, said he had never set foot in either Schuylerville or Saratoga County.

The officer, affected by Sandy's passion and sincerity, made a critical decision, detaining George while efforts were made to determine the truth. Subsequent investigation, including contact with Saratoga authorities, confirmed that the murder of Mary Pelaccia had never been solved, and that George Constanzo, the only suspect, had vanished.

Despite protesting that his surname was Gallinelli, George was taken north to Ballston Spa and brought before Town Justice Wendell Townley

> **George Constanzo Will Stand Trial Monday for Woman's Murder in 1920**
>
> New York Man Is Charged with Killing Mrs. Mary Palaccia in Schuylerville More Than 10 Years Ago—Justice Brewster to Preside
>
> DEATH PENALTY IF CONVICTED

> **Arrest Man For Murder 10 Years Ago**
>
> Husband of Dead Woman Recognizes Alleged Killer in New York City

on charges of vagrancy, to which he pleaded guilty. Townley sentenced him to ten days in the county jail, allowing local authorities time to revive the decade-old case and determine if they had the right man.

While George was held in custody, he maintained that he had never been to Saratoga County. But Mrs. Angeline Macero, Mary Pelaccia's sister, visited the jail, viewed an inmate lineup, and confirmed his identity.

After a decade of freedom, George Constanzo was indicted by the grand jury on a charge of first-degree murder. At his arraignment, Constanzo entered a plea of not guilty, fully cognizant that conviction carried the death penalty. The trial was set for January, but was delayed until March 30, 1931, allowing time for the return of the district attorney, John B. Smith, who was familiar with the particulars of the case.

The line of questioning pursued during jury selection indicated the prosecution would rely heavily on the testimony of fifteen-year-old Ralph Pelaccia, who had witnessed the crime as a four-year-old boy. After two days, a jury was seated, and Sante Pelaccia, along with his extended family, began reliving the nightmare of more than a decade ago. Ralph's well-being was of particular concern as the coroner, the undertaker, a town physician, and the constable offered explicit accounts of the grisly crime scene and his mother's wounds.

The weapon was described as a solid piece of wood about two and a half feet long and two inches square, with a nail protruding near one end. Dr. Edward Callahan testified that the cause of death was a fractured skull, resulting from a beating with a club, leaving the right side and top of Mary's head crushed, and the "brain protruding from the skull."

Constable Harold Myers, who had been summoned to the Pelaccia home within minutes of when Mary was found dead, described the scene:

> ... lying on her back on a bed in a bedroom on the second floor, her head battered in, and the bed clothing pushed to the foot of the bed, and the body nude.

Mary's parents, the DeFabios, took the stand and claimed that in front of three other witnesses, Constanzo had threatened to kill their daughter if she didn't repay ten dollars she owed him. The comment was made, they said, just three days before her murder.

Investigators testified to what they had learned about Constanzo's whereabouts following the murder. After draining his bank account, he had gone to Saratoga, and then to Portland, Maine. When he finally settled in New York City and found employment, George assumed the alias Fred DeRuga, "because it was shorter than Constanzo," as he put it. In his pocket at the time of his arrest, officers found an employment slip bearing the DeRuga name.

Although George claimed innocence, no alibi was offered. His principal defense was the suggestion that many fights had occurred between the Pelaccias and their boarders, and that any of the people involved had motive enough to kill Mary.

The strongest move on Constanzo's behalf was an aggressive effort to ban Ralph Pelaccia from the witness stand. The defense attorneys claimed that Ralph's age at the time of the murder would have rendered him "incompetent to testify." Therefore, he should likewise be declared incompetent ten years later.

It was a strong argument, but Judge O. (Osceola) Byron Brewster addressed the issue by performing a cursory examination of Ralph to determine his capabilities. In the judge's estimation, the fifteen-year-old, doing well in his first year in high school, fully understood the gravity of taking a legal oath and testifying honestly. The motion to bar Ralph from the witness stand was denied.

After the teenager described the gruesome story as he remembered it, the

---

TESTIMONY MAY START TODAY IN BALLSTON COURT

State Claims Defendant Attacked and Killed Woman at Schuylerville 10 Years Ago

HER YOUNG SON WITNESS

Youth Who Lay Beside Mother When She Was Killed Will Take Stand defense, as promised, went to the attack, disparaging his memory of events a decade ago. Efforts were made to upset and confuse him, but Ralph simply stuck to his story. When he stated that it was the defendant he saw at the head of his mother's bed, Judge Brewster turned to him and again asked, "Now, are you sure that was George Constanzo you saw there?" There was no delay in the reply: "Yes, sir."

The judge then asked how he had come to know Constanzo. Ralph said he had seen him once before, when George came to the house, looking for Mary. Ralph had answered the door, telling Constanzo that she wasn't home, when his mother was, in fact, in another part of the house.

The defense emphasized that Ralph was barely four years old at the time, and that the murder had happened more than ten years earlier. They added that the child's identification of the killer was based solely on the man's general facial characteristics—yet Ralph had failed to notice or recall a prominent scar on Constanzo's face.

The Judge pressed further. "Do you think you might be mistaken as to who that man was that night in your mother's bedroom?"

"No, I don't believe I could be mistaken."

"When you saw George, was there a light in the room?"

"Yes sir."

Brewster questioned him further, and a vigorous cross-examination by the defense followed, but Ralph remained firm in his answers.

George's attorneys called Mrs. Nicholas Sullivan, who said the Pelaccias and Constanzo seemed friendly with each other at the party held just hours before the murder, a sentiment confirmed by others. Mrs. Seri Petrolio, who lived in the other half of the tenement, added that she heard nothing unusual that night from the Pelaccia household. While that may have been true, its value wasn't clear. Whether or not there was noise, there was no denying that Mary had been murdered that night.

Several others took the stand, most of them testifying through an interpreter. But at the end of the day, there was no denying it: Ralph Pelaccia

Prosecution Rests in Murder Trial

RALPH PALACCIA, SON OF MURDERED WOMAN, IDENTIFIES CONSTANZO

Fifteen-year-old Youth Tells Court and Jurors He Was Awakened by Noise and Saw Defendant—Deputy Sheriff Testifies had been the star witness for the prosecution.

Final summations were offered on the morning of Friday, April 3, the trial's fifth day. The defense again focused on attacking the testimony of Ralph, for reasons stated earlier. By 2:00 PM, the jury began deliberating.

After a few breaks to receive further instructions from the Court, the jury emerged after nearly ten hours, informing the judge that they were deadlocked—eight voted for first-degree manslaughter, while four opted for acquittal. Brewster told them to continue deliberating, but he eventually was forced to declare a mistrial. A re-trial was set for early June.

On June 8, 1921, for the second time in recent months, George Constanzo, 49, stood before Judge Brewster on charges of first-degree murder. But there would be no second trial. His offer of a guilty plea to first-degree manslaughter was accepted. At long last, nearly eleven years after his mother's murder, Ralph Pelaccia's memories of that horrible night had been confirmed.

On the following morning, the judge passed sentence, imprisoning the defendant for a shorter period than expected, considering the brutality of the crime and the killer's status as a fugitive for more than a decade. Brewster cited mitigating factors in his decision, including the young age of the principal prosecution witness.

Other influences on the Court's ruling remained confidential, but surprisingly, he referred to Constanzo's state of mind at the time of the killing. Since the murder happened two months after his removal from the home, it wasn't clear why it was acceptable for Constanzo to have been in such a high state of agitation.

> The sentence the court feels itself obliged to pronounce in your case is to outward appearances disproportionate to the grade of the crime whereof you have been convicted by the allowance of your plea. Especially is this true in view of the atrociousness and brutality of the act that apparently caused the death of the deceased. I do not feel at liberty to announce now fully the reasons that have caused the permission of your plea, and results in the sentence to be pronounced.
>
> The long lapse of time since the commission of the crime; the difficulty met with in the proof thereof; the extraordinary situation presented with reference to a pivotal witness for the prosecution on account of non-age; the result of the first trial, and the study which has been

made of you, as associated with the acts, which stamp you as having been under the influence of an overpowering emotion, and which indicates that, while probably you were legally sane, yet another personality so possessed you as to explain somewhat the fiendish maniacal character of your act.

All this and other considerations are answerable for your conviction of the lesser degree of homicide than that charged, and partially explains the sentence of this

> **Manslaughter Plea Entered By Constanzo**
>
> Prevents Necessity of Second Trial on Charge of Slaying Schuylerville Woman

court, which is that you be confined in Clinton Prison in Dannemora, at hard labor, for an indeterminate period, the minimum of which shall be not less than five years and the maximum not more than ten years.

Constanzo's crimes included breaking and entering; terrorizing a young child; brutally murdering a young woman; fleeing successfully as a fugitive for ten years; changing his name to avoid capture; lying to investigators about his past in Saratoga County; and putting the county through the cost of a trial before admitting his guilt.

Five to ten years hardly seemed enough.

9

A Murder Victim Goes to Court

The jury and spectators were treated to a full view of King's face and his scalp, revealing the extreme damage caused by the hatchet attack.

Among the front-page items to appear in the March 21, 1913, edition of the *Essex County Republican* was a report that William King of Crown Point had been struck and killed by a passing train. The article corrected a rumor circulating a day earlier that the village had witnessed its third murder in the past three months.

The accident report was a terrible story, but not terribly uncommon. Hundreds of North Country residents had been killed in similar mishaps.

Initial reports said that King "was found lying beside the D&H tracks Thursday morning, decapitated." He had been seen drinking during the previous evening, and it was concluded that King had been walking along the tracks and was struck by a train, or was perhaps in such a drunken stupor that he lay on the rails and suffered the horrible consequences.

The body was discovered at around midnight by local resident James Wolcott, who reported the find to the telegraph operator. After returning to view the scene, about a quarter mile north of the Crown Point station, the two men summoned the coroner.

The following day, as word spread, a number of residents visited the site, commiserating over the loss of a local citizen and lamenting the high death toll caused by the abuse of alcohol. The coroner suggested that foul play might have been involved in King's death, an idea scoffed at by locals. King's affinity for alcohol was well known, and residents had no desire to see Crown Point's reputation further sullied by another homicide.

Four days after the initial fatality report, an entirely new version of the story revealed that King's death was anything but an accident. After the coroner's autopsy findings were finalized, a full confession had been obtained from a local man, Fred Crossman. King's death had been correctly linked to alcohol, but his end was even more gruesome than the earlier report of decapitation by train.

The investigation revealed that a few gallons of whiskey had arrived by train for Silas Stafford, and the trio of Stafford, Fred Crossman, and William King had repaired to an old houseboat that had been pulled ashore. (The old boat was known to locals as "the shanty.") The three men proceeded to imbibe heavily and were soon thoroughly intoxicated.

It was believed that Crossman had planned the gathering, for there had been bad blood between him and King for some time. Having once lost a fight to King, Fred had sworn on several occasions that he would one day get revenge. March 19, 1913, turned out to be that day.

According to Crossman, angry words were spoken between the two men. King then struck him across the head, knocking him backwards against a wall. The two exchanged blows, eventually crashing into furniture and tumbling to the floor. Crossman managed to get King in a chokehold and used his free hand to rain blows on King's face. Finally, warning his captive to behave once he was set free, Crossman released his grip.

The men rose to their feet, and King stormed from the houseboat.

That could have been the end of it, but it wasn't. Crossman's signed statement revealed the grisly details of what happened next. After telling Stafford he was going to "finish the job," he exited the shanty, grabbed a short-handled, single-bit axe (hatchet), and began following King, who was walking along the railroad tracks.

Coming upon him from behind, Crossman swung the blunt side of the hatchet heavily against the side of King's face, knocking him to the ground. Billy screamed for him to stop, but Crossman inflicted several blows to the head with the hatchet blade and then left King for dead. Returning to the shanty, where Silas Stafford was asleep, Crossman went to bed.

In the morning, he and Stafford awoke early and decided to get more rum from Vermont. Before rowing across the lake, they encountered a local man, Charlie Wolcott, who informed them that Billy King was dead. The two men went to view the body along the railroad tracks, and Stafford then headed for the lakeshore to borrow a boat for the trip to Vermont.

Crossman, who had returned to the shanty to wait for Stafford, noticed some congealed blood on the hatchet. Using an old rag, he wiped it clean, and then joined Stafford in crossing the lake to Vermont, where they shared several more drinks.

The weary Stafford, still well under the influence of so much alcohol, went to sleep, only to be shaken awake later by Fred Crossman. Although they were hardly in a sober state, the two men talked about King's death. Stafford vaguely promised to speak in Fred's defense should any suspicions arise about his involvement. Comfortable in having secured an alibi, Crossman then returned alone to Crown Point.

Arriving back at the shanty, Fred was told by a neighbor he should "skidoo" because the authorities were looking for him, but his reply was, "I ain't done nothin' to skidoo for." Noting that he was still "pretty drunk and tired," Crossman went inside and slept. Shortly after, both he and Stafford were arrested and held in jail, pending the results of the coroner's inquest.

Those were the facts of the story as sworn to in a confession bearing Fred Crossman's signature. As ugly as it all sounded, the coroner's reconstruction of the crime, based on available evidence, was much worse. Crossman's seemingly graphic description was apparently the toned-down version of events.

According to the coroner, the initial blow with the hatchet's blunt end had fractured King's skull. The "three or four blows" Crossman said he made with the hatchet's blade were somewhat of an understatement. The coroner reported a dozen cuts on King's scalp. The victim also had a shattered shoulder, an injury that occurred after his death. It was presumed to have been caused when the body was struck by a passing train.

Although serious wounds had accumulated from the beating, the choking, and more than a dozen blows with the hatchet, the coroner ruled that none of those injuries had caused Billy King's death.

His demise, instead, had resulted from internal injuries, the worst of which were five broken ribs, a ruptured kidney, and a ruptured spleen. Those wounds and other internal damage were caused by Crossman's boots when, after beating King with the hatchet, he jumped heavily on the man's prostrate body. He then laid King's corpse on or near the rails, in a position he felt would suggest the man had been struck by a passing train.

That final step appeared to have been a gross miscalculation on Crossman's part, for the body was found very close to the rails. The impact from a train would surely have caused any object to be cast some distance away. With suspicions raised by the location of the body, the coroner had begun to look for other potential causes of King's many cuts and bruises.

The trail eventually led investigators to Fred Crossman. Following the coroner's report, the investigation, and the confession, Crossman was charged with first-degree murder, while Stafford was released on bond as a material witness.

First-degree murder carried a penalty of death, and to avoid that fate, Crossman needed help. He enlisted the aid of former District Attorney Patrick J. Finn to present his defense. Finn was already a busy man, having been retained by two other Crown Point residents who had recently been charged with murder.

An unrelated occurrence brought further pain to the King family just two weeks after William's death, when the body of his brother, George, was found floating in Lake Champlain. George had disappeared five months earlier while fishing. No one knew for sure what had happened to him, but suspicions that he had drowned were confirmed when his decomposed body surfaced in the lake.

> **JURY PANEL FOR A MURDER CASE**
>
> Crossman to Be Tried at Elizabethtown September 29
>
> **ACCUSED OF KILLING WM. KING WITH AXE**
>
> FIRST WHIPPED HIS VICTIM IN A FIGHT AND THEN PURSUED HIM TO HIS DEATH IS ALLEGATION

Due to the unusually busy court schedule addressing multiple murder cases, Crossman's trial was delayed until the fall. On Monday, September 29, jury selection began at 1:00 PM. By Wednesday night at 11:00 PM, the entire trial was over.

Among the evidence presented were two signed confessions that clearly stated Crossman's guilt and were overwhelmingly damning in their content. The defense also presented a shocking, attention-grabbing exhibit—William King's head. The jury and spectators were treated to a full view of King's face and his scalp, revealing the extreme damage caused by the hatchet attack. Of all the morbid court moments in New York State history, the appearance of the murder victim's head six months after his demise surely ranks near the top of the list.

After two days of testimony, the jury concluded deliberations within six hours, but confusion arose momentarily when their findings were declared in court. The foreman responded to the judge's usual query with the word, "Guilty," and it was assumed the crime was first-degree murder. A polling of the jury revealed they had opted for second-degree murder, convicting the defendant, but saving him from execution.

The following morning, Crossman was sentenced to an indeterminate life term, with the possibility of parole after twenty years. He was hustled off to Dannemora, while Finn, dissatisfied with the decision, served notice that an appeal would be filed.

It was more than a year later that Finn, assisted by attorney Harry Owen of Port Henry, began to make some headway in his quest for a new trial. By January 1915, the case had reached the Appellate Division of the New York State Supreme Court. Finn and Owens' strongest argument was that Crossman's confessions had been obtained using "third-degree tactics." The confessions were the predominant factor in his conviction. The defending lawyers contended that, since coercion was used, the confessions should not have been admitted as evidence.

Bolstering their case was one other very important fact: the only witness to the events leading up to King's death, Silas Stafford, had not been called upon to testify. Although he had been held as a material witness, Stafford was suddenly released by District Attorney Fred LaDuke just prior to the commencement of the trial, and was subsequently unavailable to appear on the witness stand.

The appeal case languished in the higher courts until September 1918, by which time Crossman had served five years in prison. Arguments were presented before a panel of judges, and in early December, the appellate court rule, 3–2, that Crossman should receive "a new trial, or such other proceedings as should be deemed proper."

Supreme Court Justice John Kellogg, who wrote the opinion, was deeply disturbed by the handling of both Crossman and Stafford as suspects. Having been drinking and carousing for two days,

Murder victim William King was the star witness at the trial of his accused killer

both men were already in very poor physical and mental condition when they were arrested. (Had they been in normal condition, their treatment after being arrested would still have been unacceptable and illegal, according to Kellogg.)

Once they were in custody, the two men were kept awake for three nights and two full days and underwent frequent, intense interrogation. A confession was prepared for Crossman. He finally broke down, signed it, and asked what would become of him. Judge Kellogg said that Crossman's question indicated he was not made fully aware of the consequences of signing the confession.

Jurors viewed the victim's skull, which was battered and bruised from multiple hatchet wounds

The judge also expressed outrage at the actions of local officials:

> ... taken from the jail illegally, and to enable the detective to force from him a confession. ... We must conclude that the district attorney and the coroner were parties to the illegal act. Certainly the detective was acting for the district attorney, and was engaged by him for the purpose of extorting a confession from the defendant and Stafford. The defendant swears that the detective visited him frequently, using threats and coarse and brutal language to him, demanding in various forms that he admit that he killed the man. Defendant always protested his innocence.

Having studied all the evidence and listened to hours of testimony, the justices announced, with great dismay, what they deemed to be the true story: King was most likely killed in the fight inside the shanty. But if that case had been presented in court by the district attorney, Crossman might well have claimed self-defense, with the potential result of no punishment.

Instead, a story was concocted (possibly by police, the DA, and the coroner, acting together), claiming that Crossman won the fistfight, and then followed King nine hundred feet down the rail line, where he attacked and killed him. In legal terms, that made it a case of premeditated murder.

The judges instead found it entirely logical that Crossman's reaction to killing King in the boathouse would have been to somehow conceal his role in the crime. That end was achieved by placing the victim's body on the railroad tracks, making it appear that his death resulted from being struck by the train. While noting "it may be that the defendant committed the crime," the justices stood strong behind the principles of American law:

> It is desirable that real criminals should be convicted. It is undesirable that the officers of the law should become criminals in trying to punish crime. It is better for the public welfare that a criminal escape punishment than that punishment should follow such illegal and high-handed action upon the part of the district attorney and his agent, the detective.
>
> ... We think it is evident that this confession was procured by threats of bodily harm, and by actual bodily harm and ill usage of the defendant, and by the promise of the district attorney, made through the detective, his agent, that if defendant would admit the murder, it would be treated as an accident and not a crime.
>
> Aside from the confession, it is difficult to say that the evidence shows that the crime of murder was committed. Upon the evidence, we are satisfied that the guilt of the defendant has not been proved beyond a reasonable doubt, and that justice requires a new trial.
>
> The conviction should therefore be reversed, upon the law and facts, and the defendant returned to the custody of the sheriff of Essex County, there to await trial or such further proceeding in this matter as may be proper.

CROSSMAN SECURES A NEW TRIAL

Alleged Crown Point Murderer Taken From Clinton Prison to Elizabethtown

---

KELLOGG'S DECISION IN CROSSMAN CASE

Judge Kellogg Says Crown Point Man Was Forced Into Making Confession

In early May 1919, Fred Crossman stood once more before Judge Borst. The district attorney who prosecuted the original case had since died. Both the new district attorney and Judge Borst were privy to the facts of the case after it had been completely re-investigated, and without the forced confessions.

It was found that William King had been killed in a drunken fight, and he had been the aggressor. The new district attorney, O. Byron Brewster, put it none too delicately:

> I am convinced that the confessions in question were partly untrue. Facts which were not developed upon the former trial, and which I dare say are not in the possession of the defendant's counsel, have come to me which impel the belief that this defendant did kill King. However, the killing resulted from a drunken row in the close quarters of the small fishing shanty; and in the altercation and conflict which led up to the killing, I believe that King was the aggressor.
>
> The traits and habits of the two men point to that, as well as other things. Crossman's one vice at that time was intemperance; King, on the other hand, was a man of ungovernable temper and quarrelsome nature. I believe that in his debauched and drunken condition, King brought on the fight, and this resulted in his being killed on the floor of the fishing shanty.
>
> After that had taken place, the enormity of the affair dawned upon this defendant, and he and his companion [Stafford] carried the body to the place by the railroad track where it was found, as developed on the former trial. ... I believe that, while this defendant killed King, that the homicide did not rise to the degree of murder or manslaughter.

Judge Borst was of like mind:

> In view of what I have learned, I am satisfied that the statement that the DA has so frankly and candidly made, is correct. That King was killed in beyond denial, and that you are connected with the killing, and that thereafter, acting naturally as a human being would act when frightened, the body was removed and placed along

the railroad track, but that the killing was done in the shanty. That, I am satisfied, is the correct statement of facts connected with your case.

King was of a quarrelsome nature, as the district attorney states, and as I am advised by other people who have interested themselves in your behalf. The result of the quarrel between you and him resulted in a struggle there, and a fight, and the death of King.

You were directly connected with the taking of the life of a human being. You have suffered and have atoned to the extent that you have been incarcerated for something over six years; you have suffered that punishment, and as you look back at it now, you can see that it all is the result of a drunken row. If you had remained sober, you undoubtedly never would have been connected with the offense, and King would undoubtedly be alive today.

It is a terrible thing to take the life of a human being, especially a man who is so ill-fitted to pass from earth to his Maker as was King, but I am satisfied that there is an element which mitigates against what was done, in your favor, and that is the element of self-defense.

None of us except yourself will ever know absolutely as to just the occurrences there, but many things point to the fact that the statements made by the district attorney here are correct. From what I know of the case and from what I have been advised, I am going to accept the statement of the district attorney.

… You are a strong, healthy man, and you are still in the prime of life, with great opportunities before you. You have suffered; that should be a lesson to you. I will accept the suggestion of the district attorney to suspend sentence upon you, which means that you will be at liberty to go and remain at large, so long as you behave yourself.

The condition that I suggest is this: that you drink no intoxicating liquor of any kind during the present year.

Crossman was released from jail and returned to civilian life. Three years later, he married and began raising a family (three children survived and two died in infancy).

In 1949, thirty years after regaining his freedom, Fred Crossman, 79, died at the Moses-Ludington Hospital in Ticonderoga.

10

A Delayed Murder?

Did a murder victim die more than eight years after the execution of his killer?

Charles Arthur Duffy of Chateaugay in northern Franklin County was an all-round good guy. Encapsulating his life into snippets of accomplishments, deeds, and significant events provides plenty of supporting evidence.

Arthur, as he was known, was born in August 1894 to a Vermont mom, Agnes, and an Irish immigrant dad, Edward, who found success as a local merchant and was widely known in the community.

Young Arthur was an excellent student, and athletically talented as well. In summer 1905, just a week before his eleventh birthday, he was among a group of boys having a good time at "the old swimming hole" on the Marble River. When seven-year-old Willie Hill was victimized by cramps and sank out of sight, Duffy swam to help, eventually bringing Willie ashore. Although the incident ended sadly when Willie failed to revive, the selfless act of rescue was a clear reflection of Duffy's character.

After graduating from Chateaugay High School, he attended Holy Cross Preparatory School in Worcester, Massachusetts, for one year, and in 1918 graduated from Catholic University in Washington, D.C., where he served as senior class president. Following two years as an instructor in the Naval Reserves at Hampton Roads, Virginia, he returned to Chateaugay and was elected chairman of the committee charged with creating a new branch of the American Legion, the John E. Harrica Post. As an active member of the Knights of Columbus, he assumed a leading role in organizing a K of C's baseball league.

In 1920, he married Evelyn Hackett, a Chateaugay schoolteacher. Following a wedding trip to Montreal about fifty miles north, they moved into a home in Chateaugay village. Arthur Junior was born a year later.

In 1922, Chateaugay lamented its loss when Arthur moved to Malone, where he and a cousin, Francis J. Duffy, took over the family's prosperous clothing store. While expanding the business, Arthur was very active in the community, organizing sports leagues, running for local political office, and generally taking a leadership role. In every way imaginable, he was a good citizen.

It was about as clean a life as one could live. How, then, in 1925, did Arthur Duffy become a key player in the first nightclub murder in Montreal's history?

It happened innocently enough during a mid-summer trip to the city with his cousin, William Fay. At about 1:00 AM on July 23, they entered the Dreamland Cabaret for a wedding-related party. Within minutes of their arrival, two uninvited men walked in. One of them brandished a gun and fired several shots into the floor. That got everyone's attention.

Patrons were ordered to raise their hands and line up along the walls. A waiter was enlisted to quickly collect all the valuables in the room. As the thieves were backing out of the room to leave, a visiting musician entered and strolled across the floor, unaware that anything was amiss until one of the burglars took aim and fired, hitting him in the stomach.

As Donald Carragher crumpled to the floor, badly wounded, Arthur Duffy couldn't take it anymore: he had to act. Grabbing a chair, he picked it up and threw it at the robber, who instantly fired into Duffy's face and fled into the street.

The bullet entered Arthur's cheek, missed the jawbone, and either exited at the base of his skull or became lodged there. Although he should have been dead, he didn't even miss a day's work. Both of the injured men were taken to Montreal General Hospital, but Duffy, unflustered and feeling fine except for the cheek wound, returned to Malone and was operating the store as usual on Thursday morning.

Carragher was not so fortunate. Surgery was performed, but the internal damage was severe, and he died seven days later. At that point, the robbery and assault case became a murder case, prompting a manhunt.

Although the name of the accomplice was unknown, the shooter was identified as Joseph Mauro, known to have used the aliases Joseph Fraust and Ernest Bizanti in northern New York. Mauro had once served prison time at Elmira for burglaries committed in Niagara Falls.

Montreal police provided circulars to lawmen across the North Country, and detectives pursued multiple leads. Persistence paid off, and within a few months, the fugitive was captured in British Columbia on

A Delayed Murder?

Canada's west coast, three thousand miles from Montreal. At the time of his arrest, Mauro did apologize for one thing, telling the detective he was sorry for not having killed Duffy.

Four months after the shooting, Arthur Duffy and William Fay returned to Montreal and testified in one of the shortest murder trials in Quebec annals—just three hours long. The jury was likewise speedy, reaching a guilty verdict in twenty-five minutes. Without delay, Mauro was sentenced to hang, and on February 19, 1926, he was executed at Bordeaux Jail in Montreal.

Arthur Duffy returned to his previously idyllic life, but in March 1928, tragedy struck when Evelyn died of pneumonia. In the following year, he remarried, taking Lucille Murchard as his second wife. She later gave birth to Arthur's second son (he also gained a stepson through the marriage).

After the partnership with his cousin was dissolved, Arthur moved to Rochester, but returned to operate Duffy Brothers Department Store in Chateaugay. He was very active in promoting the business and expanding its offerings, but in the fall of that same year, he began struggling with illness. Always healthy, strong, and athletic, Arthur was suddenly housebound for two weeks with unusual symptoms. The onset of powerful, debilitating headaches forced him to seek expert help at the Royal Victoria Hospital in Montreal. A series of X-rays revealed a brain tumor, and surgery was deemed necessary.

> **Mauro Hanged in City of Montreal**

Six hours into the operation, he expired. Doctors said the large tumor had been growing for a decade or more. Coincidentally or not, it was ten years earlier that Mauro had killed Carragher and shot Duffy in the face. Anecdotal evidence suggests that the bullet remained in his head all those years, but no official record provides confirmation.

It was odd enough that Arthur Duffy lived in Chateaugay, but was shot in Montreal and died in Montreal, particularly when the two events were separated by nine years. It was also highly unusual to have been shot

> **C. ARTHUR DUFFY OF CHATEAUGAY DIES IN MONTREAL**

> **Died Nine Years After Being Shot**

nearly point-blank in the face and returned to work just hours later.

If Arthur's untimely death was due to complications from the long-ago shooting, he was actually a homicide victim (there are many similar instances on record).

And if that was the case, the murderer, Mauro, was executed more than eight years before the death of his second victim.

11

Decades of Depravity

> In Glens Falls ... this murder occurred ... in a section of the city in which saloons and houses of prostitution are plentiful, and these places are frequented by only low-lived, degenerate, depraved persons, who have no respect for their character or the laws of God or society.

Select details of a person's history can be revealing, especially when viewed in perspective. Take the case of Warren County's Beecher Faber. He was known to have tortured and killed animals; frequented local saloons; was a heavy user of alcohol, cocaine, and morphine; and spent periods of confinement in various institutions in Warren County, Washington County, Rochester, Albany, Elmira, and Dannemora.

That's quite the resumé, but add one more fact to put it all in perspective: Faber accomplished all that and more before his twenty-second birthday. And he would do plenty more in the years to come.

Attorneys who defended him for various crimes as an adult pointed to an incident from Faber's youth (he was accidentally struck in the head by an axe) that led to his "disability," which manifested itself in constant criminal activity. Others—some who knew him, and some who pursued justice for his crimes—said he was just a bad seed.

Beecher was born in Glens Falls on July 10, 1878, one of Joseph and Matilda Faber's ten children. Records indicate that when the Fabers married, Matilda was between 11 and 14 years old (early documents give her age as 12 when her first child was born).

By the age of ten, Beecher had already been in plenty of trouble for lying, stealing, and a host of other offenses, the worst of which was torturing and killing cats and gouging their eyes out. "Worst" is subjective, of course. For his parents, the last straw came when he set fire to the family home, at which point they relinquished all hope of controlling his behavior.

That offense at the age of twelve landed him in the Rochester

Industrial School (reform school) for four years. Release from Rochester was obtained through rehabilitation, but when he was freed after four years, Beecher hadn't changed, returning to a life of crime without missing a beat. He was finally caught robbing a milk peddler and sentenced to three months in the Albany Penitentiary.

Immediately after release from Albany, he was arrested for petty larceny and sentenced to thirty days in the Warren County jail. Shortly after being freed, Faber was incarcerated again for another crime. He broke the lock, escaped his jail cell, and hid in a nearby room, where he was recaptured, leading to potential grand jury charges for escape. In the meantime, he was again released, whereupon he robbed a patron in a local bar and was locked up again.

When the grand jury indictment was confirmed, he submitted a plea of guilty in July 1897 (two days after his eighteenth birthday) and was sentenced to three months in the county jail. About a month after his release, Beecher teamed up with a partner in robbing a local real estate office and a grocery story. Uncertain that the charges would stick, local lawmen held the pair on vagrancy charges, for which a judge sentenced them to four months in the Albany Penitentiary.

If ever an individual appeared to be pure, unadulterated trouble, it was surely Beecher Faber. He was well known to lawman and jailkeepers across the region. By this time, he had already become a heavy drinker, and a drug user as well, particularly favoring morphine and cocaine.

In 1899, shortly after once again being released from Albany, Beecher and a partner stole gum, candy, and canned goods from a grocery, and several valuable items, including silverware, from a trading-stamp store. A business office was also burglarized, and for lack of $1000 bail ($27,000 in 2012) the two men were confined to jail.

While incarcerated, his partner confessed. Two months later, several of the items, including the silver, were located and traced to the two men. Faber finally relented, admitting to the crimes. Both men entered guilty pleas in court and were sent to the Elmira Reformatory.

But for Faber, it was immaterial. By all previous indicators, the likelihood of his reforming was miniscule. After serving nearly two years at Elmira, Faber was set free just shy of his twenty-second birthday. He remained true to form, returning to a life of crime, but managed to avoid legal trouble for a few months.

In early November 1901, he and another man, carrying guns and plenty of cash, caused a ruckus at the Champlain Hotel in Fort Edward. After leaving the hotel bar, they were involved in a fight on a nearby bridge, during which several shots were fired in the direction of the hotel.

A month later, Faber entered the same hotel and spoke confidentially to owner Thomas Garrigan, asking if he owned a gun. Beecher explained that he had scouted the local bank, and only one man was left on duty during lunchtime. With Garrigan's help, they could rob the bank and split the take. The oblivious citizenry would offer little resistance.

After listening, Garrigan became incensed, yelling at Faber to get out of his hotel. As he left, Beecher grabbed a pepper-sauce bottle and threw it at the man's head. Garrigan fired a beer glass in reply, striking Faber on the back of the neck. He departed, shouting a vow to soon return.

And he was good to his word. Beecher went down the street to the hardware store to purchase a revolver. The clerk handed him one for inspection, along with a box of cartridges, and Faber proceeded to load the gun. Then, when other customers entered the store, he sneaked out.

Walking to the canal bridge, he showed no regard for the men standing in front of Garrigan's and simply opened fire, taking four quick shots at the barroom door. He then calmly strolled to the nearby Adelphi Hotel, where he was arrested minutes later. Under questioning, and displaying his usual disregard for the law, Beecher told the sheriff he was a professional thief. He was jailed on assault charges: by sheer luck, no one had been struck, although he narrowly missed Garrigan.

In the Fort Edward village jail, while awaiting transfer to the Sandy Hill facility, he added to his criminal repertoire, committing arson by setting fire to the blankets and other materials in his cell.

Addressing the shooting incident at Garrigan's, the grand jury returned an indictment on first-degree assault charges. Despite a lengthy and varied criminal record, this was Beecher's first offense as an adult. But his reputation was widely known, and the days of reformatories and local jails were past. In late March 1902, Faber was sentenced to four and a half years at "Little Siberia," Dannemora's Clinton Prison.

In early 1906 he was released, and if consistency was a virtue, there was no doubt that Beecher Faber was heaven sent. On April 5, 1906, nearly four years to the day that his sentence began, Faber was the subject of a Glens Falls manhunt for stabbing a local man, Glen Bacon. The two had argued at a pair of local establishments, and with a head wound that was bleeding heavily, Bacon had gone to police and accused Faber of stabbing him (a doctor suggested it looked more like a blunt-force injury). Bacon was held on intoxication charges, but Beecher was still on the loose.

Within twenty-four hours, he was brought before a judge on charges of second-degree assault. A grand jury indictment followed, virtually ensuring Faber's return to prison, but he was eventually released on bail, and the case dragged on in local courts for more than six months.

Beecher, meanwhile, was a busy man, wooing a young girl from Fort Ann. Edna Nelson, 19, had left home to work for what she called a prominent Glens Falls family. From "prominent" to Faber's lifestyle was a huge stretch, but Edna became the focus of his attentions, and whatever criteria she might have had for a mate, Faber somehow fit the bill. Against the wishes of her parents, the two were married.

That marriage license was Edna's ticket to the seedy side of life. She soon found herself with steady alternative employment: Beecher became her pimp, selling her wares to all takers. On several occasions shortly after their wedding, Edna was arrested for prostitution (the official charge was "being a disorderly person").

Meanwhile, Faber's latest case, (the stabbing of Glen Bacon in April 1906) had languished in court for some time. Finally, frustrated by the lack of clear evidence, the district attorney moved for dismissal. But true to form and consistent to a fault, Beecher was back in court about a month later, in January 1907.

And this time he wasn't alone. Edna was again brought in on prostitution charges, much to the displeasure of Judge J. Edward Singleton, who had already handled many cases involving the Fabers. During her appearance, it was revealed that Edna's married life included beatings and forced prostitution by her husband. The court had heard enough, ordering Faber confined to the Albany Penitentiary.

Beecher was incensed at the punishment, and while exiting the courtroom, he physically attacked Singleton, vowing to kill him. The prisoner struck the first blow, but the judge, fully capable of handling himself, gave better than he got. Faber was soon on his way to familiar haunts in the Albany lockup.

Singleton, hoping to turn a young girl's life around, ordered Edna home to her parents, with a warning to stay away from Glens Falls. If she disobeyed and again appeared before the court, the judge promised her a three-year stint in the House of Refuge for Women in Albion, New York.

When Faber completed his sentence and was released, he immediately went after Edna, forcing her to return with him to Glens Falls, where they resumed their previous sordid activities. And soon enough, they found themselves right back in Glens Falls court.

In late July 1907, both he and Edna were at Halpin's saloon, plying their trade, when a disagreement resulted in the terrible beating of bar patron Morris Ryan, courtesy of Faber. After an all-night search, Beecher was arrested at his father's Crandall Street home. Edna's parents were notified, and both George, 64, and Ida, 52, showed up in court, pleading for mercy on her behalf. Both said they had no knowledge of their daughter's illegal activities until they were contacted by the court. They attributed most of her bad behavior to the influence and brutality of Beecher Faber.

The judge was sympathetic to their pleas. Retreating from his promise of three years at Albion for any further offenses, he instead sentenced Edna to one year at the House of the Good Shepherd in Albany. If she behaved for the first six months there, she would be freed early to return to her parents' home in Fort Ann. For her part, Edna, who had just turned twenty-two, promised to stay away from her friends in the underbelly of Glens Falls and to seek an annulment of her marriage.

And George Nelson, disgusted at what had become of Edna's life, told the court that Faber would one day regret mistreating his daughter.

Edna behaved as instructed and, in January 1908, was released to the custody of her parents. Faber, also out of jail, tried repeatedly to see her, but Edna rebuffed him. George Nelson notified local authorities of his son-in-law's presence, and in early February, when Faber went to Fort Ann to get Edna, police forced him to leave the village under threat of arrest.

Beecher left as ordered, but at the age of twenty-eight, and with nearly two decades of criminal activity under his belt, he wasn't about to turn over a new leaf. Returning to Glens Falls, he fumed over the problems with Edna, and ten days later, decided to act.

On Thursday, February 20, at 3:00 AM, he went to his brother's apartment and took a raincoat, $40 in cash, and a handgun. Before departing Glens Falls at 10:00 AM, Beecher showed his usual disregard for any legal consequences, boasting openly that he was heading to Fort Ann, and once there, he would kill the entire Nelson family. Coming from anyone else, it might have sounded like bravado, but from Faber, it was nothing but ominous, and altogether believable.

A short time later, after arriving in Fort Ann, he stopped to imbibe plenty of booze at a local hotel, where he further bragged of his mission before proceeding to the Nelson residence. George, Faber's father-in-law, refused to allow him inside, but Beecher forced his way into the home, took Edna upstairs, and locked the door. George called local lawmen.

Two constables soon arrived and, after assessing the situation, told Beecher to come out or they would break the door down. It was a tense situation, defused only when Faber relented and opened the door. But when the officers acted to place him under arrest, Beecher resisted, forcing them to subdue him.

Finally, with calm restored, the group headed for the front door. Then, without warning, Faber pulled out a revolver and turned, with the intention of shooting George Nelson. At sixty-five, Nelson was more than twice Beecher's age, but the old man was quick to react. Whipping his own gun quickly into position, he fired before Faber could get a shot off.

Beecher dropped, badly wounded. The bullet struck his shoulder, penetrated a lung, and lodged in his ribs. By the time they reached the sidewalk in front of the Nelson home, Faber was unconscious. A doctor was summoned to treat his injuries, and he was then placed on the noon train to Glens Falls.

Considering what Faber had put Edna through for the past few years, it could have been (and might well have been) a very satisfying moment for George Nelson. But good citizen that he was (and a victim of circumstances, as well), George turned himself in to the local justice of the peace, who release him, pending an assessment of Faber's injuries.

At about 4:00 PM, Beecher awakened in the hospital and gave police a statement, but his condition was failing. Doctors said that he was too weak for them to remove the bullet, and that either way, he was very unlikely to survive.

By midnight, his condition was listed as critical. Twenty-four hours

> **FABER RECEIVED WHAT HE COURTED**
>
> ---
>
> **Threatened Family and Was Shot Himself.**
>
> ---
>
> **VICTIM CANNOT RECOVER**
>
> ---
>
> Sensational Affray in Fort Ann—Man Attempts to Kill His Father-in-Law and is Shot by the Latter.

later, there was still no improvement—he remained conscious, but barely alive, prompting a media death watch with newspaper headlines like CANNOT SURVIVE and LINGERS AT DEATH'S DOOR.

Despite his condition, Beecher asked frequently for Edna to visit him. With all that had gone before, especially his terrible history with the Nelson family, it hardly seemed a possibility, even as a dying wish.

But Mrs. Beecher Faber did go to the hospital to see her husband, if nothing more than to spend his last moments with him. Within days, they reconciled, much to the horror of the Nelsons, although the news hardly seemed relevant in light of Beecher's impending death. But reconciliation wasn't the only big surprise for the troubled Nelson family. Faber, once written off as hopelessly injured, began showing signs of recovery. Edna announced she was moving back in with her husband once he was released from the hospital.

Against all odds, his condition continued improving, and a week later, Faber survived surgery to remove the bullet, which was found to have flattened against a rib. Edna roomed with relatives in Glens Falls so she could visit him daily.

The Fort Ann community was shocked when, on March 8, George Nelson was arrested and charged with first-degree assault for shooting his son-in-law. During his arraignment the next day, several witnesses testified to the public threats Faber had made against the Nelson family. Perhaps the most supportive comments came from none other than Edna Faber, who said the gun was accidentally discharged by her father due to nervousness in a very tense situation. Even more surprising, she reminded the court that Beecher had served time in Dannemora, and "was an all-round bad man" who had led her into the world of prostitution.

Justice Willard Robinson had heard enough. Faber's attorney argued that Nelson should be held for the grand jury, but Robinson rejected the plea with a stunning but highly praised comment as reported by the *Glens Falls Morning Star*:

> ... I ought to hold you for the grand jury because you *didn't* kill Faber.

It was certainly inappropriate wording, coming from a judge, but the sentiment received wide support from Fort Ann residents, many of whom greeted George Nelson at the depot when he returned home.

Three weeks later, Faber was sufficiently recovered to appear in a Fort Ann courtroom, where he faced charges of assault filed by the two officers who had arrested him at the Nelson home. But for Faber, it was business as usual. A little jail time meant nothing to him. Upon release, he returned to a life of drinking, drugs, and crime, and was in and out of court whenever the law caught up with him.

Later that same year, he was again sought for second-degree assault related to an incident in Jack Ryan's Fourth Ward Café. Faber, on the run to avoid capture, was arrested in Schenectady and brought back to Glens Falls for arraignment.

According to investigators, Beecher had fought with the cafe owner on November 21 and caused a deep wound to Ryan's head by striking him with a weighty, iron cuspidor. As he had done many times in the past, Joseph Faber paid his son's bail, which was set at $1500 ($36,000 in 2012).

In the ensuing weeks, as Ryan and his wife prepared legal action, they received several warnings from Beecher, including one unequivocal death threat, but they appeared firm in their stance.

Following two court delays, the case came before a judge on January 13, 1909. Jack Ryan, perhaps intimidated by Faber, did not identify him as the assailant, but Maude Ryan exhibited no such ambivalence. As a result of her testimony, Beecher was ordered held for grand jury action in lieu of $1000 bail, which again was paid by his father, allowing Beecher to retain his freedom.

With statements like, "She will never testify against me again," Beecher continued to publicly vow he would get even with Maude. Ten days later, it became clear that Joe Faber had made another bad investment. On Glens Falls' infamous West Street, known for its shady characters and wild saloons, Beecher did the unthinkable. Free on bail and bent on revenge, he calmly strolled into Ryan's establishment and opened fire.

Jack Ryan was nowhere to be seen, but his wife was behind the bar. Faber fired twice, hitting Maude both times, and sent a third round into bar patron John "Kip" Kelleher, as everyone else dove for cover or ran for the door. The uproar brought Jack Ryan rushing from another room. As he appeared, Beecher turned the gun towards him and fired once. Following one more shot (apparently at random), he calmly exited the bar.

Faber's aim at the bar owner was dead on, but Jack Ryan was alive, uninjured, and very fortunate to be both. By a great stroke of luck, the tray he was carrying had deflected the bullet. Others were not so fortunate.

Doctors, police officers, and the district attorney were soon on the scene. Witnesses were questioned while the victims were tended to and rushed to the hospital. There was no doubting the identity of the shooter, and officers knew from experience where to look first—at the home of his father, Joseph Faber.

There, seated at a table, they found Beecher, who acted totally oblivious to their questions and denied any knowledge of the affair. Despite those claims, he was handcuffed and taken to the city jail. Arraignment was delayed pending confirmation of the victims' condition. Initial reports suggested that, without complications, they would survive.

Investigators initially found several people willing to testify about the details of the shooting, but when it was learned that neither victim was expected to die, many of them withdrew the offer. A murder conviction might well have put him away for life, but a lesser charge meant he would one day walk the streets again, a frightening prospect.

> **DESPERADO RUNS AMUCK;**
> **SHOOTS MAN AND WOMAN**
>
> Enters Saloon in True Arizona Style, Shooting Right and Left--Proprietor's Wife and a Patron Receive Bad Wounds--Victims In Parks Hospital--Faber Arrested

Beecher Faber was the most feared man in Glens Falls, and in light of the revenge shooting at Ryan's bar, there was little doubt that he would do the same to anyone else who dared testify against him.

Meanwhile, Maude Ryan, shot in the arm and stomach, and John Kelleher, shot in the back, lay in the hospital, their condition the subject of much speculation. On the second day after the shooting, doctors expressed the opinion that Maude was improving and would probably survive, but that Kelleher might not make it.

A day later, that situation was reversed. Surgery was performed on Maude, but in the hours following the operation, her condition was reported as critical. Kelleher, with a bullet believed to be nestled in one of his lungs, began to show marked improvement. Faber remained jailed in solitary confinement while the drama played out.

Four days after the shooting, it became evident that he wasn't going anywhere anytime soon—Maude Ryan died from her wounds. The autopsy revealed that one bullet had penetrated her liver and stomach, while the other had entered her wrist and exited at the elbow. Formerly Maude Richardson, she left behind both parents and eight siblings. The Wevertown native was just twenty-five years old.

The officers told Beecher nothing of her passing, but shortly after Maude's death, he became visibly agitated. An unknown person had been seen at the rear of the jail, and it was surmised they had spoken to Faber through the window's bars. He was moved to a secluded cell and watched closely amid concerns he might try suicide if he knew of Maude's death.

Maud Richardson Bump "Ryan"

Without apparent reason, Faber paced back and forth for an hour. He then requested reading material and was brought newspapers and books, but couldn't seem to concentrate. He asked for water, and during the next five and a half hours, thirty-five more glasses were brought to his cell.

The erratic behavior prompted guards to check on him every five or ten minutes. Shortly before midnight, unusual groans were heard from the direction of his cell. An officer rushed in to find Faber hanging from his belt, suspended just above the floor. The belt was cut, and Beecher appeared to have suffered only minor neck abrasions, a diagnosis that was confirmed by the jail's physician.

Some suggested that the suicide attempt, combined with the oddball behavior exhibited earlier in the day, was a ploy to prove his insanity and thus prevent any future possibility of facing execution.

Although no mention was made in reports at the time, the extreme nervousness and high state of agitation might well have been a result of weeklong imprisonment, causing withdrawal symptoms. Besides being a heavy drinker, Faber was a habitual abuser of both cocaine and morphine.

The following morning, Beecher was taken to court, where he was granted an adjournment on the grounds of his right to counsel. The attorney of his own choosing was out of town at the time.

The delay was by no means unusual, but it was his selection of J. Edward Singleton that astonished many observers. Faber had appeared before former Police Justice Singleton many times in the past, and it was Singleton who Faber physically attacked in the courtroom for sentencing him to the Albany Penitentiary back in 1907.

When that occurred, the judge responded by pummeling him. And yet, instead of seeking revenge, a Faber staple, Beecher now turned to his former foil as the man who could save him from the electric chair. His explanation was simple, telling a reporter, "Singleton is quick, and he can see points where I can't." Beecher also confirmed that he had experienced extreme insomnia, sleeping barely an hour each night. The doctor finally allowed him a dose of opiates, after which he slept soundly.

At his initial court appearance, several witnesses testified to Faber's actions on the evening of the shooting. Most compelling of all was the story told by Jack Ryan, recalling that after their fight, Beecher had made several death threats by telephone. In one call, Faber said:

> Don't you cross my path. It's the electric chair for me anyhow someday, and I would just as soon die now.

Fearful of further trouble at the time, Jack said he'd be satisfied if Beecher simply stayed away from the bar. Faber agreed—sort of—by saying, "All right, but when we meet, it will be a case of who sees first," which meant that when they finally met face-to-face, it would be a question of who managed to get the drop on the other. Anyone with knowledge of Beecher's past knew better than to take such a statement lightly.

After the initial hearing, Faber was ordered moved to the county jail at Lake George to await grand jury action. Moving the area's most notorious criminal of the past decade attracted a lot of attention. More than two thousand citizens gathered to watch the transfer at the Glens Falls jail. The local guards were happy to see him go, having wearied of the constant suicide watch and catering to the prisoner's odd requests, which at times made them feel like Faber's employees.

Beecher was always concerned about his appearance, but at the Glens Falls lockup, he had been denied the use of a razor for fear of a suicide attempt. At Lake George, the guards took it a step further and shaved him themselves. Their intent was to monitor Faber closely at all times, and for good reason. He had commented earlier that escape from the county jail would be easy, and they didn't want him embarrassing the facility.

As a preventive measure, he was confined to his cell at all times and denied the usual privilege of using the hallway for exercise. A wooden barrier was placed in the corridor to bar other exercising prisoners from approaching his cell.

Conspicuous in her absence from all of this was Faber's young wife. Although Beecher and Edna had reconciled during his recovery in the hospital, they had another falling out when he was later arrested in Schenectady. While they were apart, she had returned to live with her parents, and he had pursued his grudge against Jack Ryan.

Just hours before shooting up the saloon in Glens Falls, he had called Edna, but she refused to speak to him. Not to be ignored, Beecher sent her an ominous telegram: "Ed: You should not have made such a mistake. Beecher Faber." Had he not been captured after shooting Ryan and Kelleher, Edna and the Nelson family might well have been his next victims.

A prominent newspaper story soon appeared, stating that Edna was still in love with her husband. Offered as evidence was a letter that she sent to the editor of the *Glens Falls Morning Star*.

> Enclosed you will find a small photo of Beecher. It is the only one I have, and for my sake, see that nothing happens to it. It is of no value to some, but to me it is. If you are going to use it in the paper, will you send me one of the papers?
>
> ... No one can make me think there is not some good in Beecher and that he has a heart. If one could only look ahead, how different things might be. ... Glad I could help you in any way, as long as he wanted me to. Remember now, I wouldn't want this picture lost for a great deal.
>
> Yours truly,
> Mrs. Edna Faber

A few days later came a correction from Edna herself:

> I see by your sketch in the *Morning Star* of Wednesday that you have taken the wrong meaning altogether of the note sent with Beecher's photo. I want it understood that I did leave Beecher, and were he free today, he would be no more to me than a stranger.
> It was not his fault that we parted, for I left him without any words and came to my home.
> Will you kindly see that this is made right, as I am not so narrow-minded as to uphold any such crime as it is alleged he has committed.
>
> Yours truly,
> Mrs. Edna Faber

In early February, two weeks after the shooting at Ryan's, Kip Kelleher was released from the hospital with the bullet still inside him. Since he had recovered, doctors believed it was best to leave the slug alone rather than risk surgery.

A week later, the county announced it would no longer keep a guard assigned to watch Faber around the clock. Two reasons were given: it was believed he had faked the earlier suicide attempt, and the expense of the upcoming trial for murder would be costly to county coffers. Removing the guard was described as a cost-saving measure. [If they were proven wrong about the need for a suicide watch, the cost savings would be far greater, but that was not announced as official county policy.]

Edna's photograph of Beecher Faber

The following day, whether coincidental or not, Faber threw a major tantrum, ripping off his clothes and throwing them out of his cell, smashing a chair, and tearing up his bed linens. It seemed as if he were trying to demonstrate that he was, indeed, insane. It was noted that an insanity defense might be his only hope in avoiding execution.

While Faber awaited action by the grand jury, a couple of news items surfaced with links that introduced his name once again to the news media. A local man by the name of Harry Bump was arrested and jailed on charges of forgery. As it turned out, the late Maude Ryan was paired with Jack Ryan, but they weren't actually husband and wife. To be with Ryan, she had left her husband, Harry Bump.

Ryan himself was also in the news. On grounds of immoral practices, the state excise commissioner closed down Michael Ryan's bar, the Fourth Ward Cafe, known informally as "Jack Ryan's Place." Jack Ryan's liquor license had been revoked two years earlier, but to avoid closing the bar, his brother Michael obtained a license, and Jack operated the bar on his behalf. The story allowed the media to replay the entire shooting incident and related developments, featuring Beecher Faber.

Meanwhile, Faber's nonchalance about his situation began to wane as the grand jury session neared. With just a few days to go, he became silent and withdrawn, facing the likelihood that one of three possible outcomes held his fate: confinement in an asylum, life in prison, or the chair.

On April 23, exactly three months after the shooting, Attorney Singleton stood by Faber's side as he was formally charged with first-degree murder. Singleton, appointed by the court due to Faber's poverty, entered a plea of not guilty on grounds of insanity. The trial was set for May 17.

Faber was in no way admired by the public, but as so often happens in sensational trials, the accused became a "rock star" of sorts, in modern parlance. Great numbers of court devotees, particularly women, attended his appearances, just as they did his transfer from the Glens Falls jail to the county facility at Lake George. His case, of course, possessed lurid elements that inspired great intrigue, from childhood crimes all the way to pimping for his young wife.

After all, few thirty-year-old hoodlums could claim two decades of criminal activity. Faber had spent many years in various jails and reformatories. He had shot people and had himself been shot. He had tortured animals, and attacked a judge in court. He was the most feared man in the region, consistently exhibiting utter disdain for the law and its consequences. What more could one ask for?

As expected, the trial opened to a packed courtroom. Among the prosecution's early witnesses was John "Jack" Ryan, who testified that Faber had phoned him with threats just prior to shooting up the bar. John Kelleher took the stand as well, followed by several other bar patrons who witnessed Beecher entering the bar, firing five shots, and backing out the door before walking calmly to his father's house.

On day three of the trial, Singleton began presenting Faber's defense, offering evidence to support his claim that Maude Ryan would have survived the incident if she had received proper medical care. The strength of that claim centered on the delay of surgery to remove the slug, by which time, he said, she was too weak to survive.

He followed with several witnesses who attested to Faber's heavy drinking and frequent use of drugs, which were blamed for his erratic, bizarre, and violent behavior. This supported Singleton's claim that Faber was temporarily insane during the bar scene, which meant he was guilty of shooting Maude, but was not responsible for his actions.

Singleton also questioned several doctors who treated the victims, but for the most part, they supported the notion that Maude Ryan died from gunshot wounds and shock, and that no treatment would have prevented her death.

At one point, he reviewed the "highlights" of Beecher's life, some of them recounted by his sister, Mary Varney. She described fits of anger with sudden recovery, frequent use of morphine and cocaine, and an incident where he poured kerosene on the floor and set the house on fire.

During the trial, Edna Faber took the stand and said that her husband forced her to have sex with other men for money, and that he always took the money from her. She said he often ingested morphine, worked only three days in all the time she was with him, and frequently beat her. Edna also verified the phone call and subsequent threatening telegram she received just moments before Beecher launched his attack at Ryan's bar. It was very damning evidence.

She also mentioned another side of Faber, one that unintentionally boosted his insanity defense. He at times had claimed to be a philosopher, a deep thinker who said his own writing was superior to William Shakespeare's. He claimed to have invented a type of airship, and promised big things in the future. Others supported her testimony with similarly bizarre stories.

> **BEECHER FABER'S TRIAL**
> **GREAT EVENT OF THE DAY**
> Prisoner Will Answer Today for the Killing of Maude Bump—Counsel Will Try to Prove That Faber Is Insane—Experts Will Testify as to Prisoner's Mentality

Both sides presented

extensive, compelling evidence by various doctors to support their cases. Most prominent for the defense was Dr. M. J. Thornton, charged by the US government with examining immigrants at Ellis Island to verify their mental condition. The prosecution countered with several noted physicians, including Dr. Palmer, who had treated more than a thousand patients at Matteawan State Hospital for the insane.

The trial was deluged with spectators, many of them women. Large crowds gathered outside, unable to enter, but fearful of missing any of the drama. The pressure in the courtroom was intense, causing Faber's mother and sister to break down crying. But for those who had followed the criminal exploits of Faber for so many years, it was hard to muster sympathy for a man who had brought so much grief to so many people.

Singleton did his best to save Beecher from execution, reaching out to the collective conscience of the jurors in his final summation, the closing lines of which were ably delivered, and powerful:

> It is your serious duty to say by your verdict whether the life of this defendant shall be taken away. It was God almighty who endowed this man with life, and you should not take it away unless you think he was sane and realized his acts. If you decide he is insane, he will be sent to an asylum, and no one will ever try to get him out.
>
> I do not believe that this man should go to the electric chair. It is immaterial to me whatever you do with him if you do not send him to the chair.

Judge Edgar A. Spencer's charge to the jury was extensive, reviewing all the testimony. It didn't favor one side over the other, but the imagery he evoked regarding a section of Glens Falls was memorable:

> Most of you men, with the exception of one, reside in the rural districts of the county and are perhaps not familiar with the dark spots, the slums of the cities, nor the habits or manners of the people living there. There have been things disclosed during the progress of this trial, extraordinary things, which no doubt have made your flesh creep as you heard them related.
>
> In Glens Falls, the beautiful young city, which boasts of being one of the best in the state, but which in reality is no better than any other city of its size, there is

a saloon where this murder occurred, located in a section of the city in which saloons and houses of prostitution are plentiful, and these places are frequented by only low-lived, degenerate, depraved persons, who have no respect for their character or the laws of God or society. It was in this locality that the saloon was located, and here, as you have heard several witnesses testify, were from 25 to 50 people congregated in three small rooms, one a barroom, another a sitting room, and the third a kitchen. And for what purpose were they there? Surely this resort was not a good place for the morals of those present.

… The defendant became addicted to liquors and drugs when quite a young boy, and it was not unusual for him to frequent the saloon kept by this Jack Ryan, a man who had been married, but left his wife and was living with another woman, who had also been married, but left her husband; but in the locality where they lived, this was not considered anything out of the ordinary, for without any doubt the place conducted by Ryan was a very bad one.

You have noticed the witnesses who frequented these resorts, who testified in the case, and noticed the marks of degradation caused by using drugs and liquor. Undoubtedly when this prisoner entered Ryan's saloon and struck the proprietor with a cuspidor, he was under the influence of liquor. After the hearing on the charge of assault, Faber made remarks to different people as to what he would do to those who testified against him.

Near the end of his comments, Judge Spencer agreed to Singleton's request that certain points about the deliberation process be emphasized, including two phrases:

> That if there is a reasonable doubt as to the sanity of the prisoner, you should give the defendant the benefit of the doubt and acquit him on the charge of insanity. It is the duty of each juror to be governed by his own opinion, although the remainder may not agree with him.

After meeting for four hours, the jury notified Judge Spencer that they could not agree. They were encouraged by him to continue the effort, but after eight hours, they were still deadlocked: eleven voted guilty of first-degree murder, and one voted for acquittal on the grounds of insanity. Spencer accepted their decision and ordered a new trial date of July 6. Somehow, Singleton had pulled it off and won his client a reprieve.

The second trial revealed no surprises. Except for two new witnesses with information supporting the statements of others, the same people were called to the stand and the same testimony was given.

One variation occurred during the charge to the jury. As he had done at the first trial, Attorney Singleton requested that certain phrases be emphasized, including the following:

> While it is the duty of each juror to discuss and consider the opinion of others, he must decide the case upon his own opinion of the evidence, and upon his own judgment.

This time, Judge Spencer balked, replying:

> I shall tell the juror that he should join with his co-jurors and should make in some respects their opinion his own. If, after discussing with his fellow jurors, he changes his mind, it is just what he should do if he can. I shall not advise a juryman to make himself a standard for everybody else. You never could accomplish anything that way.

In suggesting that a juror should "make in some respects their opinion his own," Spencer appeared to depart from the basic tenet that each juror should form his own opinion. Singleton registered his objection, which was denied by the court, but was noted in the record.

On Saturday, July 10, 1909, after less than four hours of deliberation, the jury returned a verdict of guilty. The first ballot was 11–1, and the second was unanimous. The court's intent was to pass sentence on the following Monday, but Singleton requested that it be done so immediately. Moments later, Judge Spencer informed Beecher Faber that he was to die in Dannemora's electric chair during the week of August 8. He had less than a month to live. As he passed the judge while exiting the courtroom, Faber uttered to him a sarcastic, "Good boy."

After bidding farewell to several family members who had gathered at the courthouse, Faber prepared for the trip north. Two weeks later,

Decades of Depravity

> **FABER SENT TO CHAIR**
>
> Jury Returns Verdict of Murder in First Degree
>
> DELIBERATED FOR FOUR HOURS

despite expectations to the contrary, Singleton filed an appeal. It was thought that after two trials, the issue had been settled, but Faber would fight to the end.

As always, the appeal served as a stay of execution, extending the number of days Beecher had left on earth. For the time being, he remained imprisoned at Dannemora, and was still there a year later, pending the results of his appeal. Finally, in October 1910, the Supreme Court rendered a verdict. Attorney Singleton had once again given his client renewed hope.

The court ordered that a new trial must be held, a decision based primarily on Judge Spencer's error in charging the jury. The upper court held fast to the concept that each juror should decide the case based solely on his own judgment.

A secondary issue was procedural: at sentencing, the court clerk failed to ask if there was any reason why sentence should not be pronounced. As a result of those two errors, and after more than a year on Death Row, Beecher Faber was going home—to the Warren County jail.

Having already paid $12,000 ($300,000 in 2012) for two trials, and now facing a third, the citizens of Warren County were outraged. The region's most notorious criminal was still costing them dearly.

All along, Singleton's goal was to save Beecher from the chair, and for the first time, it looked like he would succeed. Rumors circulated that a deal was in the works, and public outcry may have influenced the decision.

Days later, it was learned that the rumors were based on fact. On October 28, and for the third time in five months, Faber appeared in court on murder charges. The terms of a deal were executed, but not without drama. He was to plead guilty to second-degree murder in exchange for an indeterminate (open-ended) sentence, ranging from a minimum of twenty years to a maximum of life imprisonment.

> **FABER WINS APPEAL**
>
> Glens Falls Desperado Granted New Trial by Higher Court.
>
> TO MAKE THIRD FIGHT FOR LIFE

As the process began, an outburst from Beecher brought an immediate halt to the proceedings. He had changed his mind! But after a brief meeting with Singleton, Faber, wearing what one reporter described as a "cynical smile" on his face, agreed to continue.

Sentence was imposed by presiding Justice Van Kirk, bringing the proceedings to a close. As he left the courtroom, Beecher Faber, arrogant to the end, turned towards Van Kirk "with a leering expression," as the same reporter put it, and said "I wish you'd see that hard labor is imposed."

He would find out soon enough. Within a few hours, Faber was once again behind the walls of Dannemora. There he would stay for a long time, eventually working in the prison library, studying law and helping other convicts with their legal pursuits.

FABER IS SENTENCED

To Twenty Years in Prison at Hard Labor.

MURDER IN THE SECOND DEGREE

Four years later, in 1914, John "Kip" Kelleher died at the age of thirty-five. There was speculation that his death at such a young age was due in part to the effects of Faber's bullet, which remained in his body, but no one knew for certain.

In 1920, a friend of Faber's circulated a petition in Glens Falls, seeking a pardon on his behalf, but there was no change in his status until early 1924, when he was transferred to Great Meadow in Comstock, a half hour northeast of Glens Falls.

In late February 1925, after serving nearly fourteen and a half years, Faber was released on parole. Newspaper reports recalled his crimes, but pointed to the successful rehabilitation of a perennial criminal who had bettered his condition while in prison. He was now forty-six years old, and had spent a good portion of his life behind the bars of several institutions. Perhaps this last, long stint had mellowed him somewhat.

Actually, using the standard established earlier by Faber, he had slowed remarkably (or had become harder to catch), taking seven months before recording his first arrest. In October, he was confined to the Saratoga County jail for drunkenness. Upon release, he was arrested and charged with robbing the cash register of the Bluebird Inn, a violation of parole that landed him back in Great Meadow Prison.

In August 1927, Faber was transferred to Dannemora after causing problems at Great Meadow, where the warden deemed him a hopelessly incorrigible criminal. No one was surprised at that assessment.

He was paroled in 1928, but was jailed again in 1930 on second-degree assault charges for using a pair of scissors to stab a man during a barroom altercation. In short order, he was back in Dannemora. It was noted frequently in the media that Faber had spent approximately thirty-two of his fifty years behind bars.

In 1934, the cycle played out once again. After transfer to Great Meadow and later being granted parole, he was jailed in early January 1935 on assault charges in connection with a fight at a rooming house. His sentence called for sixty days in the county lockup, during which time Faber filed a writ of habeas corpus, arguing the case himself based on the knowledge he had accumulated while working in the Clinton Prison library. The writ was denied, and Faber was resigned to serving out his sentence, unaware that a member of the state parole board had meanwhile issued a warrant for his arrest.

By the end of February, due to the recent parole violation, he was re-arrested immediately upon release and returned once again to Great Meadow Prison, where he remained in 1940, a sixty-two-year-old prisoner with a criminal record dating back five decades.

12

Evil Personified: Neighbor in a Trunk

A ghastly odor filled their nostrils. Although repulsed by the smell, they lifted the black cloth shielding the contents, revealing the back of a human leg.

In early November 1886, in the settlement of Brownville, a few miles northwest of Watertown, Mary Brennan was awakened by sounds in the dead of night. Although she was 78 years old, Mary still did housework and was capable of taking care of herself. Alarmed by such noises at 2:00 AM, she climbed out of bed, got dressed, and went to investigate.

As she stood near a window, the glass pane suddenly shattered across the sitting-room floor. Someone reached in, grabbed Mary, and pulled her outside, where she gamely battled four attackers. Resisting against such odds was futile. She was beaten to the ground, and her face was dragged across coarse gravel during the struggle to escape. Badly wounded, she cried out for help as one of the attackers knelt on her chest, frisking her and demanding money.

The commotion awoke the neighbors, some of whom ran to Mary's aid, scaring off the thugs. Though she was badly bruised from the beating and suffered cuts from being dragged through the broken window, it appeared Mary would recover from her injuries. Her son Patrick ("Patsy" to his friends) and his wife Sarah lived nearby, providing a place for Mary to stay while she recovered.

Within a week, two suspects, Edward Duke and Charles Steele, were arrested and charged with assault in the first degree. It was then learned that the victim's condition had worsened, and she appeared to be fading, perhaps due to internal injuries. The district attorney brought both young men before Mary, who identified them as her attackers. The judge set bail quite high at $3000 ($72,000 in 2012), enough to keep Edward Duke locked up. Steele, however, met bail and gained his freedom.

Three days later, Mary Brennan died.

The district attorney upped the charge to first-degree murder, and Steele was taken into custody. Acting quickly out of necessity, the coroner empaneled a jury and began an inquest, leading the entire group to Patrick Brennan's house to view Mary's body. Later, a number of witnesses were heard, including Patrick's wife Sarah, who tended to Mary's multiple cuts and bruises for days after the attack.

The third and final day of the inquest lasted nearly eight hours. Among the evidence presented was the coroner's report on Mary's injuries:

> A careful post-mortem examination was made of the body by my direction. It revealed many bruises and slight wounds and the fracture of several ribs. The medical examiners were certain that the injuries had produced her death.

Near the end of testimony, the defense presented several witnesses who swore that the two defendants were elsewhere when the crime was committed. Despite those claims, it was fully expected that Steele and Duke would face first-degree murder charges, and certainly nothing less than manslaughter.

Hours later, to the dismay of Patrick Brennan and the residents of Brownville, only five of nine grand jury members believed the two men to be guilty. Four others concluded that Mary's injuries had been caused by unknown persons. The coroner's official report ended with one sad, disappointing line: "These verdicts did not justify me in issuing a warrant, and my connection with the case came to an end."

With no indictment, no one paid a price for Mary Brennan's death. No one, that is, except her son Patrick, who would suffer more grief and tragedy in his lifetime than one man could be expected to bear.

Sarah and Patrick Brennan had only one child, a daughter, Mamie, who turned three years old when her grandmother died. In April 1901, at the age of seventeen, Mamie died. Patrick took it hard, but Sarah was devastated. Since she and Patrick were in their mid-forties (life expectancy then was about forty-seven), there were no more children in their future.

For the appropriate term of mourning (usually a year), Sarah wore a black dress in memory of Mamie, and did so in April of each year thereafter.

Six years later, in May 1907, the Brennans of Paddy Hill greeted new neighbors James and Mary Farmer, who moved into the old Barton House building next door (it had previously been a hotel and tavern). Mary, five months pregnant at the time, became friends with Sarah. They routinely visited each other's homes, despite the obvious great disparity between the couples' financial means.

The most visible evidence of this was in the general appearance of the two properties. The neighboring lots were a study in contrasts. The Brennans, longtime residents of Brownville, had a home neatly kept both inside and out. The yard was well maintained, featuring flowers and shrubbery, and the fence around the property was, like the house and barn, nicely painted. Conversely, the old Barton House, now occupied by the Farmers, had worn and chipped paint, broken windows, and a dirt yard littered with bottles, cans, and other debris.

Like many communities within small towns, Paddy Hill was a place where everyone knew everyone else. The rumor mill disseminated local "news," whether gossip or factual in nature. Gossip is often based on elements of truth, a fact that caused consternation for Patrick Brennan when, in late 1907, he began hearing through the grapevine that his wife had sold the family home to the Farmers.

The story was repeated enough to Patrick that it soon became irritating. He confronted Sarah, who denied that any such deal was in the works. Comfortable that neither of them was behind the rumor, they could only wonder about the source. Further mention of it by neighbors became little more than an annoyance.

On the afternoon of April 23, 1908, Patsy (Patrick) discovered that there might be something to the rumors after all. Arriving home at the end of the workday (he was a boiler operator at the Remington mill), Patrick found the door locked and the house key not in its usual hiding place. When he had left for work that morning, Sarah said she had a dental appointment with Doctor Huntington in Watertown. Patsy assumed she may have gone visiting after the appointment, so her absence was no cause for alarm, although the missing key was a mystery.

Finding the barn also locked, he used a hammer to remove the hasp, and then used a ladder from the barn to access a second-story window of the

Mary Farmer

house. While Sarah was away, Brennan passed the time working around the property until the voice of Jim Farmer came from across the fence. Unemployed for some time, Farmer had just returned home from down the street, where he was working on building a cement sidewalk for a relative.

Their conversation, as related by Brennan, follows:

> Farmer: Don't you know that I own the place now?
> Brennan: No you don't!
> Farmer: Yes, the place is mine, all right. I bought it last October, and you can see the deed at the county clerk's office. I paid $2100 for it.
> Brennan: That's funny. My wife never said anything about it, and you neither have said anything about it all these months.
> Farmer: I didn't think there was need of it. Mrs. Brennan has been paying me $2 a week rent for it, but I've decided now that I'd like to move in and enjoy my property.

It seemed unlikely that with prolonged unemployment, the neighbors had the means to purchase a home, but Farmer and his wife provided Patrick with the details. It seemed that Sarah had sold the property to them, spent extravagantly on new clothes, and had left town for Duluth, Minnesota, wanting nothing more to do with her husband.

The new owners were saddled with the awkward task of breaking the news to Patrick, who was both stunned and heartbroken, especially after twenty-five years of marriage.

He returned to work the next day, but coming home on Friday was as traumatic as the previous day had been. That night, a local constable served him with a notice of ejection. Adding insult to injury, the Farmers informed him that they had also purchased the entire contents of the home, producing a bill of sale to prove it. He would be forced to vacate the house, taking nothing with him except for his own clothing.

Brennan was devastated and thoroughly confused at such a sudden, disastrous turn of events, and wanted more than ever to learn the story behind it. He checked the train station, but no one had see Sarah leave. The Farmers told him she had since changed her mind about Minnesota, and instead had gone to Watertown, asking that all her goods be sent there to the home of James Rattray.

That night, Patrick complied with the ejection notice and left his property behind. Traveling to Watertown, he paid a visit to Rattray, who said he knew nothing of Sarah's whereabouts. Perhaps she had gone to Duluth after all.

Acting on his own suspicions, Brennan went to the office of Dr. Huntington, where he learned that for the first time ever, Sarah had missed a dental appointment. Still uncertain what to do, but knowing he had to do something, Patrick met with local attorney Floyd Carlisle. At that point, two days had passed since Patrick had last seen Sarah.

Once privy to the details of the story, Carlisle made some inquiries. What he learned added even more to the mystery. A woman presenting herself as Sarah Brennan, but matching the appearance of Mary Farmer, had appeared at attorney Frank Burns' office in January and executed a deed, transferring the former Brennan property to Peter J. Farmer, the four-month-old son of Mary and James Farmer.

What's more, the transfer was from Mary Farmer, who, as the deed reflected, had purchased the property from Sarah Brennan six months earlier, on October 30, 1907. Perhaps Patrick Brennan had been legally evicted after all, and Sarah had indeed left him.

Meanwhile, on the morning after the home was vacated, the Farmers moved in. A few local men were hired to help move the contents from one home to the other, mostly personal goods stored in heavy trunks and boxes. There was no need to move most of their furniture. Since they had purchased the Brennan house and contents, they now owned furnishings of much higher quality than the Farmers' previous home.

When the move was completed, Mary Farmer sent a message to the priest, informing him that his presence was required at the Brennan home. Assuming someone might be gravely ill or in need of counseling, Father Penteur arrived quickly, only to find that the Farmers had purchased a home, and Mary wanted him to perform the traditional blessing. He did so, but with some reluctance. After all, they hadn't even settled in yet.

Frustrated and suspicious from the results of his own investigation into Sarah's disappearance, and upset at the loss of his home, Patrick finally turned to other resources. District Attorney Fred Pitcher listened to Brennan and agreed there were several problematic elements to the story.

Two days after the Farmers moved in, Sheriff Ezra Bellinger began an investigation, venturing to the home with six other men: Patrick Brennan, Undersheriff Charles Hosmer, Chief of Police Gaylord Baxter, Deputy Sheriff Samuel Gates, Sergeant Edward Singleton, and Attorney Floyd

Carlisle. The plan was to question the couple about the property deeds and to find out where Sarah Brennan was, in hopes of relieving the sudden turmoil that had beset Patrick Brennan's once idyllic life.

When the men reached the Farmer residence on the Hounsfield (south) side of the Black River, Mary recognized the sheriff and allowed the group inside. In response to questions about the deeds, she explained the transactions. The property was purchased for $1200; the contents of the house were purchased for $67; part of the money came from boarders that she housed, added to weekly savings from her husband's income; and she had received around $700 after the death of an uncle in Buffalo.

At first denying she had copies of the deeds, Mary acquiesced under pressure from Chief Baxter, who said he knew she possessed the documents. Attorney Carlisle examined the first deed and showed Mr. Brennan his wife's signature, eliciting an instant denial from Patrick—it was definitely not her handwriting.

Then came the kicker—the signature of Sarah Brennan on the first deed matched the handwriting of Mary Farmer's signature on the second deed, the one transferring the property to her infant son, Peter. But Mary had an explanation at the ready. When they arrived at the attorney's office together, Sarah Brennan had forgotten her glasses, so Mrs. Farmer signed Sarah's name at her request.

It was a very plausible story, except for one important detail. Francis Burns, the attorney in question, had already confirmed that a lone woman had handled the processing of the deeds.

Comfortable that some type of fraud had been committed, the district attorney forged ahead with more questions while other investigators began looking around the house and the property. Since the Farmers had just moved in two days earlier, there were many packed boxes and containers scattered about. One of two trunks was wrapped in clothesline, "to prevent breakage of the fragile contents," as Mary explained.

There were also three large, heavy, wooden boxes that aroused the officers' suspicion. Upon opening them, the men were surprised to find all sorts of clothing, towels, and other goods with price tags still attached. Included was a quantity of women's clothing, although most of it was much too large for the diminutive Mrs. Farmer. They could only surmise that the goods had been shoplifted and/or stolen from clotheslines (very common crimes for the times).

The two trunks, stacked in a summer kitchen at the rear of the house, also attracted the men's attention. When asked about them specifically, Mrs. Farmer said the top trunk was hers and the bottom one was Jim's. Mr. Farmer shot back, "That's a damn lie. The top one is mine and the bottom one is yours."

When asked about the contents of the hefty trunk bound in clothesline, she said it contained books. The men removed the rope, but the trunk was locked, and Mary was unable to find the key, which apparently had been misplaced during the moving process.

Jim Farmer handed the sheriff a hammer and said, "Bust her open; just take the damn hammer and bust her open." Bellinger did so, but it was still too dark to see the contents. Lighting a match, he moved in closer as some of the men peered with him into the darkness.

A ghastly odor filled their nostrils. Although repulsed by the smell, they lifted the black cloth shielding the contents, revealing the back of a human leg. Moments later, the full remains of Sarah Brennan came into view, face down in the trunk. The back of her skull was badly crushed. Blood was everywhere, and in such quantity that some had leaked onto the floor through the corner of the trunk.

Sheriff Bellinger turned quickly and, in his own words, "snapped the handcuffs on [Mr.] Farmer," who stared into the trunk and said, "I did not know she was in there."

Patrick Brennan was horrified, and with disbelief in his voice, reportedly said to Farmer, "My God! Did you do this?" The two men had known each other since childhood.

"As God is my witness, I did not," was his response.

There was no doubt the body was that of Sarah Brennan: with her lay a medallion, once the property of her beloved daughter Mamie, who had died at seventeen. The black cloth proved to be the mourning dress Sarah wore each April in memory of her lost child.

Mary Farmer was ordered to view the trunk's contents. She did so, but refused to talk any further. Persistent questioning and the sight of Sarah's mangled remains soon weakened her resolve. In a stunning turnaround, instead of learning where Patrick's wife was living, the men listened incredulously as Mary Farmer confessed to a brutal murder.

Her first comments suggested the workings of a demented mind. Mary and Sarah liked each other, she said, and Sarah was going away. So, to keep her from leaving, Mary dispatched her with an axe. It was as simple as that. She took the investigators next door to her former home, where she described what had occurred that fateful morning.

Later, as the interrogation continued, Mrs. Farmer said the truth may as well be known: her husband had killed Sarah. When Mary walked into the house that day, James had Sarah on the floor and said, "There, goddamn her, I've fixed her now," after which he threw Brennan's lifeless body into the storage trunk.

No matter which story was true, a search of both properties turned up plenty of evidentiary items tying the Farmers to the crime. As Mary talked, confirmation of her statements was found in one of the houses. A typical example was the broad-brimmed hat Mrs. Brennan wore when she visited the Farmer home that day. Mary said they later burned it in the stove, which is where investigators found the framing of the hat intact, with many burned remnants still attached.

The news about other physical evidence wasn't as good. Everything that had become tainted with blood during the murder and the disposal of the body had been burned by Mary, a job that investigators found she had performed thoroughly. Forensics in 1908 was hardly what it has become today, and a hundred years ago, the average policeman may not have noticed tiny specks of blood spatter, if any, in fact, remained.

But with several items of physical evidence, along with copious circumstantial evidence, the case against the Farmers appeared strong. Mary's multiple and conflicting confessions would have to be sorted out in the days to come.

Coroner Charles Pierce, assisted by several physicians, examined the body to determine the cause of death. Three cuts on the wrist were indicative of Sarah Brennan's desperate efforts to ward off blows. The only other distinctive wounds were to the head, which was a dreadful mess.

The list of injuries was sickening: a broken left jaw; several cuts on the cheek; both lips sliced apart; a huge gash stretching across the forehead, above both eyes; a severed left ear; and three deep gashes behind where the left ear should have been.

Investigators searching both homes for additional physical evidence were finally rewarded with success. Despite the thorough job of cleaning, Mrs. Farmer had mistakenly stowed away a bloodied apron. Neighbors identified it as one she was seen wearing on the day of Sarah's visit. Further circumstantial evidence was compiled, but the effort soon appeared unnecessary. From a jail cell, Mary Farmer was telling her entire life story.

Most of her youth was spent in Buffalo, and from 1901–04, she

Evil Personified: Neighbor in a Trunk

worked several jobs as a domestic. Jim Farmer, now a paperhanger, was a sailor on the Great Lakes at the time, and became acquainted with Mary during frequent stops at the Buffalo docks. In 1905, Mary, 26, and James, 44, were wed at Buffalo, and within a few months moved to Brownville. Admittedly a heavy drinker, Jim had trouble maintaining employment, and the couple struggled to make ends meet.

In spring 1907, with Mary several months pregnant, they relocated to Paddy Hill and befriended their new neighbors, the Brennans. Mary soon hatched a devious plan to steal away the Brennan's property, and barely six months after their arrival at Paddy Hill, she managed to remove the deed from the home of her newfound friend, Sarah Brennan. Boldly passing herself off as Sarah, Mrs. Farmer transferred the property to herself. A few months later, she signed her new property over to Peter Farmer, their four-month-old son.

In early April 1908, Mary asked if she could accompany Sarah to a dental appointment with Watertown's J. Frederick Huntington, the dentist who for the past decade had cared for Brennan's teeth. When Sarah's appointment ended, Mary consulted with Huntington about correcting some faulty work done on her teeth in Buffalo. Before the women left the office, two appointments were booked: Mary Farmer for April 21 and Sarah Brennan for April 22.

The dental arrangements would prove crucial to investigators in tracking Farmer's evil, detailed plan and reconstructing events from the day of the murder. Mary did attend her April 21 appointment, but when it ended, she didn't pay, instead claiming she had forgotten her paybook (checkbook) at the office of attorney Brayton Field. After assuring Huntington that she owned a home, had money in the bank, and that payment would be no problem, Mary went on her way. But the dentist was skeptical. Following his instincts, Huntington called Field, who said he wasn't aware that Mary possessed such a paybook.

On the following day, during Sarah Brennan's dental appointment, Huntington inquired about Mary's claims of money, property, relatives working at the hospital, and other topics. Sarah confirmed that they were all fabrications, and warned Huntington that he might have difficulty securing payment for the work he had done. Said Sarah of Mary Farmer:

> She has lied so much about different matters that I do not believe her. She is not the class of a woman I care

to associate with, but she is my next-door neighbor, and I like to keep on good terms with my neighbors.

Sarah's crown work required a follow-up visit on the next day, April 23, and that appointment also became crucial to eventually determining her whereabouts. Before going to the dentist, she had made the fateful decision to stop in for a visit with Mrs. Farmer.

The details of their conversation were never revealed, but in light of the past few days' events, they likely touched on the subject of Mary's avoiding payment to Sarah's longtime dentist, and her frequent lies about financial assets.

Whatever words may have passed between them, Sarah Brennan never made that follow-up dental appointment. According to Mary Farmer, the two women quarreled that morning, and then something happened:

> Mrs. Brennan came to my house. She said something, and in my insane madness, I struck her over the head and killed her. ... My God, why did I do it? I must have been tempted. I never thought of it until the moment. ... My husband never knew of the murder until the day you opened the trunk.

When Mary told the story, she was advised that an admission to murder carried a mandatory death sentence. She professed not to care and continued with the narrative, describing how she cleaned up the bloody aftermath and put Sarah's body in the trunk.

On the day of the murder, Mrs. Farmer was seen carrying the baby on repeated trips to her husband's workplace down the street, and one time also carried a package. Mary's confession shed light on the nature of those forays. The wrapped package in question held the Brennan's black pocketbook containing deeds, insurance policies, and other papers.

On another trip, Mary approached James and said, "Here are the keys. If you don't see Mrs. Brennan by four o'clock, you never will again." Handing him $12, she explained that Sarah had paid the rent and left town (but the $12 had actually been taken from the dead woman's body).

Mary claimed she didn't tell her husband about the killing, in part because he often drank, and she feared he would at some point blurt out her secret. It was best to tell no one and dispose of the body, which she apparently had planned to do. A newly opened box of chloride of lime was found in the vacant Farmer home. It was suspected that the powerful disinfectant was intended for use in covering up the odor of decomposition, but events had played out in unexpected fashion, and Mary hadn't yet had an opportunity to finish the job.

Until the trunk was discovered by investigators, it appeared she planned to cut the corpse into small parts while Jim was away and gradually get rid of them, possibly by tossing them in the nearby river.

The local priest's involvement added a macabre touch to the story. Poor Father Ponteur, for several years well acquainted with the struggles of the Farmers, was called upon to bless their new home. He expressed reservations, but Mary insisted, even retrieving the holy water needed for the ceremony. To his own horror, Ponteur now realized that he performed the ritual blessing while, at that very same time, the bloodied corpse of Sarah Brennan lay festering in the next room.

Although Mary's retelling of the tale seemed plausible and sincere, DA Pitcher wasn't buying all of it, particularly due to one disturbing fact: when the Farmers first took over the Brennan home, and Sarah was missing, they offered Patrick the opportunity to board with them. Pitcher's suspicion was that the Farmers had agreed on what to do (kill Sarah), but not on when or how to do it.

Once the deed was done, Pitcher opined, the offer to Patrick was a trap, and had he accepted, he would have met the same fate as Sarah. Perhaps, then, the body remained in the house only because the job was not yet finished. Pitcher's feeling was that Mr. Brennan narrowly avoided joining his wife in the trunk.

Even with a full confession, there was still plenty of work to be done. Coroner Charles Pierce issued his findings after an inquest of several days:

> Upon view of the body of Sarah Brennan of the town of Hounsfield, Jefferson County, N.Y., April 27th, lying dead in a trunk in her former home ... and after carefully examining and inquiring into all circumstances attending the death of the said Sarah Brennan ... I do say: That the deceased came to her death by wounds on the head inflicted by one Mary Farmer ... in a back middle room of what is known as the old Barton House, the home of the said Mary Farmer, situated on what is known as Paddy Hill ... on April 23, 1908, between the hours of 8:30 and 9:30 in the forenoon.

> That the said Sarah Brennan came to her death by said wounds produced by said Mary Farmer with a hammer, hatchet, or similar instrument. Witness my hand at the city of Watertown this 8th day of May, 1908.

Notably, James Farmer was not mentioned at all. It was left to the grand jury to decide whether one or both Farmers should be indicted.

A week later, the results were in. Among those to testify were many of the Brennan's neighbors on Paddy Hill. One reported how carefully Mary Farmer had supervised the moving of the trunk, while others described the clothes Sarah Brennan wore when she entered the Farmer home, never to be seen alive again. Peter Farmer, seventy-five-year-old father of James, testified that on April 23, Mary had brought a black pocketbook to his daughter's (Alice Doran) house, where Peter lived, and hid it beneath a chair cushion. Patrick Brennan confirmed that the pocketbook in question was Sarah's.

In the end, the grand jury brought indictments against Mary and James Farmer for murder in the first degree. At their arraignment, both asked for court-appointed representation due to a lack of financial resources. James entered a plea of not guilty and specifically requested that Brayton Field be assigned to his case. Mary entered no plea and left the choice of attorney to the court.

The DA's office planned to pursue both Farmers, but in separate trials, beginning with Mary. The prosecution's case against her was by far the strongest, and it offered hope that along the way, further damning evidence against James would be uncovered. Likewise, the defense attorney for James Farmer would closely follow Mary's trial in search of testimony that might help exonerate his client.

The first trial began in mid-June, 1908. Representing Mary was E. Robert "Bob" Wilcox, a very capable lawyer and fiercely protective of his clients' interests. A fine example of his aggressive posture came shortly before the trial began with this comment:

> ... the scales of justice have been demolished, the constitution has been trampled, and the Goddess of Liberty stripped of her gown ...

The offense prompting his hyperbolic tirade seemed innocuous enough: a visit to the jail by attorney Floyd Carlisle (who was assisting

DA Pitcher) and Doctor Somers of Ogdensburg for a second mental examination of Mary Farmer. Wilcox's statement served notice that he would be endlessly vigilant in protecting Mary's rights.

And he was, every step of the way. Perhaps grasping for any possibility in the face of such great odds against his client, Wilcox was an obstructionist throughout the proceedings. He raised exceptions and objections constantly, preventing any continuity of testimony.

It was annoying to spectators and just about everyone else, including Justice Rogers, who admonished him frequently, but to little effect. There was no doubt that Mary Farmer had an absolutely tenacious advocate in the courtroom.

Wilcox's principal task was to save her from the electric chair, and it wouldn't be easy. Mary's confessions (there were now five different versions) were very detailed. Much of the trial testimony focused on providing confirmation of her statements. This put Wilcox in the unusual position of trying to refute the words of his own client and somehow prove her insanity.

He pushed hard in an effort to prove that perhaps Sarah Brennan had left her husband because they weren't a happy couple. As evidence, he cited the fact that they did not sleep in the same bed together. Patrick Brennan himself admitted on the stand that separate sleeping arrangements had been in place for the past eleven years. Wilcox probed the relationship between Patrick and Sarah as far back as 1881, using incidents from the distant past to demonstrate a lack of closeness. Perhaps he was just being thorough, but the tactic sometimes smacked of desperation.

With most of the evidence in, the defense was left with three main points to hammer home. First was their claim that Sarah Brennan had transferred the property to her friend, Mary Farmer, in order to avoid the threat of losing it in a slander suit by one of their Paddy Hill neighbors, a Mrs. Baker.

Second was their assertion that the murder occurred during a fight between the two women, so it wasn't of a degree requiring the death penalty. As evidence of the supposed fight, they cited bruises to Sarah's face, and cuts and scratches to Mary's hand and arm.

Third, and the option with the greatest potential, was the idea that Mary Farmer was insane. Gradually, as the defense case weakened, the insanity angle was explored in greater detail. Many neighbors and relatives were called to the stand, sometimes offering stories that seemed only tenuously linked to the issues at hand.

One example was a nephew who worked in a store, and from whom Mary purchased "three wash tubs of the same size, three dust pans, and more than one mop." The odd purchase, he said, and the fact that she never looked him directly in the eyes, led him to judge her as irrational. Cross-examination revealed that the nephew was unaware his aunt was running a boarding house, which made the purchase seem sensible after all.

Another witness told of Mary putting her husband's clothes in the refrigerator (bringing a smile to her face for the first time since the trial began). Surely the average person would consider such behavior a sign of dementia or some other serious mental issue. No rebuttal was offered, but the prosecution could have mentioned that a helpful household hint of that era was to spray clean clothes, roll them up, and place them in a refrigerator, which would help prevent mildew until time was available for ironing them. Instead, Mary's actions were offered as further proof that she had lost her mind.

During the discussions of insanity, much greater weight was ascribed to the testimony of several professional witnesses, including prominent psychiatrists and psychologists who attested to Mary's unstable mental condition. And, as usual, the prosecution presented a like number of impressive doctors who earnestly claimed she was nothing but normal.

Dr. Royal Amidon talked extensively with Mary, who described for him some members of her family: a grandmother who was a criminal, and forced her grandchildren to steal for her; a father who beat the children for stealing; a father and mother who were both insane; an uncle who died in insanity; an aunt in an insane asylum in Buffalo; an insane cousin; and a brother and sister who had "fits." In fact, Mary said she also experienced the same fits, followed by periods where she exhibited odd behavior but retained no memory of it. In Dr. Amidon's opinion, Mary Farmer had never been sane, and suffered from "hereditary degenerate insanity."

The prosecution countered with no fewer than three doctor witnesses of their own—Somers of the state hospital at Ogdensburg, and Barnette and Deane of Watertown—certifying Mary as completely sane.

There were discussions of ringing in the ears, color-blindness, imperfect vision, and slight facial deformities that some doctors linked to insanity, but others said were completely unrelated. Mention of unusual conditions was introduced, including circular insanity, described as rotating through repeated periods of depression, rationality, and excitement.

In a nod to the growing world of forensics, Dr. Isabel Meader, a chemist and "microscopist," testified to the areas of the home cleaned by Mary Farmer, but still yielding quantities of human blood. Among the bloodied items she identified were matting, a towel, a strip of cloth, and a door casing. Bits of human flesh were found on clothing owned by the Farmers, and a shoe taken from the trunk bore a bloody fingerprint.

When he took the stand, all eyes were riveted on Dr. Henry Dean, who performed the post-mortem examination. To illustrate his findings, the bloody trunk was brought into the courtroom and placed on exhibit. Dean opened it to reveal the bloodstains, after which he described Sarah's clothing and her many injuries. His determination was that she died of external wounds.

Irony played a role when Patrick Brennan took the stand. During one exchange, he identified the hatchet used to kill Sarah as his own, one that had been given to him by a Paddy Hill neighbor.

At the completion of testimony, a dinner break was taken prior to final summations. When everyone returned for the afternoon session, seated in the witness stand was a mannequin, dressed in the clothes worn by Sarah Brennan on the last day of her life. Defense Attorney Wilcox, already upset with use of the bloody trunk as a dramatic backdrop for prosecution testimony, protested strongly. The judge ordered the mannequin's removal.

During final summations, the prosecution's review seemed to ensure Mary's guilt, stressing that the brutality of Sarah's death and the mutilation of her body was no accident. The intent, they said, was to dump the corpse into the river. Even if it was recovered and examined, it would be difficult, if not impossible, to identify the victim.

The defense had much less to work with but left no stone unturned, finally focusing on Mary's sanity as the key issue. Wilcox finished with an impassioned plea:

> I am coming to another great and all-important point. Through Christ's teachings, men learned that it was not right to kill the insane. Is she insane? She surely is. [Turning toward Mary Farmer] Is that the face of an intelligent person? ... Gentlemen, you may send her to the electric chair, but you will never sleep after that. Your conscience would not let you. ... You said you would give her the benefit of every reasonable doubt, and there is no doubt she is insane.

If there is that doubt, you cannot take from her, her life. I ask that the law of this great and glorious republic be followed, and that you do by this woman what is just, and send her to an institution for the insane.

Three hours later, the jury returned and the foreman announced the verdict: "We find her guilty as charged in the indictment."

When the judge pronounced the mandated penalty of death, Mary Farmer was scheduled to become the second woman in New York State to die in the electric chair. She was ordered confined in Auburn prison to await execution during the week of August 2.

For officials at Auburn, it was unclear how to proceed. Temporarily, at least, Mary would be held in the women's wing of the prison. She was supposed to be on Death Row, but there were two problems: Death Row was in the men's section of the prison, and the cells were all filled.

Solutions to the unique situation were discussed, but there was no great sense of urgency. The sentence was unlikely to be carried out anytime soon. An appeal was expected, which carried with it a stay of execution until such time as the appeals court rendered a decision.

Perhaps more important was another unusual issue—the possibility that Mary would be called as a witness in her husband's murder case. His trial was expected to begin several months after Mary's scheduled execution date. If for no other reason, it appeared the state would have to keep her alive to be available as a witness.

Within three weeks of her conviction, Mary's attorney, Bob Wilcox, filed an appeal, delaying the execution until at least late November. A few days later, Wilcox received a letter from Mary (it had already been seen by

> **CONDEMNED TO DIE**
>
> A VERDICT OF GUILTY PRONOUNCED UPON MRS. FARMER.
>
> **FIRST WEEK IN AUGUST**
>
> Sentenced by Justice Rogers at Watertown to Die in the Electric Chair in Auburn as a Penalty for the Death of Mrs. Sarah Brennan.

Auburn Prison officials). The missive contained a confession—the sixth, for all those who were keeping score. But Wilcox said it differed from her previous confessions in that it implicated others in the death of Sarah Brennan. He described Mary's letters as confusing and hard to understand, leaving him convinced more than ever of her insanity.

Wilcox hated to lose, and he was obviously still trying Mary's case in the media. The ultimate goal was to avoid execution of his client. If he could prove her insanity, there was a chance her sentence would be commuted to life in prison.

While in Auburn, Mary had written only once to James at the jail in Watertown, where he awaited his own date in court. On October 19, shortly before her appeal was to be heard, the trial of James Farmer commenced.

It didn't take long for the prosecution to suggest his culpability in the plot to snatch away the Brennan's property. It was previously believed that the deed irregularities were known only to Mary Farmer, who had acted alone, but a new twist was revealed. Alice Doran, sister of James Brennan, testified to the innocent role she played in the matter. In doing so, she unintentionally implicated her brother in the scheme.

After Mary Farmer fraudulently obtained the deed, using impersonation and forgery, it was given to James, who admitted to reading the particulars, but said he paid no attention to the signature. Within a few days, James asked Alice to take it to the county clerk's office for recording. On her way there, Alice looked at the document. Alarm and suspicion engulfed her when she viewed the signature. Deeply concerned, she visited the Burns legal office and inquired about the deed. They provided a description of the woman who had signed the transfer, and it matched Mary Farmer, not Sarah Brennan.

Alice called James, who went to Watertown and listened to her concerns. She wanted nothing to do with the affair, suspecting something was amiss. Alice then asked James if Patrick Brennan was aware that his home was being sold, and James replied that his own nephew, Roy Farmer, had told Patrick about the deal. Alice remained skeptical and refused to become involved, but James professed faith in his wife. Taking the papers from Alice, he handled the recording of the deed himself.

The entire episode suggested that if James didn't know anything was wrong with the deed earlier, he surely should have been alerted by the suspicions of his sister.

Many of the same witnesses in Mary's trial were also called to the stand in James' trial, including the priest, several law officers, and a number of friends, relatives, and neighbors. Some of them verified instances of drunkenness by James. Others testified that James told them he had purchased a property on Paddy Hill. That last item of information was important, for if James Farmer mentioned the purchase to several of his friends, wouldn't he have also mentioned it to Patrick Brennan?

The idea that he drank and was often inebriated was actually a defense ploy, suggesting that James was loose-tongued at times and may have told friends of a real estate transaction that was otherwise kept secret by Mary. Still, there was no explanation of why he never mentioned the purchase to the owner's husband, who was his friend and next-door neighbor.

Another co-worker said that, while at work, a completely sober James Farmer told him in fall 1907 that he had purchased a house on Paddy Hill, and that the entire contents were included because the owners of the home were moving away.

Even children testified, in this case reporting events that occurred when they babysat the infant, Peter, in the Farmer home. One youth was present at the blessing of the house, watching as Father Ponteur sprinkled holy water in the room where Sarah Brennan lay dead in the trunk.

Unlike the packed-house crowds at Mary Farmer's trial, Jim's was often lightly attended. On some days, the courtroom was only about half filled, and many of those present were witnesses waiting to testify.

Seated at the defense table and receiving plenty of media attention was an unexpected attendee. Robert Wilcox, who defended Mary Farmer and now fought to save her from the chair, was there for two reasons. Most importantly, he hoped to hear new evidence that might help Mary, but he also suggested many questions that were used by the defense team during the earlier trial, and that might help Jim's cause.

One witness, Dr. Isabel Meader, who offered forensic information against Mary Farmer, also did the same against James. At issue was a pair of blue pants worn by Jim on the morning of the murder. Although he was pouring a sidewalk that morning, he admitted going home at the start of work in order to change out of his blue pants. Meader testified that in her opinion, hairs found on those pants matched hairs taken from the corpse of Sarah Brennan. Also on the pants was a morbid morsel:

> ... a little fragment of human flesh, about the size of a pinhead, which was not diseased and which came from at least an eighth of an inch below the surface of the body.

Thus far, it was the only physical evidence tying James to the murder. He was suspected of involvement in the plot to kill Sarah, but all the other evidence pointed to Mary having committed the actual homicide alone.

The defense spent much of its time attempting to prove that the Farmers had sufficient financial resources to purchase property, therefore negating any need for a nefarious plan to steal the Brennan's home. In light of those claims, it's curious that the prosecution failed to note an alternate viewpoint: if the Farmers were doing so well financially, why were they both entitled to court-appointed representation, which is generally granted in cases where defendants have meager resources?

Another argument lacking in credibility was the explanation for transferring the deed to his four-month-old son, Peter. That came about, said James, when he realized the life-threatening dangers of his job working on the anchor ice at the mill. No other citizens with dangerous occupations, whether farmers or lumbermen, made similar bequests to their children, but James and Mary saw fit to make Peter Farmer far and away the youngest property owner in the county.

Much attention was also paid to the events of April 23–25. The defense claimed that Mary killed Sarah late Thursday morning, and then spent a lengthy period cleaning the mess. At 1:55 pm, she visited Jim at the sidewalk job and purportedly said, "Here are your keys. Mrs. Brennan has gone away. Go and tell Patsy." Rather than go to the mill to see Brennan, Jim waited until Patrick came home late in the afternoon to inform him that the Farmers planned on taking over the property.

On the following day, while Patsy was at work, Jim and Mary secured an eviction notice, which was served on Patrick that evening. The next day, Saturday, was an eventful one as well. The Farmers moved in, hiring locals to carry the heavy goods next door, including the trunk holding Sarah Brennan's body. Jim hit the bottle early and, by several accounts, was under the influence all day.

One neighbor testified to James' reply when asked where Mrs. Brennan was: "I don't know, but she'll never come back to live with Patsy." At the time, Mary Farmer was crying and pacing the floor, apparently in reaction to Jim's drinking. Another possible explanation for her nervous behavior was posited: her murder victim was in the next room and starting to decompose.

Despite the chaotic situation, Mary sent for the priest that afternoon, asking him to bless their new home. Jim saw an opportunity and tried to interest the reverend in purchasing the organ that came with their new house. The priest declined, but played on it briefly, prompting Mary Farmer to comment that it was the first time the organ had been played since the death of Mamie Brennan several years earlier.

After ten days of trial, the moment arrived for final summations. Unlike the sparse crowds from earlier in the proceedings, hundreds battled to gain entrance to the courtroom, leaving dozens frustrated outside.

The DA couldn't have asked for better visual aids. Behind him sat the ominous, bloodstained, black trunk, and on the table by his side were Sarah Brennan's bloodied clothes and other items of physical evidence. Pitcher spent much of his time disparaging the defense arguments about the Farmers' income, and dismissing the idea that Jim was ignorant of events surrounding their takeover of the Brennan's property.

For their part, defense attorneys revisited the Farmers' income issues, stressing that Jim was just a hard-working, longtime local who happened to marry a woman capable of committing unthinkable acts.

Justice DeAngelis was meticulous in addressing each issue to be decided by the jury. Several times he emphasized that only they could decide what was in James Farmer's heart when certain events occurred, like the recording of the deed and the eviction of his neighbor.

A few odd circumstances occurred on the trial's final day. The date was October 30, 1908, exactly one year from the day Mary Farmer executed the forged deed, which had set the entire sequence of events in motion. And the jury for Jim's trial deliberated from 11:30 AM to 2:30 PM, almost exactly the times that Mary's jury was out.

The results were no different, providing a third coincidence of sorts. James was found guilty of first-degree murder and sentenced to be electrocuted during the week of December 13.

Soon, both Farmers were on Death Row at Auburn Prison.

Two weeks later, it was Mrs. Farmer who was making headlines. With both trials ended, an interesting story, previously kept confidential, was revealed. Prior to Mary's trial, one arm of the investigation into her past led to Binghamton, where one Mary Burnes, an employee at Binghamton City Hospital, used fraudulent means to obtain a deed to some valuable property. When the scam was discovered, Burnes managed to escape to Buffalo, where she worked as a domestic under the names Mary Ann Bree and Mary O'Brien. (It was later determined that Burnes was somehow connected to an institution in Troy, possibly as an inmate.)

> # FARMER MUST DIE.
>
> ## Wife Now Awaits Execution in Auburn Prison.
>
> ## MURDERERS OF MRS. BRENNAN
>
> The Man Had All Along Pleaded That He Had No Hand in the Crime, But he Jury Held Him Equally Guilty With His Wife.

Headline proclaiming James Farmer's guilt

Mary Burnes' employment at the hospital occurred around 1903. Photographs of Mary Farmer were shown to an employee who had worked closely with Mary Burnes, and the response was shocking: they were undoubtedly one and the same person, a fact confirmed by a hospital physician who also knew Burnes. Had Mary Farmer not been awaiting execution, she would have faced prosecution on the Binghamton charges.

Patrick Brennan also surfaced briefly in the news when, nine months after his wife was murdered, he married Emma Snyder of Brownville.

In early 1909, the appeals court heard arguments in connection with Mary's case, and on February 12, the lower court's decision was affirmed. Mary Farmer's execution was scheduled for the week of March 29.

Robert Wilcox, though supremely frustrated, battled on. Visiting Binghamton and Buffalo, he secured affidavits from several of Mary's former co-workers and employers, attesting to her erratic behavior over the years. Some employers said Farmer was a hard worker and much appreciated, while others told of her extravagant claims, like ownership of large, expensive homes and rental properties (none of which proved true).

He also obtained an affidavit from Father John Hickey, who regularly tended to Mary's spiritual needs at Auburn. Hickey felt Mary was insane and should not be executed. With those statements in hand, Wilcox hoped to convince Governor Charles Evans Hughes to commute Mary's sentence. The question to be addressed was a difficult one—was she a deceitful, inveterate liar, or was she mentally impaired?

Wilcox tried every plea imaginable, but the governor was no pushover, posing many difficult questions to the attorney. Why appoint a commission to look at her possible insanity? Hadn't that been addressed during her trial? Are you saying she was insane, or did she become insane in prison? What information do you have that was not brought before the court of appeals? There were no good answers to the governor's questions.

His resources depleted, Wilcox pleaded for mercy. At the very worst, he said, Mary was guilty of manslaughter (to which no death sentence was attached), and her insanity was partly evidenced by having kept a decomposing corpse in her home. Wilcox also voiced the claim of many activists who said women should not be subjected to execution.

Governor Hughes reasoned that the idea of transferring the property to the infant indicated Mary's sanity, and added that the law provided no protection to criminals based on sex. Being female should not excuse punishment, and the penalty for first-degree murder was death.

Exactly a year earlier, the governor had sent infamous murderer Chester Gillette to his death. Once again, with trust in the court's work and belief in the defendant's guilt, he declined to offer clemency. Mary Farmer would die, and Robert Wilcox was devastated.

To the press, he said, "I shall take no further action. There is none that I can take." Despite that statement, the never-say-die attorney continued fighting to the end. As required, he provided the district attorney with seven days notice of further action he would be pursuing. But as Wilcox admitted, it was a futile gesture. Mary's execution was imminent:

> The governor's decision was not handed down in time to allow me the necessary action. If I had eight or ten days, I might be able to do something. Now it seems to be all over and I can do nothing but let her be judicially murdered. The woman is insane without question, and she did not recognize me in the slightest degree when I entered her cell.
>
> According to most reports, Mary spent some time reading in her cell, but during nine months of imprisonment, she mostly did nothing.

> All of her three guards admit that she did a tremendous heap of silent meditation that at times made the silence hideous, and in at least one instance caused the resignation of her guard, Mrs. Seymour Squyer, who said: "I simply cannot stand it. She never talks."

Just five days before Mary Farmer's scheduled execution, a remarkable story surfaced: Patrick Brennan had won back his property. That information was revealed during media review of an appellate court ruling on attorney's fees. One of the cases cited was Brennan's property suit that had been settled in fall 1908. It was an unusual bit of litigation, if for no other reason than the identity of his opponent—one-year-old Peter Farmer, who still held the deed to Patrick's former home.

Brennan had asked the court to invalidate both deeds, since Mary Farmer's trial had proved that the first one was forged. The court concurred. Representing the interests of Peter Farmer was attorney John Conboy. In another odd coincidence, Conboy had in recent years acted on behalf of the Farmer property. The home that Jim and Mary Farmer first bought, next door to the Brennans on Paddy Hill, was once known as the Barton House, an inn and tavern established by Robert Barton around 1895. Barton eventually filed bankruptcy, and it was Conboy who handled the final disposition of the property.

As the day of reckoning for Mary Farmer neared, preparations were finalized. Dr. Edwin Spitzka, who handled the post-mortem of Leon Czolgosz, assassin of President McKinley, was retained to perform the autopsy of Mary Farmer. Robert Wilcox, who battled so hard to save her from the chair, offered what comfort he could. He described young Peter's development, and encouraged Mary to go to the chair calmly, and with dignity. He also urged her to consider making a statement that could help save her husband's life.

Mary Farmer had asked about James, and the prison warden finally agreed to one last meeting between them. They hadn't seen one another since Mary left the jail at Watertown nine months earlier. With less than twelve hours to live, she was taken to Death Row, where James soon joined her. A reporter described their final encounter:

> Facing death at dawn, the woman showed no evidences last night of collapse, though the last words between herself and husband, separated in their parting

interview by heavy bars and an impenetrable screen, were affecting to the two women attendants and the captain of the guard. As the law does not permit it, there was no farewell embrace when the time came for separation. When the steel door of Mrs. Farmer's cell closed and James Farmer, weeping, was led away, the woman fell upon her cot and wept for a few moments, and then began to pray.

To prevent James from hearing his wife's last moments when she left Death Row and was taken to the chair, he was temporarily relocated to another wing of the prison.

Bob Wilcox reported that in his last meeting with her, Mary promised to make a confession absolving James of Sarah Brennan's murder. Although no specifics were offered, Father Hickey later announced that he had obtained some very important information from Mrs. Farmer. It was to be released only after her execution.

Just a few hours later, Mary Farmer became only the second woman in New York State to die in the electric chair. At 6:00 AM, she was removed from her cell. Fifteen minutes later, she was pronounced dead.

Shortly after, Father Hickey released Mary's notarized statement:

> My husband, James D. Farmer, never had any hand in Sarah Brennan's death, nor never knew anything about it till the trunk was opened. I never told him anything that had happened. I feel he has been terribly wronged. James D. Farmer was not at home the day the affair happened; neither did James D. Farmer ever put a hand on Sarah Brennan after her death.
>
> Again, I wish to say as strongly as I can that my husband, James D. Farmer, is entirely innocent of the death of Sarah Brennan, that he knowingly had no part in any plans that led to it, and that he knew nothing whatever about it.

Two months later, armed with Mary's last-minute confession, attorneys Field and Kellogg argued before the New York State Court of Appeals that the verdict against James Farmer must be set aside. They had filed the appeal based on other issues, but Mary's confession had considerably strengthened their case.

The DA presented strong evidence as well: that James was within

Evil Personified: Neighbor in a Trunk

MARY FARMER OWNS TO CRIME

Confesses Murder Details on Eve of Her Execution.

WILL MEET HER DEATH TODAY

three minutes walk of his home when the murder was committed; that he profited by recording the forged deed; that some of his hair was found in the trunk; and some of his clothing had been stained with human blood.

In October, the court announced a reversal of judgment. Although it was a split decision, Jim Farmer would have a new trial. One justice strongly disagreed with the finding, but the crux of the decision held that James should have been charged as an accessory, at worst. In effect, the high court had found James Farmer not guilty of murder in the first degree.

The DA had fully expected Farmer to follow his wife to the electric chair. Now, the most he could do was charge James with two crimes: forgery, and accessory to murder. The defense attorneys were fairly salivating at the prospects of winning freedom for their client. In early November, James Farmer was returned to the county jail at Watertown, and in mid-December, the murder indictment was official quashed.

On Christmas day, he received an unforgettable gift: freedom. Although James still faced charges, several relatives joined in paying his bail bond, allowing him to join them for Christmas dinner. It was nothing short of a stunning turnaround, and the rarest of events: after nearly two years of incarceration, including fifty-three weeks on Death Row, a defendant was given another chance in court.

And it wasn't long in coming. On February 21, the parade of witnesses began once again in what was basically a replay of the first trial. But the mood was decidedly different. Since his return, James' family and much of the community had been supportive. During the trial, Farmer was portrayed as a lifetime local man who had been victimized by the evil deeds of his wife.

There was a new panel of jurors, but little new evidence and few new witnesses. The result, however, was an entirely new verdict. On the evening of March 1, 1910, after only one vote by the jury, James Farmer was pronounced not guilty of being an accessory to murder. The packed courtroom erupted in celebration. The cheers and thunderous applause

Looking into the eyes of Mary Farmer, murderer

were quelled only by a long, insistent pounding of Judge Edgar Emerson's gavel, and a threat to fine those who disobeyed the call to silence.

The defense moved to quash the remaining charge of forgery, but Emerson opted to hear arguments from both sides later in the week. After court was adjourned, Farmer accepted congratulations from dozens of attendees and shook hands with each member of the jury.

The DA expressed doubts about pursuing the forgery charge, and after meeting with Judge Emerson, the case was abandoned. James Farmer was a free man. He moved in with his sister, Alice Doran, and her husband, Michael, who had been caring for young Peter Farmer, now nearly three years old.

Patrick Brennan died in 1918. His funeral was held in the Paddy Hill home he once shared with Sarah, whose murderer was the only woman among forty-eight individuals to die in Auburn's electric chair.

Thirty years after her death, Mary Farmer maintained a presence of sorts in the Jefferson County Courthouse. Inside the court railing, the first chair on the aisle's west side was known as the "Mary Farmer chair," the one she had sat in during her trial. On the seat's underside, her name had been written in red ink. Long a curiosity, the chair remained in use for decades.

The infamous trunk that held Sarah Brennan's body, and once sat as mute but powerful evidence in the courtroom, was also the subject of morbid attention. Several individuals tried to purchase it over the years, until Willard Moore, courthouse custodian, burned it.

The old Barton House, which became the Farmer home and the scene of Sarah Brennan's murder, was occupied off and on, beginning in 1911. It was a combination home and grocery store when it burned in 1945.

13

The Candy Killer

A gift for her husband: chocolate to die for.

For Herman Farr, a forty-year-old town of Champlain employee (in northeastern Clinton County, New York), Wednesday, May 20, 1925, was just like any other workday. He rose early, cleaned up, ate breakfast, and packed a lunch. It was still between 6:00 and 7:00 AM, so he tended to a few chores before heading off to join his crew at the local sandpit.

A couple of hours into the morning shift, Herman raided his lunch pail for a snack and unexpectedly found a few sweets inside. Although he hadn't packed any candies, he certainly recognized them, having purchased a bag of chocolate drops the day before as a gift for his wife, Bessie. As a thoughtful gesture, she must have tossed a few in with his lunch, providing a special treat for the morning break.

His appetite temporarily appeased, Herman returned to work, but a short time later, he began feeling ill. Cramps, muscle spasms, and a queasy stomach forced him to stop for rest, but as the symptoms worsened, his co-workers became alarmed and called the local physician.

Dr. George Allen of Champlain soon appeared on the scene and found Herman in deep distress. "Doc," he said, "I've been poisoned." Allen gave him some medicine and drove him home, but on the way, Farr vomited twice. When they arrived, Bessie ran outside and heard her husband say, "Dearie, I'm awful sick." She and Dr. Allen supported him as he walked to the house. They positioned him on a cot, and the doctor gave Mrs. Farr directions on what dosage and timing to use for his medications.

Around mid-afternoon, Allen returned to find his patient in dire straits, beset by violent, painful convulsions that doubled him in half involuntarily. Although Herman remained conscious, he was clearly in agony. The horrible symptoms attacked him mercilessly throughout the night, and the next morning, he could bear no more. Just twenty-four hours after experiencing the first painful symptoms of the mysterious illness,

Herman Farr breathed his last. Two young girls were rendered fatherless, and a young wife became a grieving widow.

The coroner ordered an autopsy, and family and friends undertook burial preparations. Dr. Allen, his suspicions aroused by the nature of Herman's symptoms and the suddenness of his death, sent the victim's stomach to the Albany police lab for analysis. Early results indicated the presence of strychnine in Farr's urine, prompting an immediate investigation, led by Champlain's police chief, Edmund Dragon.

It was soon learned that William Hogge, owner of a drugstore in Champlain, had sold 25 cents worth of strychnine to a woman on May 8, and he believed the buyer was Bessie Farr. The woman claimed she had borrowed some strychnine from a local man to poison some nuisance foxes, and wished to replace it. She requested an ounce, but the druggist had less on hand, prompting her to inquire if more would be available soon. Their conversation, unusual in nature, remained clear in his memory.

Investigators also discovered that Mrs. Farr had summoned local insurance agent Arthur Gokey to her home on April 8, just six weeks before Mr. Farr's death. At that time, a life insurance policy for $2000 ($25,000 in 2012) was taken out on Herman, with Bessie as the beneficiary.

It wasn't a huge amount of money, but with investigators quietly branching out in several directions, information was developed that Bessie may have had another motive for getting rid of her husband. The Farr family lived in Wilfred Boudreau's home, and the rumor mill had been buzzing about a possible romance between Bessie and Wilfred. The Farrs were known to have battled fiercely at times, and Bessie was often seen going for drives with Boudreau.

In the meantime, further test results from Albany confirmed suspicions that Herman had died from strychnine poisoning. Three days after Farr's death, armed with the lab and insurance information, plus the romance angle, authorities arrested Bessie on suspicion of foul play. Boudreau denied any knowledge of what had transpired, but he was also taken in and detained as a material witness.

Both were held overnight, and on Monday, Bessie was questioned extensively by Sheriff Day and District Attorney O'Connell. She continued denying any knowledge of how her husband had died, but hour by hour, additional bits of information gleaned during the investigation were revealed by the detectives. Bessie finally realized they were onto her, and by Monday night, she had signed a full confession, admitting to replacing the candy's innards with poison and putting it in her husband's lunch pail.

The question was, why?

When details of her confession were released to the media, the public was both fascinated and appalled to learn about Bessie's background. Her youth was spent in Mooers Forks, about ten miles west of Champlain. Her current age was given as thirty-six, an error that was repeated in newspapers across the country when the sensational murder story was picked up by the Associated Press. The false age may have been Bessie's effort to prevent her past life from undergoing intense scrutiny.

At the time of the murder, she had actually just turned twenty-eight, and her daughters were thirteen and twelve. A quick calculation reveals that motherhood began at a very young age. It was also mentioned that she was adopted, but that information was a bit misleading.

Bessie was born to a pair of twenty-year-olds, Joseph and Alvira Mesick, on April 13, 1897. When Alvira died in March 1899, Bessie and Joseph remained on the family farm with Joseph's parents and three brothers. His younger brother, Amos, married in 1904 and took over operations on the farm. Joseph remarried a year later, left the farm, and went on to raise a large family, but Bessie did not join him, instead remaining with her aunt and uncle, grandmother, and two cousins on the family farm.

It was an unusual path, but atypical events were a staple of Bessie's life. She claimed to have married at age twelve (to Herman Farr) and to have given birth to a child when she was thirteen, followed by a second when she was fourteen. While there are some errors and discrepancies in various official records, there is also plenty of evidence supporting her claims. Even erring on the side of caution, Bessie Farr was, at the age of fifteen, the married mother of two young daughters. The family moved from Mooers to Altona, and then to Champlain.

Foregoing an education to marry and raise a family, especially at such a young age, led to a difficult life. While talking to the district attorney, Bessie referred to "the drudgery and monotony" of cleaning, cooking, and caring for children. She was, after all, a child herself in many ways. Physically, she was a full-grown woman, but was otherwise described as having the mentality of a twelve-year-old.

Her neighbors in Champlain told of loud fights during which Bessie often threatened her husband's life. But during her confession, Bessie described frequent beatings by Herman, leaving her bruised and scared. The children, she said, were frightened of him as well.

CHAMPLAIN WOMAN CONFESSES SHE POISONED HER HUSBAND

Mrs. Bessie Farr Breaks Down Under Grilling Of District Attorney O'Connell; Admits Placing Strychnine In Chocolate Drop She Put In Husband's Dinner Pail; Another Arrest May Follow.

WOMAN DENIES POISONING MAN

Mrs. Farr Champlain is Accused of Giving Husband Chocolate Drop

On May 28, 1925, conflicting headlines appeared in the Bessie Farr case, a story carried nationally after gaining the attention of the Associated Press

The DA and the sheriff were satisfied with Bessie's confession, which established further motive beyond the suspicion that she had killed him for the insurance money.

The following morning, she spoke with Attorney Harold A. Jerry, who would represent her in court. Shortly after, Bessie recanted, claiming to have no knowledge of what might have caused her husband's death, and denying the suggestion that she had planted poison in his lunch. The confession, she said, came out of fear caused by the relentless badgering during questioning, just as her husband used fear and intimidation to keep her in line. Bessie reaffirmed her love for Herman and said that despite the beatings and abuse, she loved him, and would never have stayed with him for fourteen years of marriage if she felt otherwise.

During a meeting with a reporter from the *Plattsburgh Daily Republican*, she explained the confession:

> They made me lie. They scared me to death. They were here, two or three of them every now and then, and forced me to say things that were not so.
>
> I loved my husband, and did call him a dear man when his remains were being lowered into the grave last Saturday morning. I have been married to him for fourteen years. He was cruel to me and often beat me, but I loved him always.
>
> I did not dare ever to say anything against him to anybody, for fear that what I said would be carried back to him, and if he ever heard that I said things about him, he would kill me. He did put poison in my food lots of times, and I would get dreadfully sick.

As further damage control, Farr also granted an interview to Quebec's *Huntingdon Gleaner*:

> They made me admit things that were not so. I wanted rest. I was tired of their questions. They dogged me all night. Every time I showed signs of weariness, they piled their questions worse than ever. Finally, to be rid of them, I told them that I put the poisoned chocolate drop in the lunch pail. But that is not so.
>
> Herman had brought me the candy. Goodness knows, he brought me things seldom enough. He seldom showed affection either for me or the children. Certainly, I wondered when he brought the candy home. He took me by surprise. But I didn't kill him for bringing me the chocolates. I don't know how the poison got there. He was happy when he left home that morning.
>
> I was happy, too. Really, his little attention had given me a new lease on life, and I dreamed of happiness that I had not had in all the years of our married life.
>
> The girls were happy, too. They were afraid of their father because of the way he had abused me on many occasions. They wanted to see me happy, and they wanted to love their father, but he wouldn't let them. He always spoiled everything by his abuse of me.

Throughout the days of Bessie's interrogation, her confession, and the subsequent reversal, Wilfred Boudreau remained in custody as a possible accessory to murder, though he remained uncharged. At all times, Bessie insisted that Wilfred was not involved in the Farrs' problems.

The story had already gained widespread attention, with bold headlines proclaiming Bessie's nickname: CANDY KILLER CONFESSES! Now, with the prospects of a trial and the story of Bessie's unusual background, interest increased. Plattsburgh photographer Kenneth Brush was commissioned by newspapers in New York City to send images of several Champlain sites associated with the story. Chocolate drops, the candy that proved to be Herman's undoing, received a massive amount of free publicity.

Due to Bessie's retraction, instead of a murder case settled by confession, the attorneys were now required to prepare for trial. On June 16, a preliminary hearing featured the testimony of William Hogge, the Champlain pharmacist, and Dr. Allen, who treated Herman for poisoning.

Much of it was compelling, covering the details of the strychnine purchase and the final, horrible twenty-four hours of Herman Farr's life.

Further damning was the testimony of Arthur Gokey, a Champlain insurance agent who sold the Farrs a life insurance policy shortly before Herman's death:

> I called at the Farr home at his request. He had little to say while I was making out the policy. Mrs. Farr engineered that part of it. She was made the beneficiary. I must admit that I witnessed nothing that indicated to me the couple were on other than the best terms. This whole case, since Farr's death, has been a deep mystery to me.

Although a claim had since been submitted to collect on the life insurance policy, the company deferred settling the matter until the court case was finalized.

On Friday, August 14, a tearful Bessie collapsed in court as the judge rendered his decision. Despite Attorney Jerry's plea on her behalf, claiming she was physically and mentally impaired when she made the confession, Bessie was ordered confined to jail without bail, pending the grand jury's consideration of first-degree murder charges.

While the defendant waited behind bars and both sides prepared to do battle, outside forces came to bear in an unusual manner. Just eight days

2 LITTLE GIRLS ARE TO DECIDE FATE OF MOTHER

Children witnesses In Candy Poisoning Of Father, Case In United States.

CHARGE OF MURDER.

Mrs. Farr, A Bride At 13, Says Her Life Has Been Continuous Drudge.

after Herman Farr died, Henry Soper of Elizabethtown, about sixty miles south of Champlain, was found dead. His wife Fannie was charged with murder, and the case ended in shocking fashion. On November 20, 1925, Mrs. Soper was found guilty and sentenced by Judge Edward Whitmyer to die in the electric chair. The execution of a woman was a rare finding, one that did not escape the attention of Bessie and her attorney—nor did the fact that the judge handling Farr's trial was Edward Whitmyer.

Two hundred jurors awaited the call to duty on Clinton County's high-profile murder case, but the call they received three days after the Soper decision was unexpected: don't come to court on Monday. No explanation was provided, but such an order likely meant that a settlement had been reached.

On November 30, 1925, Bessie Farr, no doubt influenced by the Soper trial outcome, avoided a potential death sentence by pleading guilty to second-degree murder in exchange for a sentence of twenty years to life.

In support of the agreement, District Attorney O'Connell said:

> While the defendant, in my opinion, is sane, there is an apparent possibility that facts might be presented upon the trial to indicate an arrested mental development which, while not of such an extent as to free her from the responsibility for her act, might have the result of influencing a jury to find a lesser degree than murder first, the crime charged in the indictment.

On behalf of Bessie Farr, Harold Jerry spoke:

> ... the elimination of a trial will cause a savings to the county of several thousand dollars. [The savings was estimated at $10,000 to $20,000—equal to $125,000 to $250,000 in 2012.]
>
> ... there is, of course, but one sentence that can be imposed upon the defendant: a minimum of twenty years, and a maximum of her natural life. But with the commutation automatically allowed by law, she can, by good behavior, become discharged in fifteen years.
>
> I trust your Honor will be able to extend even further leniency, and consider yourself justified in recommending her parole after serving not more than ten years. This, I believe, will meet with the ends of justice.

When it was over, Bessie professed confusion about the reference to her mental capabilities. As far as she was concerned, she had never been given a chance.

> I don't know what they mean when they say, "arrested mental development." I never knew anything but work. I never had time to think. Now that I have plenty of time, it drives me mad to think what has happened.

For someone who had known nothing but motherhood for fully half of her young life, it was difficult to say goodbye to her daughters. Since Herman's death in May, the girls had stayed with Mr. and Mrs. Edward Dragon (as Champlain's chief of police, it was Ed who had led the investigation of the Farr case). Bessie felt that living with the Dragons was the best option for the girls, far better than their previous circumstance.

> Herman had some insurance. It amounted to about $2500. They can use that to get some learning. That's one of the things I never had. They said I killed him to get that money. They lie. I wouldn't touch a penny of it. If I did get any of it, it would be the first money I ever had in my life.

In a final interview before departing for Auburn Prison (in central New York State), Bessie was asked about her suspected paramour, Wilfred Boudreau, who was present in the courtroom when she entered her guilty plea. Direct questioning prompted a brief, open exchange:

> REPORTER: Do you love Boudreau?
> BESSIE: I did.
> REPORTER: Was it worth it?
> BESSIE: When it first started, it seemed like the only happy thing in my life. But it didn't go on that way. Looking back at it, I reckon it didn't.

The day after her guilty plea, Bessie was accompanied by both the local jail matron and the sheriff as she boarded the 9:57 PM train: destination, Auburn. Attorney Harold Jerry was there to see her off. Standing discreetly off to the side, seemingly unnoticed by Bessie as she crossed the boarding platform, was Wilfred Boudreau, who watched her board the train. But she knew he was there, honoring her request from the previous day when they visited at the jail.

While talking later with reporters, Boudreau said he planned to return to New York City where he once worked. As one writer put it, he "could not stand the averted glances and whispering tongues of the people at Champlain."

Upon Sheriff Day's return from the trip to Auburn, he reported that Bessie had broken down and wept when they parted. His description of the women's facility was surprisingly upbeat:

> The prison itself is as pleasant as such a place could well be. Each woman has a cell to herself, with outside light. For a few hours a day, there is work to be done in the clothing shops, after which the women are allowed to mingle together.
>
> Every good day, they are supposed to exercise outdoors, where there are tennis courts and places for other less violent outdoor sports. There is also a school for those who want to attend and secure a better education.
>
> In the evening there are moving pictures and radio entertainments. The women are locked in their cells at 8:00 PM. The entire prison is immaculately clean.

The lives of Bessie's daughters, Hattie and Della, took different paths after beginning with so few advantages. When the prospects of their mother's trial loomed, the two girls, prospective witnesses to life in the Farr household, were described by the press as "very intelligent and well-behaved, giving every evidence of careful training."

Hattie later attended St. Anne's Convent in Montreal, but Della was placed in the Rome State School, a facility "for helpless, unteachable idiots" and delinquents. All sorts of "afflictions" (as they were called) were eventually addressed at the state school, including mental illness, teen pregnancy, criminality, retardation, and others. Among Della's problems was illiteracy. According to school records, she had not recently attended school, and at the age of eighteen, she was unable to read or write.

When Della was in Rome in 1930, her mother was just seventy miles west in another state institution, Auburn Prison, where she worked various jobs. Considering the method Bessie had used to kill her husband, it was somewhat ironic that she was entrusted with the job of waitress in the warden's residence.

After serving her time (fifteen years due to a reduction for good behavior), she returned to the North Country, settling in Rouses Point, just four miles west of her former home in Champlain. Daughter Hattie (O'Lena) also lived in Rouses Point, where she had worked as a cook in Anctil's Restaurant since 1934.

Bessie passed away in April 1961, a week shy of her sixty-fourth birthday. Hattie died on the job at Anctil's Restaurant in January 1972.

14

Passion, Poison, Prison

Alice began talking, and what she revealed more than confirmed Horicon's neighborhood gossip mill, which was now operating in high gear.

On the morning of Sunday, June 23, 1927, in the town of Horicon, west of Lake George in Warren County, Byron and Alice Frasier, a married couple of twenty-eight years, shared their plans for the day. Alice's routine was to share a window-shopping trip with her sister, Maggie Rising. Byron, after a long week's work at Brant Lake, planned to drink his customary bottle of homemade wine, do a little gardening, and then catch a long nap. He had just arrived home on Saturday night, but was to return to Brant Lake by 4:00 Sunday afternoon.

The two visited as Alice, 41, changed her dress and Byron, 55, poured a glass of wine. The homegrown batch tasted a bit sour, and the two of them agreed it might have been left standing in the sun too long. As she left for her sister's home about two miles away, Alice told Byron he would find jellyrolls and other goods in the pantry when he was hungry.

The trip to Horicon was the usual good time for the ladies, and they didn't arrive back at the Frasier residence until late afternoon, at about the time Byron was supposed to leave. Entering the kitchen, they were greeted by a shocking sight. Byron lay sprawled on the floor, face down, his neck bloodied from a head wound. They could only surmise that he had suffered a stroke, striking his head on the stove as he fell. Although he was bloodied, Byron's head injury didn't appear serious enough to have caused his death.

The women called Dr. Howard B. Swan of Chestertown, a Warren County coroner, telling him what they had found, and of the suspicion that he had suffered some type of spell. When Swan arrived at the scene, Byron Frasier had clearly been dead for some time. His tightly clenched fists and the positioning of his limbs suggested a victim who had died in agony. After examining the body and noting other telltale signs, Swan said nothing to the women of his suspicions, but notified the sheriff and the district attorney that something appeared to be amiss.

A state trooper, Sergeant Dewey Lawrence, arrived on the scene, followed by the sheriff and DA. While Lawrence looked around the home for evidence, a man showed up and began visiting with Alice. A few questions addressed to neighbors revealed the man's name: Stephen Baker, a local who had been working regularly at the Frasier home. Some of them suggested that Mrs. Frasier and Baker were romantically involved.

Meanwhile, the sheriff and DA questioned Alice, who denied any knowledge of the reason for her husband's sudden demise. As far as she knew, he had suffered some type of attack, fallen from his chair, struck his head on the stove, and died.

The victim's body was removed and an autopsy was performed by two physicians under the supervision of Coroner Swan. By Tuesday, although further lab testing was needed, both doctors had arrived at the same conclusion, confirming Swan's suspicions: Byron Frasier had died a horrible death from ingesting a fatal dosage of strychnine. The question was, where had it come from?

Investigators went immediately to the Frasier home and again questioned Alice extensively. She stood firm, claiming no knowledge of what had happened to Byron while she was away all day, shopping with her sister. But as other bits of information accumulated, more and more the evidence pointed to someone within the Frasier home.

That night, Sergeant Lawrence remained in the farmhouse to ensure nothing was disturbed before a detailed search could be conducted by police investigators. All was quiet until after midnight, when noises from someone moving about alerted him. He slipped outside, pausing briefly for his eyes to adjust. Spying a figure moving through the darkness, he followed discreetly behind until the person stopped, dropped to the ground, and appeared to move a large rock.

Lawrence pulled his gun, turned on his flashlight, and ordered the person to stand. Training the light upward revealed the face of Stephen Baker. In one of his hands was a bottle, and the sergeant had a pretty good idea what it held.

Both Alice Frasier and Stephen Baker, 51, were arrested and held in custody for the murder of Byron Frasier. Although it appeared the killers had been captured, there was a whole lot more to the story, as authorities would soon find out. Alice began talking, and what she revealed more than confirmed Horicon's neighborhood gossip mill, which was now operating in high gear.

Baker, it seems, was much more than a hired hand. He and wife Grace (Bolton) Baker had six children, with current ages of 28, 24, 21, 19, 17, and 11. But two years ago, in early February 1925, after thirty years of marriage, Grace left Stephen and filed for divorce, having endured gossip, innuendo, and suspicions about her husband's supposed dalliance with a local woman, whom Grace named in the divorce papers as a co-respondent. That woman was none other than Alice Frasier.

The high-profile, contested divorce of the Bakers was a rarity that attracted the attention of folks across Warren County. Many residents were called to testify before a packed courtroom as to the plaintiff's and defendant's character (or lack thereof), and to offer pertinent details, which kept tongues wagging in nearby communities.

> **TAKE NOTICE**—Whereas, my wife, Grace, has left my bed and board without just cause or provocation, I do hereby forbid all persons harboring or trusting her on my account as I shall pay no debts of her contracting after this date, February 10, 1925. Stephen Baker, Horicon, Warren county, N. Y.

Alice Frasier took the stand, ironically, on her twenty-sixth anniversary, swearing that she and Stephen were nothing but friends. Byron's testimony offered at least partial corroboration of Alice's statements, but in the end, the judge granted Grace Baker a divorce and ordered Stephen to pay alimony.

Stephen objected to the alimony requirement, and on different occasions found himself jailed briefly for not paying. He also continued spending time at the Frasier residence, even working there while Byron was away (which happened frequently). In fact, in the days prior to Byron's death, while he was on the job at Brant Lake, Baker was working at the Frasier home and spending nights there. He had only left Saturday afternoon, just hours before Byron arrived home.

Byron and Alice quarreled frequently over the attention paid to her by Baker (her eager reciprocation was also an issue), and they did so again that night. While such shenanigans were not unheard of, marriages of twenty-eight and thirty years duration added an unusual element to a story line that was more commonly driven by youthful passions.

Alice could not control her ardor for Stephen, a fact that eroded her marriage and led to nefarious planning. At some point in May, she purchased a quantity of strychnine from a Chestertown drugstore and bided her time. In June, after the better part of a week with her illicit lover staying overnight, she could wait no longer.

To ensure the job was done thoroughly, she poured a quarter of the strychnine container into a bottle of Byron's homemade elderberry wine while he was out of the house briefly on that fateful morning. He came back in and immediately began imbibing as they discussed their plans for the day. The wine had a decidedly sour taste, but that didn't stop him from drinking it. He reminded Alice of his four o'clock departure for Brant Lake, which she acknowledged in her confession with the words, "… but I knew he would never go."

A cold, heartless sentiment indeed, but there was more. She nearly didn't leave the house soon enough, admitting that while crossing the field leading to her sister's home, Alice could hear Byron coughing, clearly in great physical distress. Unmoved, she kept on walking as her husband of nearly three decades began suffering a slow death of unimaginable pain.

Later that day, after the body was found and authorities were notified, the interrogation of Alice lasted well into the evening. While everyone else left the Frasier home late Sunday night, both Baker and Alice were allowed to remain there. She told Stephen what she had done, and together they took the empty wine bottle and hid it beneath a rock. But after investigators, armed with the autopsy report, returned on Tuesday and again questioned her for hours, Alice was worried. Fearing the bottle would be discovered, she asked Baker to remove it that night, a process that was interrupted by the presence of Sergeant Lawrence.

At all times during questioning, and in her two confessions, Alice insisted that Stephen Baker knew nothing of the murder beforehand, and had only helped her hide the wine bottle after the deed was done. Alice admitted having loved Baker for the past three years, and her reason for committing the crime was straightforward: she couldn't have Stephen if she had Byron, so Byron had to go.

Frasier was held in the Lake George jail on charges of first-degree murder, but Baker, accused as an accessory, was freed a week later when his father came up with

$5000 bail. Baker still had plenty of reasons to worry about the immediate future. An accessory conviction carried a maximum sentence of five years in prison, and who knew what Alice might say on the witness stand when facing the death penalty?

With great public interest in the case, the Frasier homestead was beset with curiosity seekers and souvenir hunters, the latter of whom were grabbing anything they could carry away. In need of money to fund her defense, Alice would, in a sense, turn one last time to Byron for help. An auction was held two weeks after his death, selling the entire contents of the farm, everything Byron had accumulated in his lifetime. A huge gathering of about five hundred people generated a profit for Alice of $1200 ($15,000 in 2012).

She then retained the services of Glens Falls attorney Paul Boyce, who promptly addressed the media. Mrs. Frasier's confessions, he said, would have little bearing in court, and neighbors and relatives of Alice would be coming forward to speak on her behalf.

But a case of sorts was already in the making, based on sympathy for the defendant. Details of Alice's past were leaked to the press, lending a "backwoods" aura to the stories published in several metropolitan newspapers. It was enough that Byron was fourteen years her senior, but that wasn't all. When they married, Alice had barely passed her fifteenth birthday, meaning Byron was almost exactly twice her age at the time.

He was also her cousin. And, as it happens, Stephen Baker was her cousin as well. Those were the kinds of juicy details the media loved and the public devoured.

Alice, meanwhile, languished in jail, very uncomfortable in her new surroundings. News in late June did little to lift her spirits. The lab results from the autopsy arrived, verifying the cause of death as strychnine poisoning. It wasn't unexpected, but the reality offered little hope for Alice's future. From other cases involving female murder defendants, the standard outcome appeared to be a plea bargain, admitting guilt to second-degree murder in order to avoid the higher charge, which carried a death sentence. Public opinion leaned towards the idea as well, uncomfortable with the concept of putting women to death, no matter what the charge.

One other option existed for Alice, that of an insanity defense, but by mid-October, that too was out the proverbial window. At the grand jury's suggestion, Mrs. Frasier was examined by professionals to determine her capabilities. A commission of three prominent specialists studied Alice, presenting their findings to the Honorable Irving I. Goldsmith, Justice of the Supreme Court:

> In the opinion of these commissioners, it is our conclusion that the said Alice Frasier is sane.
>
> That said Alice Frasier is mentally deficient (moron) with an intelligent quota of 55, and although she is chronologically forty-three years of age, her mental age is eight years and ten months, while her basal age is but six years.
>
> That while her mental age and judgment is that of a child eight years and ten months, she has the emotional instinct of an adult, with the judgment of a child.
>
> That judgment of said Alice Frasier is therefore defective, and was at the time of her alleged crime, because of her mental defect.
>
> We do believe that because of her act, she is a social menace and should be placed in confinement for a period of at least twenty years, by which time her sex cravings will be at a minimum, and her childbearing period will have terminated.

Justice Goldsmith set an appearance date of November 3, when Alice would be presented two options: pursuing a jury trial, or pleading to a lesser charge. Stephen Baker was also in the news, entering a plea of not guilty to charges of being an accessory to a felony. His bail was increased to

MRS. FRASIER HAS CHILD'S MENTALITY
Woman Charged With Murder Is Declared Sane But "Social Menace" by Commission

MRS. FRASIER MAY MAKE GUILTY PLEA
South Horicon Woman Expected to Admit Murder in Second Degree and Escape Chair

$7500, with a court date to follow Alice's appearance.

On November 3, Alice ended all speculation by entering a plea of guilty to second-degree murder, earning her a sentence of twenty years to life—but she wasn't going anywhere just yet. A cell in Auburn's Prison for Women awaited, but she was temporarily housed in the county jail at Lake George, pending service as a witness in the Stephen Baker case.

Nine days later, she was back in court. Baker fought to the bitter end, hoping for a charge of tampering with evidence instead of accessory to murder. To bolster his claim, Alice testified that she was no longer in love with him, and that his only aid to her was in lifting the rock so she could hide the bottle, and then later moving it at her request.

Character witnesses also appeared on Baker's behalf, but it wasn't enough. He was found guilty and given the maximum punishment of a $500 fine and two and a half to five years in Clinton Prison at Dannemora. But there was still hope for a reversal. His attorney, James Kiley, served notice of appeal and requested a certificate of reasonable doubt (noting that a question of law still existed). The application was granted, and Baker was released on bail.

It had been an eventful two weeks in November. Alice Frasier was convicted, testified in Baker's case, and was shipped off to Auburn Prison. Stephen Baker was convicted, but freed on bail and hopeful of keeping his freedom. And his ex-wife, Grace Baker, married John R. Bennett.

As with several of the other players in this story, there were a few oddities connected to the new joining. Bennett, 62, was sixteen years her senior—and had previously been married to Grace's sister.

Following delays, Baker's case was heard by the Appellate Court, New York's highest. Kiley argued that the jury erred because Baker had done nothing beyond concealing evidence. The court was buying none of it, and in late May, they ruled unanimously against Baker, citing the law:

> … a person who assists a murderer to conceal evidence which might connect the slayer with the crime is an accessory after the fact.

Since the ruling was unanimous, there was no further possibility of appeal. Rather than wait for the court order, Baker visited the county treasurer and paid his fine.

Exactly one year and one week after Byron Frasier's death, both defendants in the case were in prison: Stephen Baker was an inmate at

Dannemora, while lost paramour Alice Frasier was serving as a cook in the Auburn Prison kitchen—presumably with access to the food, but not the drinks.

15

Victim of a Historic U.S. Range War

Eight slugs were found in Giles' corpse, more than enough to kill him, but perhaps just the right amount to send a message.

By an odd coincidence of "twos," a pair of brothers, born two years apart in Franklin County, New York, were involved in two unusual murder stories separated by nearly two thousand miles. One story was linked to two places called Dickinson. Both stories made national headlines, and neither was ever solved.

By far the more famous of the two cases was the 1903 murder of millionaire Orrando Dexter in the Franklin County town of Santa Clara. Dexter's beautiful, expansive estate (purchased in the 1990s by Shania Twain and Mutt Lange, who built a recording studio on the shore of Dexter Lake) was managed by superintendent Azro Giles. Azro was on the scene shortly after Dexter was shot and killed. [A chapter of the author's award-winning book, *Oliver's War: An Adirondack Rebel Battles the Rockefeller Fortune*, covers the incident.]

The lesser known of the two stories involved his brother, Orlando Giles. Like the Dexter story, it included murder, mystery, and intrigue, with a dose of courtroom shenanigans and a potential western range war thrown in for good measure.

Like Azro, Orlando was born in Dickinson, New York. Most of the first four decades of his life were spent in northern New York, passed in ordinary fashion. During those years, he pursued various interests: serving as assessor and political party delegate; farming; operating a creamery and butter factory; running a boarding house and sportsman's resort; and operating a store.

In 1891, he ran into some trouble with a civil suit, and an arrest warrant was issued. To execute it, the sheriff visited Giles' store at Dickinson Center, but when he entered, Orlando stepped into a nearby room and closed the door. The sheriff followed, only to be greeted by "a Winchester in his face and a threat to blow the top of his head off," as one reporter put it.

Although he managed to disarm Giles, another opportunity arose for his prisoner to secure a weapon. With Orlando once again wielding a gun, the sheriff judiciously withdrew.

Hours later, he was back with reinforcements. After a chase, Giles was wrestled to the ground, put in a chokehold, and arrested. Appearing in court, he was released on $500 bail.

Two weeks later, as many other North Country folks had done, the Giles family (wife Alice and two children) headed west, eventually settling in South Dakota, midway between infamous Deadwood (130 miles south) and Dickinson, North Dakota (70 miles north).

Along the shores of the North Grand River, north of the Black Hills, Orlando, now in his early forties, developed a successful ranching operation. It was beautiful country, famed for spectacular scenery, but notorious as well. The Giles ranch was located east of where a national incident had occurred just a year earlier, the Johnson County War in neighboring Wyoming, one of the truly deplorable incidents in American history. At issue was the open-range concept, where cattle roamed without fences. The large ranchers opposed smaller ranchers and homesteaders, accusing them of cattle rustling. Eventually, owners of the big ranches took the law into their own hands, developing an actual hit list and sending hired guns out to eliminate the suspected rustlers.

People were killed, and on direct orders of President Benjamin Harrison, federal troops finally intervened—but they did so to protect the killers, who were eventually set free and never prosecuted. Those siding with the victims were incensed at what amounted to government endorsement of vigilante justice, and the issue remained extremely volatile.

In that tense atmosphere, a year after gunmen in Wyoming killed a suspected rustler, the bullet-riddled body of a small ranch-owner was found on May 11, 1893. It was Orlando Giles.

In the ensuing days, headlines predicted a renewal of the Wyoming range war, and citizens were outraged. There was little doubt in anyone's mind that the cattlemen were responsible for the murder. Eight slugs were found in Giles' corpse, more than enough to kill

> **EIGHT BULLET HOLES IN HIS BODY.**
>
> A St. Lawrence County Man Killed by Neighboring Ranchers in the West.

him, but perhaps just the right amount to send a message.

Justice was demanded, but there was no easy solution. Ominous newspaper stories from Nebraska and the Dakotas appeared as far east as the *New York Sun*, which addressed the issue:

> The authorities were requested to investigate the murder, but they were intimidated by rough characters, and no arrests have been made. Scouts are on the range every day, and no one can ride out without seeing a horseman on a hill, quietly taking in the country with the aid of a telescope.
>
> Nothing escapes their vision, and it would be impossible for the stockmen to get a crowd together to clean out the rustlers without attracting their attention. The rustlers say they will not leave, although notice has been served on them to depart.
>
> The natural consequence is that a war may be the outcome of the murder of Giles. The cattlemen are determined to break up the rustlers, who, on the other hand, are equally determined to stay in the country.

It was rumored that Giles had not been an innocent player in events leading to his death. From his ranch in South Dakota, within a few miles of the North Dakota line, he had reportedly taken regular trips north to Dickinson in southwestern North Dakota to sell cattle. Yet it was observed that his own herd seemed to maintain its head count, despite sending so many cattle to slaughter.

From the *Bismarck Tribune*:

> The present trouble between cattlemen and cattle rustlers north of the Black Hills bids fair to result in open warfare. The other day, a small stockman named Orlando Giles was found dead near his ranch on the North Grand River. Giles had only a small bunch of cattle, but he had been hauling dressed beef to Dickinson all winter without materially diminishing his own herd.
>
> For some reason, he never exhibited any hides of the numerous animals he was slaughtering. There were many cowboys who were convinced that he was killing other people's cattle for his individual profit, and this belief was the cause of his sudden taking off [killing].

Just as Giles was from Dickinson Center (southwest of Malone), the town of Dickinson, North Dakota, also had direct ties to New York's North Country. The place was a railroad stop initially known as Pleasant Valley Siding, but was changed a year later to Dickinson in honor of Wells Stoughton Dickinson of Malone, owner of vast tracts of land there prior to Dakota statehood. Wells was a prominent entrepreneur and politician, and had traveled to the Dakotas as a land agent, helping to settle the area. Other Dickinson family members from Malone and Moira also settled in Dickinson, North Dakota, most notably Horace, who became a leading citizen of the growing township.

In support of the cattlemen's claims that Orlando was a rustler, a newspaper story cited Giles' recent letter to the folks back home. In it, he purportedly mentioned that "there were 40 nice fat steers, not branded, and ownerless, not far from his ranch, and that he might 'run them in.'"

The same article was repeated back home in Franklin County, New York, but the actual letter was never produced, casting doubt on its validity, and suggesting it may have been nothing more than a disgraceful tactic to further dishonor the victim and justify his murder.

Overshadowed by the furor was that a mother in New York had lost a son, Alice Giles had lost a husband, and two young children were orphaned. Investigators probed further, but came up empty. Somebody had to know something, but nobody was talking.

The story languished for well over a year, until December 1894, when a shocking announcement was made: Alice Giles and an accomplice had been arrested for the murder of her husband. Sensational headlines described a love triangle that resulted in the ruthless killing of Giles in order to take his land, his cattle, and his wife.

The accused was William "Billy" Davidson, who had stayed at the Giles home since Orlando's death. Authorities claimed to have overwhelming evidence that Giles had been on his way home from Dickinson when Billy and Alice encountered him on the trail, deciding then and there to bring their plan to fruition and do away with him.

Both were taken to the Butte County jail and arraigned later in Deadwood. Their hopes of making bail dissolved as the state's attorney recounted his version of the crime to the sitting judge. Alice and Billy, he said, had ridden out to meet Orlando on his return trip from Dickinson. Davidson shot him while he still sat in the wagon, and then made him walk to a remote place, where he was shot again, which spooked Orlando's team of horses. After retrieving them, Davidson returned and pumped six more slugs into the victim. As proof that Alice was present, the attorney cited the prints from a horse whose stride suggested an animal tired from a long run. The prints, they said, matched those of Alice's saddle horse.

The attorney also dismissed the popular belief that cattlemen had slain Giles, noting that the body was not found on the main trail, which is where the men would have left it as a warning to other rustlers.

Finally, it was reported that since the killing, Davidson had lived at the Giles home and had continued selling the family cattle under his own name to Chicago dealers.

It was all circumstantial, with nothing in the form of actual proof, and the judge agreed that there were also jurisdictional questions. Despite those issues, he ignored common procedures and ordered Billy and Alice locked up until the grand jury could address the charges.

The case eventually came to trial in June 1895, more than two years after the killing. In short order, Billy Davidson was found guilty and sentenced to ninety-nine years in prison. Alice, meanwhile, remained in jail, awaiting trial on charges of accessory to murder.

The results of Davidson's conviction were lambasted by *The Independent*, a newspaper based in, of all places, Deadwood, reputedly one of the most lawless towns in the West, and perhaps its murder capital. The editors pulled no punches:

> *The Independent* does not believe that Davidson is the murderer of Giles at all. We believe that Giles was murdered at the instigation of the very men who have been most active in the prosecution of Davidson. We believe certain cattlemen in Butte County, like those in Wyoming, are inclined to take the law into their own hands, and when they think a man is inimical to their interests, they find a way to remove him.

There would soon be much more to write about. In early July, Mrs. Giles was acquitted, even though the case against her was described as far more damning than the one presented against Davidson. Editorials across the state ripped the decision, noting that the defense managed to get one man on the jury whom "they could rely on to hang it."

It was hard to dispute that claim. The jury initially stood at ten for conviction and two for acquittal, but after thirty-six hours, the ten reversed their votes, making it a unanimous verdict of not guilty. Alice Giles was free to go. Jurors were afterward heard saying they "had to get home to cut the hay," and that voting for acquittal prevented a hung jury and saved the county from an expensive retrial. So much for justice.

The *Deadwood Independent* was relentless in seeking to expose the laughable trials of both Billy and Alice for what they were, citing all manner of irregularities.

> ... Some of the true inwardness of the Giles murder trial at Belle Fourche has already developed. On Saturday last, Judge Plowman was informed that the defense had proof that the jury which convicted Davidson was copiously supplied with whisky during their deliberations. The bailiff who had charge of the Jury was brought into court and charged with contempt in permitting this whisky to be smuggled into the Jury room. Witnesses were produced, among them a saloon keeper, who admitted that he had sold the bailiff whisky for the use of the jury. The bailiff was sentenced to ten days in jail.
>
> ... Now, is that not a fine state of affairs to exist in a case where human life was at stake! The further the *Independent* goes into the Giles murder case, the deeper is its conviction that the prosecution is rotten as the devil, and that an innocent man has been convicted of a murder which was committed by an agency that has been very active in prosecuting him.
>
> ... There was not one particle of evidence against them, but the sheriff, court officers, and grand jury were all in the interests of the cattle men, and it was a foregone conclusion from the beginning that Davidson and Mrs. Giles must be convicted in order to cover up the tracks of men who were the real murderers of Giles.
>
> ... We shall discuss the matter more at length as soon as we can obtain a transcript of the evidence. We have received letters from Butte County, saying that we are injuring our paper by the course we are pursuing in this case. We confess we never stopped to think of the effect upon our business where the life or liberty of an innocent man or woman is concerned, and if we ever do, we hope a mob will come and throw our paper, plant, and fixtures into Red Creek.'

It was a noble, righteous stand, reflective of the role that media once played in America, a checks-and-balance, hold-their-feet-to-the-fire type of investigative journalism that is so wanting in modern times. The *Independent* continued digging in the interest of justice, fighting a system that clearly favored those with money and power.

And it paid off. Relentless pursuit of the truth for more than two years after the verdict yielded results. In September 1897, Billy Davidson was removed from the penitentiary and returned to Belle Fourche, on the northern fringe of the Black Hills, for a new trial, as ordered by the Supreme Court.

He remained there for six months, and in March 1898, the Seventh Circuit Court heard his case. Or at least they *prepared* to hear his case.

A jury was chosen, but as the trial was about to commence, the state announced that they were not prepared to prosecute. By law, the judge ordered an immediate verdict of acquittal. After serving more than two years of a ninety-nine-year sentence, Billy Davidson was a free man.

The *Deadwood Independent* maintained that cattlemen were responsible for the killing, a belief shared by many. The newspaper was certainly the driving force behind a full investigation of the kangaroo-court proceedings and the retrial of Davidson.

The Orlando Giles murder was never solved.

16

The Four Accidental Confessions

When he turned once again towards Abad, he was greeted by a pistol's muzzle and an order to put up his hands.

In the early decades of the 1920s, drifters were common among the male population, men who moved from place to place, looking for work and eking out a living along the way. Crime was a frequent component of such lives, which is one reason there were laws passed against loitering and other seemingly harmless pursuits. Folks caught loitering were routinely jailed or summarily run out of town.

Still, drifters were common, and they filled an employment niche for seasonal businesses and some of the more physical jobs, like mining and road construction. In 1924, Jose Ramoz, 22, and Jose Cayugal, 20, natives of Spain, made their way across the eastern portion of the North Country in classic drifter mode. Along Lake Champlain's western shores, they found employment at Port Henry before hooking up with a road construction crew at Willsboro. When a strike ended those jobs, they went back to Port Henry and found work in the mines. Hard luck struck again with a general shutdown of mining operations.

They left the area and went south to Glens Falls, where they met fellow countrymen Emil Abad, 33, and Perez Cabio, 22. Cabio had only recently immigrated to the United States, but Abad had done so back in 1911. He had previously worked in Toronto and Buffalo, and once owned a pool hall in Schenectady, a business he had sold a year earlier.

The four decided to combine their efforts, but it was not standard employment they were looking for. A decision was made to pool their assets and buy a car, which would allow them to commit robberies and make hasty escapes.

Abad, Cabio, and Cayugal went north again to Port Henry, purchasing an automobile there for $220 (they paid $140, and Abad signed a note for the remainder). Returning to Glens Falls, they held a strategy session of sorts. Two days later, based on what they had recently seen in Essex County, the men headed north to the small villages on Lake Champlain.

At Port Henry, they boarded overnight. The next day, June 23, they drove to Whallonsburgh and scouted the countryside, returning to their room shortly before daybreak on the twenty-fourth. Later the same day, they drove north again, but ran into trouble with a flat tire. Repairs were made at Lott's Garage (owned by Melvin Lott) in Westport, and the foursome paid the bill with their last dollar.

Indecision was replaced by desperation, and with all their money gone, it was now or never. A target was agreed upon, and the men headed for Willsboro, delaying their arrival until well after darkness. Shortly before midnight, June 24, they parked the car but left the engine running, with Ramoz at the wheel. The three other men walked two hundred feet down the street, each carrying a concealed, loaded revolver.

Abad and Cabio entered the Willsboro restaurant operated by John Gonzales, while Cayugal stood watch near the door, ready to handle any trouble that might develop. Abad asked for cigarettes, and Gonzalez, standing behind the counter, reached back for them. When he turned once again towards Abad, he was greeted by a pistol's muzzle and an order to put up his hands.

Instead, Gonzalez appeared to panic, moving away from Abad towards the rear of the room, but still behind the counter. Cabio made an effort to cut him off, repeating the order to raise his hands. There was no response, and fearing Gonzalez was reaching for his own gun, Cabio fired once, striking him in the chest.

This was hardly going as planned. Stunned at the outcome and completely neglecting the goal of robbery, all three men bolted for the door, raced for the car, and sped out of town.

They left behind a badly bleeding victim, but despite being shot by a .32 caliber pistol at near point-blank range, Gonzales was somehow still alive. Struggling mightily to the upstairs apartment, he called out to his wife, "Robbers!" before falling to the floor, unconscious.

A local man returning from work, Arthur Mero, had seen the three men enter the restaurant and noticed Ramoz behind the wheel of the getaway car. Authorities were notified, activating the sheriff's department and the state police, who began searching

> **WILLSBORO MAN SHOT BY BANDITS**
>
> Resisted Attempt to Rob Him; Probably Fatally Shot; Assailants Unknown

the countryside for "a Buick touring car with four foreigners," considered armed and dangerous.

The crew of would-be robbers had few options. To escape quickly meant sticking to the main highways, of which there were few in the 1920s. They drove to Westport and Elizabethtown, and then turned south, but once again experienced the bane of early automobile days: a flat tire. Assuming that police were in pursuit, they decided to keep going despite the blown tire, which slowed their progress considerably.

At about 3:00 AM, the men were captured near the bridge at Schroon Falls, about four miles north of Schroon Lake village. They offered no

The four men who robbed John Gonzalez. Clockwise, beginning at the top left: Jose Martin Ramoz, Jose Arco Cayugal, Lucius Perez Cabio, and Emil Abad.

resistance and had no weapons, claiming to have discarded them in the mountains during the escape attempt.

All four were jailed on robbery charges, pending identification by the victim, but they all offered full confessions, differing only slightly in detail. On Thursday, the second day after the shooting, reports from the Champlain Valley Hospital in Plattsburgh indicated Gonzales was improving and doctors were hopeful for a full recovery.

But late Sunday afternoon, everything changed. John Gonzales died, and those confessions to assault and attempted robbery became confessions to first-degree murder.

There were few options before them. They could recant and go to trial, but with the risk of conviction came the penalty of death. It was a high-stakes gamble: what were the chances a jury would believe four individuals who had confessed to a crime, but then each altered their stories after the victim (and only other witness) died?

In early October, all four were indicted by the grand jury on charges of first-degree murder. At arraignment, they all pleaded not guilty.

Attorneys Elmer Vincent of Ticonderoga and Fred Torrance of Ausable Forks represented the quartet. Their best legal advice was to avoid the great risk of trial and instead offer a plea to a lesser charge. It wasn't a sure thing, but there were several factors in their favor: their young ages; their clean records; their readily offered confessions; and their proper behavior while held in jail for the past four months.

On October 20, Justice John Crapser accepted four pleas of guilty to second-degree murder, resulting in the rarest of outcomes: one bullet fired by one man sent four defendants to prison for twenty years to life at hard labor.

And no strikes or work stoppages would be affecting *those* jobs.

17

Wickedness in Warren County

Suicide seemed unlikely, if for no other reason than one question: if Anna had taken her own life, why would she hide the bottle in the ashes after taking the poison?

Over a century ago, one of the most notorious figures in Warren County (and there were many) was a slippery character by the name of Timothy Hill, a man who became a suspect in two completely unrelated murder cases.

Born in 1861 in the town of Horicon on Lake George's western shore, Hill became involved in crime at a relatively young age, with disastrous results. In 1886, when he was just twenty-five, Clinton Prison at Dannemora became Timothy's new home for nearly eight years, courtesy of an armed robbery conviction. He also served six months in the Albany Penitentiary, but escaped prosecution for a number of other crimes due to a lack of hard evidence. He was a tough guy to pin down, and people were loathe to testify against him for fear of repercussions.

On June 21, 1895, more than a year after Hill was released from Dannemora, elderly Horicon resident Amasa Mead was busy tending to daily chores on his property near the intersection of Rock Avenue and Pucker Street (names that still exist in 2012). Living alone since his wife Mary passed away twelve years earlier, the sixty-eight-year-old farmer had long settled into a routine that included frequent church activities, caring for his cows, and tending to his property.

After a trip to Chestertown to prepare the church for Sunday services, Mead ran some errands and returned home by early evening, with time enough left for a light dinner and the customary evening prayers before retiring for the night.

At around noon the following day, a passing neighbor, Mrs. Horton Cooper, noticed Amasa's cows roaming the barnyard. On her return trip a few hours later, the cows were still out, which was a bit unusual. Concerned that the old man might have taken ill, Cooper sent her young son to check on him. The boy came racing home to report that Amasa was lying on the kitchen floor. After confirming that something was indeed wrong, Horton alerted several of the neighbors, who soon discovered several elements of criminal activity at the scene.

Pools of blood trailed away from where Amasa's body lay, the victim of a shotgun blast. The shooter had passed through the alcove to the front door and taken aim through the door window. The subsequent blast had killed Amasa and littered the kitchen with pieces of shattered glass.

Two theories were floated: Mead had been shot while seated at the table, finishing his meal, or had knelt for his nightly prayers and been slain while praying.

The usual list of authorities was summoned, and an autopsy revealed that twenty-one large buckshot pellets had struck the victim. The damage was terrific in such close quarters: eighteen pellets entered one lung, while some passed through both, and two others penetrated the heart, severing an artery. The high number of pellets indicated that two shots had been fired, probably simultaneously, suggesting the work of a double-barrel shotgun. Death had come quickly, perhaps instantly.

Although a quantity of money was found in a bureau drawer, robbery was believed to have been the motive. It was widely assumed that Mead kept an appreciable amount of cash stored at home, and the thief may have simply missed the concealed bundle.

Potentially critical evidence was found in the alcove: pieces of wallpaper that had been used as shotgun-shell wadding to seal the pellets tightly in place.

A preliminary investigation revealed that some Pucker Street boys had been seen walking in the area the previous day (Friday), and one of them was carrying a gun. On Sunday, four youths were brought in and questioned extensively, but were later released.

Further digging led quickly to a plausible suspect: Timothy Hill. Police detained him based on several bits of evidence. Key among them was the discovery that wallpaper in a room of the building where Hill lived (as a boarder) matched the spent piece of wadding found on Mead's kitchen floor. It wasn't revealed if he was being held as a witness or suspect,

ARRESTED FOR MURDER.

TIMOTHY HILL CHARGED WITH THE ASSASSINATION OF AMASA MEAD.

but to all appearances, Timothy Hill, recent Dannemora inmate, was in a heap of trouble once again.

The sheriff, district attorney, and assisting lawyers spent the ensuing days examining witnesses and piecing together the events leading up to Mead's death. A very tight lid was kept on the proceedings, allowing investigators to pursue each new lead.

Hill, meanwhile, remained at Lake George in the county jail. On July 2, based on evidence that had been accrued in the eleven days since the killing, Justice Potter order him arrested and charged with the murder of Amasa Mead.

Among those questioned during the investigation were five witnesses who testified to seeing Hill cross a bridge in the direction of Mead's home on the evening of the murder. An investigator had since walked the same route to determine whether that jaunt allowed enough time for Hill to commit the crime and return to his starting point. It was concluded that he had ample time, as laid out in the scenario provided to the media:

> Hill was seen to take a shotgun from the house of Samuel Tobin of Horicon, with whom he boarded, on Thursday, the day before the murder. He carried it to the residence of Mrs. James Kelly, a widow woman living on the corner near Round pond.
>
> He loaded the gun at her house on the afternoon of June 21, the day of the murder, and left there about 7:30 o'clock that evening, taking the gun with him. He returned to the home of his brother, Benjamin Hill, about 10:30 o'clock that night.
>
> Five different witnesses swore that they saw Hill cross the river bridge at South Horicon Friday evening, and that he was going in the direction of Mead's residence. On the Monday after the murder, Sheriff Collins found a double-barrel shotgun at the Tobin house. Both barrels had apparently been recently discharged.

In mid-July, while the defendant sat in jail awaiting grand jury action, an incident occurred that emphasized his notorious reputation. A shooting through the window of a local business occurred while a night watchman was on duty. It was noted in the media that Timothy Hill might have been the prime suspect were he not already locked up.

Authorities continued to probe for solid information in the murder case, but the wallpaper connection was the only physical evidence thus far. Although much of what they had was convincing, it could only be characterized as circumstantial. Many people suspected that Timothy Hill had killed Amasa Mead, but no one could offer any concrete proof.

Jay Hill, a cousin of Timothy, was also a suspect. Local lawmen put a Pinkerton detective on the case, but after trailing Jay for several months, nothing was found to justify an arrest.

In November, the grand jury convened to hear the entire collection of testimony from more than two dozen witnesses. As feared by investigators, no indictment was returned, and Timothy Hill was set free.

Although he was suspected of various crimes in the years following the Mead case (which was still considered unsolved), there was insufficient evidence to bring charges against him. A decade later, another member of the Hill family made headlines.

In September 1906, Timothy's brother Powell was on a bender, something the Hills were quite familiar with. At Hague, where he worked in the mines, Powell picked a fight with brothers William and George Barker, a pair of blacksmiths. It was described as the classic knockdown, drag-out fight, lasting for nearly an hour. Powell suffered a severe beating and died days later from his injuries. When the grand jury considered the case, it failed to indict.

Imbibing led to frequent problems for the Hill family, and in March 1908, Timothy's loose tongue from too many drinks resulted in a bizarre story that landed him in jail, accompanied by his cousin, Jay.

While thoroughly inebriated at Horicon's Central House, Timothy suddenly shouted to the crowd that he wanted to confess something that had been eating at him for thirteen years. Back in June 1895, while at home alone, he had taken his gun down from the wall and loaded it. In walked his cousin, Jay Hill, who borrowed the gun, only to return a short time later, frantically describing how he had shot Amasa Mead through the window of the man's front door.

The district attorney, informed of the drunken rant, heard the story repeated by a now sober Tim Hill. The court took immediate action, ordering the arrest of Jay on suspicion of murder, and locking up Timothy as a critical witness. Dozens of those who had testified in the original case were subpoenaed and questioned about the events of more than a decade ago. The charges made by Timothy were taken very seriously, but in an ironic twist, the evidence and testimony also implicated him as the possible perpetrator, just as it had in 1895. His alcohol-fueled revelation now placed him in the unique position of both chief witness and prime suspect.

It was never determined what the motive was behind his accusations, arising more than a decade after the crime. His reputation made it laughable to suggest a guilty conscience was the cause. The fact that it all came out during a drunken spree suggested a feud between cousins, and a motive of revenge, but no one knew for certain. Whatever the case, Hill had needlessly placed himself in jeopardy. The case against Timothy back in 1895 was much stronger than the argument that Jay was somehow involved, which is why Jay had been detained for questioning at the time, but was later released.

Following six weeks of investigation, the grand jury reviewed the evidence, failing once again to indict. For the second time in thirteen years, Timothy Hill was released from jail, avoiding prosecution in the Mead murder, which was relegated forever to the file of unsolved mysteries.

Trouble was the featured story line in Hill's life, and three years later, he became embroiled in another major controversy that threatened to imprison him for life.

In 1911, Timothy had taken up with a woman from Minerva, Anna Loveland, but this wasn't your typical love story with glowing prospects of settling down and living happily ever after. Anna was more than just Hill's girlfriend: she was also Mrs. Morris Loveland. A wife for fifteen years, she was mother to four surviving children, ages 13, 11, 8, and 6. Hill had known the Lovelands for at least two years.

None of those potentially mitigating factors dissuaded Timothy, who continued to pursue her. Despite their rocky relationship, Anna moved in with Hill, leaving her family behind. The two of them found boarding nearby with an elderly couple, William and Emeline O'Donnell. During the next two months, Anna confided her many relationship difficulties to the O'Donnells, but outwardly, Hill and Loveland seemed happy together.

On Thursday morning, August 10, the two were busy digging worms in preparation for a fishing trip. After returning to the house and washing her hands while chatting with Mrs. O'Donnell, Anna left the room, but suddenly collapsed near the doorway. A shout of "Auntie, I fell and I can't get up" brought Mrs. O'Donnell quickly to her side. She tried to raise Anna to her feet, but Loveland's body was spasming wildly, and then became uncontrollably rigid.

Emeline called out to Hill, who rushed in, picked Anna up, and carried her to a sofa. Observing her distress, he said, "Melt some lard, quick, she's taken poison." Mrs. O'Donnell prepared a mixture as ordered, but Loveland was dead before it was ready.

Timothy ran out to the roadway, where he had seen a man working on his car. Recognizing him as Dr. John Owen of Newcomb, Hill asked if he was a coroner, explaining that, "A woman has just died in my arms."

Owen rushed to the house and examined Anna, concluding that she had indeed died of poisoning. Highly suspicious of the circumstances, Owen called Dr. Breen of Olmstedville to assist him with the autopsy. Meanwhile, the coroner investigated the scene, collecting pieces of potential evidence. His thoroughness was rewarded when, while digging through the bucket of ashes from the cook stove, he found an empty strychnine bottle.

Questioning the O'Donnells and Hill revealed that Anna had spoken of the jealousy and other problems in her new relationship, but in the hours before her death, she had been in good spirits. Suicide seemed unlikely, if for no other reason than one question: if Anna had taken her own life, why would she hide the bottle in the ashes after taking the poison?

As it had in the past, the finger of suspicion pointed directly at Timothy Hill, who soon found himself in very familiar surroundings: a cell in the county jail. Anna's stomach was sent to Albany for analysis, which substantiated the theory of death by poisoning.

An August 28 hearing did nothing for Hill's defense. Both Morris Loveland and his brother, Jack, testified that Hill had strychnine in his possession, purportedly to kill foxes, and that Anna had previously expressed a fear of poison. Even more powerful was the statement by William O'Donnell, her landlord, to whom Anna had confided that Timothy would kill her if she went back to her husband or went with any other man. O'Donnell also said the situation in the house had become intolerable, to the point where he told the couple one morning they could no longer live there and would have to move out. The morning in question? August 10, just hours before Anna died.

Coroner Owen took the stand and testified to his role of being summoned by Hill to the O'Donnell home, where Anna lay dead, and to finding

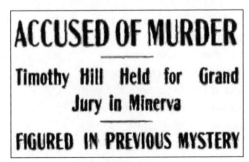

the bottle in the stove's ashes, adding that in a suitcase belonging to Hill, he found a label from a strychnine bottle.

It was powerful stuff, but just like the Amasa Mead case sixteen years earlier, it was considered largely circumstantial, this time due to one important fact: unlike Mead's death, Loveland's could have been a suicide.

Still, it was enough for the court to order Timothy confined until the grand jury could consider a charge of first-degree murder. Hill, assuming he was being detained as a witness, exploded in anger when he was arrested. The rebellion continued later at the Raymond House in Minerva, prompting his immediate removal to the Essex County jail in Elizabethtown, fifty miles north. He would remain there for eight months.

In November, a grand jury indictment became reality, and in early 1912, a trial date of May 6 was set. The evidence against Hill was strong, and defense attorneys R. B. Dudley and O. B. Brewster faced the difficult task of keeping their disreputable client out of the electric chair.

As the trial opened, the audience and jurors learned about the Hill-Loveland relationship, including the jealousy and threats. The facts that had been disseminated in the media were now laid out in the courtroom. Several experts testified to the certainty that strychnine had been used, and how effective, horrible, and quick a killer it was.

Family, friends, and acquaintances testified, but few were as effective as Emeline O'Donnell, or as affecting as Frederick Loveland, Anna's young teenage son. O'Donnell, 83, eloquently recalled events from the day of the murder, and the shaky relationship of her two tenants. And Fred brought tears to the eyes of many as he described the broken marriage of his parents, Anna's abandonment of the family to be with Timothy Hill, and her frequent drinking.

The reference to alcohol was important to the prosecution. Both O'Donnells testified that Anna had ingested whiskey from Hill's bottle that day, and Dr. Owen added that a broken liquor bottle was found in the O'Donnell's yard. Toss in the testimony about the strychnine bottle and the label that was found, and it was difficult to see a path to acquittal.

The defense team of Robert Dudley and Byron Brewster, a smart, tenacious pairing, faced a formidable task. Although nearly every bit of evidence pointed towards their client's guilt, their intent was to win. Rather than focus on improving the weaker parts of their case (and *most* of it was considered weak), they focused on the one strength: suicide.

Experts were brought in, stating that Anna Loveland may have died from a seizure and not from poisoning. That testimony provided a counterpoint to the claim by prosecution experts that strychnine poisoning was the cause of death. Then, during questioning and cross-examination of each witness, the two attorneys took every opportunity to emphasize that no one had actually seen Anna drink from the liquor bottle, and no one had seen Hill give her anything that could have held poison. The suggestion was that Anna, understandably stressed over her shaky relations with Hill, his frequent threats, the separation from her children, and the pending eviction from their living quarters, had finally decided to end it all.

Since the poison took perhaps fifteen minutes to begin showing its effects, Anna could have ingested it while digging worms, and then placed the empty poison bottle in the kitchen ash pail when she washed her hands. Other scenarios were proffered, each with a singular purpose: to establish reasonable doubt. Even if Loveland did, in fact, die of poisoning, the strychnine could have been self-administered. If that possibility was perceived by the jury as sufficient to break the chain of events as outlined by the prosecution, perhaps Timothy Hill wasn't a murderer after all.

Unlike modern times, trials of old didn't drag on for weeks or months. Just two days after proceedings opened in the Loveland case, the jury began deliberations. And less than two hours later, it was over.

In his charge to the jury, Justice Henry Kellogg explained that in a case of poisoning, there was no middle ground—either Hill did it, or he didn't—and if he did it, there was only one feasible intent: to kill. For that reason, they could reach one of only two possible conclusions: guilty of first-degree murder, or acquittal.

The first vote was 9–3 for acquittal, but the judge had left them no wiggle room, taking the option of a lesser charge off the table. Following his orders to the best of their abilities, they came to a decision and returned to the courtroom. Cheers erupted among Hill's friends in the courtroom when the jury foreman uttered the words, "Not guilty."

Jurors said afterward that they felt handcuffed by the situation. They wanted to punish Hill, but were not comfortable invoking the death penalty. And for that reason, they had no choice but to set him free. Just twenty-four hours after he stood before the jury and faced the specter of death in the electric chair, Timothy Hill was back home in Horicon, a free man.

Although he was the prime murder suspect in the deaths of Amasa Mead and Anna Loveland, neither case was ever solved.

18

Merciless Murder for Meager Money

> The entrance to the house, the kitchen, and the dining room were splattered with bits of blood, brain, and skull pieces. Both the sheriff and coroner called it the worst murder case they had ever seen.

A century ago, it was common during the Christmas holidays for North Country lumber camps to empty, at least briefly. In 1909, in far northeastern New York, the men of Altona (Clinton County) took a welcome break after several weeks in the woods.

Near the settlement of Purdy's Mills, the camp cook, Adolphus Bouvia, closed down operations on December twenty-third. Widowed a year earlier, he planned to return home and spend time with family, friends, and neighbors, some of whom worked with him on the lumber jobs.

A week later, when Bouvia missed the local New Year's celebrations, there was some concern. The fifty-six-year-old lived alone on the sparsely populated road connecting Jerusalem and Jericho, two of the many local settlements with biblical names.

On January 2, two friends called on him, but there was no sign of activity around the home. The front door was padlocked, and there was blood and bits of bone near the entrance. They surmised it was from a rabbit or some other game Bouvia had killed, but doubts surfaced in their minds. The water barrel had been tipped over, which was difficult to account for other than a struggle having taken place.

The men returned the following day with a variety of keys, and after some effort, they were able to open the padlock and enter the house. The scene that greeted them wouldn't soon be forgotten—blood and brains on the kitchen floor, leading to the dining room, where a ghastly sight awaited. Before them lay Adolphus Bouvia, frozen stiff in a pool of congealed blood—and a good portion of his head was missing.

The sheriff and coroner were summoned, and an investigation

began, but it didn't take long to arrive at a likely suspect. Several pieces of information suggested that local resident John Kinney was responsible. When it was discovered that he had given $110 ($2500 in 2012) to his brother-in-law, Arthur Lashway (who later returned it), police began searching for Kinney. His family was destitute, and for him to possess even one-tenth that much money would have been highly suspicious.

It was learned that on the previous day, Kinney had begun moving his family about ten miles south of Altona to Morrisonville. He was arrested there by Sheriff Robert Nash, and just hours after the body was discovered, Kinney was back at Bouvia's house, facing questions from the coroner.

> **MURDERED WITH AN AXE.**
>
> Lifeless Body of Adolphus Bouvia Found in Altona.

The suspect had already denied to Nash that he knew anything of the murder, but admitted having stopped at Bouvia's home early that morning to drop off a table he had borrowed more than six months previous. Because the hour was so early, he had left the table outside for Adolphus to find when he got up. The table was, in fact, where Kinney said he left it.

When pressured by the coroner, Kinney said he had seen Bouvia and the man's nephew, Frank "Pork" Lafave of Plattsburgh, walking towards the victim's home on the night of December 30. About a half hour later, Kinney again encountered Lafave as he returned from the direction of Bouvia's home. "I have killed uncle and have got his money," Lafave said, and then gave him half the cash, about $110, to guarantee his silence.

That, Kinney said, is why he at first denied any knowledge of the crime when Nash arrested him, fearing he might be charged with Lafave's terrible deed. To support that claim, he provided the name of a second witness who had seen Lafave on the road that day—Kinney's own mother. Authorities were well familiar with Lafave, who had been a resident of the county lockup on a number of occasions.

By evening, after sitting in jail for hours, Kinney decided that his first story wasn't good enough after all. Part of his alibi had already been disproved, and in embarrassing fashion—his mother, when questioned, said she couldn't confirm having seen Frank Lafave because she didn't know him. Kinney then modified his story, becoming less insistent that Lafave had committed the crime and admitting his own grudge against Bouvia, who, he said, was quite interested in Kinney's wife.

This newest alibi would soon suffer a fatal blow. Shortly after midnight,

Lafave was taken into custody at the home of Mr. and Mrs. Albert Eaton of Chazy, about ten miles east of Altona. Lafave worked at nearby Miner Farm as an electrician, and said he hadn't been to Altona in at least two months. The Eatons confirmed that he had not left Chazy for the past three weeks, and was at their home on the night of Bouvia's murder.

Lafave was held, not as a suspect, but as a witness, while the coroner moved forward with the inquest. Plenty of circumstantial evidence incriminating Kinney was presented by locals, beginning with George Trudeau, Peter Lashway, Orville Spinks, and Elrie Parrott, the four men who had found Bouvia's body.

Trudeau, friend and neighbor of Bouvia, said that on Sunday, January 2, Kinney visited Trudeau's home to return a gun he had borrowed some time ago. Later that same day, Trudeau called on his neighbor, only to find the house locked and blood and bone spattered about the doorway.

Elrie Parrott, a neighbor who had accompanied Trudeau to Bouvia's, described the same scene. When they left, Parrott said they soon crossed paths on the highway with John Kinney and his wife.

Peter Lashway and Orville Spinks, friends and co-workers of the victim, accompanied Trudeau and Parrott to Bouvia's home on Monday when they discovered the body. They also reported seeing John Kinney in the process of moving his furniture to Morrisonville.

The men described Bouvia's body, which they said appeared to have been struck three times with an axe. Still fully dressed in an overcoat and other outdoor wear, he was apparently attacked just outside the house and dragged inside to the place where he lay. Bouvia's cap was cut in several places, indicating he was still wearing it when the axe struck his head.

When officials arrived, they found an empty wallet in Bouvia's pocket and several coins scattered across the floor, suggesting robbery as the crime's motive. The money missing from the wallet was eventually linked to Kinney, thanks to one important detail. Bouvia had recently been paid by several individuals, who later confirmed they had included gold certificates (special bills imprinted with the notation "Gold Certificate" at the top) in their payments. Several such certificates were found among the recovered money.

As the inquest continued that afternoon, Adolphus Parker, Kinney's uncle, left the proceedings and visited the jail. At one point, his nephew reached through the bars, grabbed Parker, and burst into tears, telling him he was in terrible trouble.

Returning to the inquest, Parker reported on their conversation. Kinney said he was "in a bad fix," and that his wife was the source of the problem. When Parker told him it was believed Bouvia had been killed with an axe, Kinney shook his head as if to say no. When his uncle said others believed a gun was used, he nodded yes.

Several other witnesses attested to Kinney having lied about Bouvia's whereabouts during the past several days. The most damning of that testimony came from Fred Bouvia, the victim's son.

> **MURDERED FOR HIS MONEY**
>
> BRUTAL CRIME COMMITTED IN TOWN OF ALTONA.
>
> **ADOLPHUS BOUVIA THE VICTIM**
>
> John Kinney Suspected and Arrested—Evidence at Coroner's Inquest Points To His Guilt—Kinney Will Probably Confess.

At around 1:00 AM New Year's morning, he left the celebration at his father-in-law's and headed to Jericho to see his dad. On the way, Fred encountered John Kinney, who told him there was no point in continuing because his father (who lived not far from Kinney) had gone to visit Fred's brother in Chazy.

George Lashway, Kinney's father-in-law, testified that John didn't support his family adequately (he and his young wife had three children), so Lashway was obliged to take care of them. In deep poverty and with nowhere to go, the family had recently moved into George's home.

Lashway then told about an unusual incident involving his son-in-law. Kinney had asked to be awakened at 3:00 AM on Wednesday, December 29, so he could go to his home (near Bouvia's) and start a fire in the fireplace. When George went out to feed the horses at about 6:30 that morning, he encountered Kinney, who said he had fallen asleep for a few hours after starting the fire. That absence identified a window of opportunity for Kinney to have committed the crime. Lashway also identified the gun that Kinney had borrowed for so long from George Trudeau and had returned on January 2.

Other testimony addressed a key piece of evidence. When Kinney was arrested and taken to the courthouse, his request to use the toilet was allowed. The next morning, an officer found a set of keys that had been disposed of in the bathroom. Among them was one fitting the padlock that sealed Adolphus Bouvia's house.

The last evidence presented at the inquest was the coroner's report, which was quite graphic. The entrance to the house, the kitchen, and the dining room were splattered with bits of blood, brain, and skull pieces. There were indications that both an axe and a gun had been used. Both the sheriff and coroner called it the worst murder case they had ever seen.

On January 5, two days after Bouvia's body was found, Coroner Carpenter closed the inquest. During the entire time, Kinney's repeated requests to speak with his wife were ignored. He asked the sheriff to bring her from Altona to the county courthouse, but it was neither a concern nor a responsibility of the county officers to do so. Those requests would later play a role in the case.

Five days after the inquest, the coroner's verdict was announced:

> That Adolphus Bouvia came to his death on or about December 29, and that death was caused by a gunshot wound, or by the use of an axe, club, or hatchet, and further, that Bouvia's death was caused by John Kinney by criminal means, with deliberate and premeditated design to effect death.

Kinney's attorneys, Patrick J. Tierney and David H. Agnew, entered a plea of not guilty, and their client was held for grand jury action. In late April, he was indicted on five counts for the one murder, as allowed by a section of the criminal code permitting multiple indictments if the final cause of death remained unclear. In Bouvia's case, the death weapon—axe, gun, or otherwise—had not yet been identified.

Little was known about thirty-four-year-old John Kinney. He was partially of Indian heritage, and his grandfather was widely reputed in Clinton County for his hunting abilities. When John Kinney was twenty-five, he married George Lashway's sixteen-year-old daughter, Lena. They had three children, but one had since died. Two sons remained.

Kinney himself had a poor reputation, a fact underscored by his own father-in-law's testimony regarding neglect of his family. The most publicized

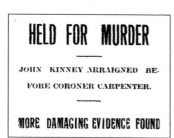

HELD FOR MURDER

JOHN KINNEY ARRAIGNED BEFORE CORONER CARPENTER.

MORE DAMAGING EVIDENCE FOUND

of his legal problems occurred at the 1902 Labor Day picnic at the nearby settlement of Jericho. Kinney and three others, including George Emery, were arrested for causing a riot. One of the victims suffered three broken ribs, three lost teeth, and other injuries, resulting in additional charges of second-degree assault.

Oddly enough, it was the same George Emery who had begun ejection proceedings against Adolphus Bouvia in early November 1909, less than two months before Bouvia was murdered.

Kinney's trial began in mid-June 1910, with speculation centering on a plea of insanity. Supreme Court Justice Edgar A. Spencer conducted the trial, which included the testimony presented at the coroner's inquest, and much more.

Plattsburgh Chief of Police Andrew Conners offered details of a conversation with Kinney, who claimed his wife's relationship with Bouvia was the cause of his problems.

> Conners: Is that the reason you killed him?
> Kinney: Yes.
> Conners: Why didn't you take more money than what you took?
> Kinney: That was all I could find.

When asked later if he had been drunk when he attacked Bouvia, Kinney said no. Many crimes of that nature were tied to alcohol abuse, but as troublesome as Kinney had been to many people, he was not known to have been a problem drinker.

Although he testified at the inquest, Kinney's father-in-law, George Lashway, was a reluctant trial witness. He admitted it was rare for Kinney to rise as early as he did on December 29, and that it was several hours before his son-in-law returned home. It also came out that the only money Lashway had paid Kinney for sawing pulpwood was two dollars, even though Kinney claimed he had received twelve dollars. It was an important point; Kinney was trying to prove that he had money of his own, and that the cash he possessed was not taken from the murder victim.

Damning testimony on that point came from other sources, including Peter Hiter, Altona's Overseer of the Poor, who testified that the town had been buying clothes and provisions for Mrs. Kinney and the children since January 11. If John Kinney had money, there would be no reason for public assistance, at least in the days shortly after he was jailed.

The evidence against him was considerable, and after nearly everyone had their say, the prosecution closed with the medical reports, which were presented with about as effective a backdrop as any district attorney could hope for. Carried into the courtroom and placed directly behind the witness stand were the front door and casing from Bouvia's house, still littered with bloodied bits of the victim's brain and skull.

As the medical experts gave testimony, his clothing was also displayed, including the blood-soaked coat and the hat with large gashes in it. But when Coroner Henry Carpenter described the inquest held at Bouvia's house, a glitch in the prosecution's case was discovered: Kinney had been asked questions before his legal rights were read to him. The judge ordered that any information provided to investigators before his rights were read must be stricken from the record.

Dr. Elmer E. Larkin, who handled the autopsy, said the victim had been dead for two or three days when the body was discovered. The fragmented condition of the skull was caused, he said, by "the explosion in the cranium due to the violent entering of the head of some substance." The damage was so severe, he said, that "the brain in the right side of the head was missing." In his opinion, a gun had been used to kill Bouvia, since it was doubtful that the body parts splattered on the outside wall had been propelled there by the blows of an axe. Dr. Owen O'Neil concurred with Larkin's findings, after which the prosecution rested.

Attorney P. J. Tierney's defense strategy came as a surprise. Instead of an insanity plea, he would attempt to prove that Bouvia had been killed by a high-powered rifle, and not a shotgun like the one Kinney had borrowed from George Trudeau. In his opening statement, Tierney said that if the jury believed him correct, they must find Kinney not guilty because the prosecution had made no mention of a rifle being in the defendant's possession, or that a rifle had been used in any phase of the crime.

Dr. William S. Buck, an expert on gunshot wounds and blood spray patterns, provided extensive testimony and physical evidence, including impact samples taken from three to fourteen feet away. Fourteen feet was the estimated space separating Bouvia from his attacker. At that distance, Dr. Buck said, the extent of the victim's skull damage could only have been attained by a high-powered rifle.

Weakening that argument were two significant issues. Dr. Buck had not actually viewed the victim's skull, and instead based his judgment on descriptions provided by the coroner and the other doctors. Further, during cross-examination by DA Arthur Hogue, it was determined that the gun used to produce Buck's physical displays was a different type from the one used to kill Adolphus Bouvia.

Frank "Pork" Lafave, whom Kinney accused of committing the crime, again testified that he had been in Chazy for two months, a fact confirmed by his hosts, Mr. and Mrs. Eaton. In rebuttal, the defense called William Laforce, an inmate in the county jail. Laforce was facing two charges of horse theft, which may have reduced his credibility as a witness. He claimed that during Frank Lafave's visit to the jail, Laforce had overheard him admitting the crime and promising revenge on Kinney for being a snitch. According to Laforce, the comment was, "Kinney, I killed old Bouvia and gave you $90." Then, on his way out, Lafave added, "John, you squealed on me, and I will get even with you yet."

Another inmate, Robert Morrison, was re-called to the stand after testifying earlier about letters he had supposedly written on behalf of Kinney. The DA pressed Morrison to admit that he had been paid by the prosecution to testify. At that point, attorney John E. Judge took the stand briefly, explaining that, just six hours earlier (at 3:00 AM), he had been dispatched to locate Morrison in Burke, a Franklin County village about forty-five miles west of Plattsburgh. Morrison was informed he would be paid fifty dollars by the county for appearing in court later that morning.

Despite the fact that many other witnesses had been subpoenaed, the defense surprised everyone by ending its case, and in early afternoon, final summations were presented. Although he had precious little to work with, defense attorney Patrick Tierney eloquently stressed that the chain of evidence was circumstantial, and "was only as strong as its weakest link. If there was a weak place in the chain, the entire fabric must fall." He also claimed that the so-called confession by Kinney had been obtained under heated, third-degree questioning. Tierney's final comments included a plea that the jury return Kinney to his family.

For the prosecution, DA Hogue took two hours to review all the evidence that had been presented. After the judge's charge and a break for dinner, the jury began deliberating at around 8:00 PM.

Sunday morning at 10:00 AM, the court reconvened for announcement of the verdict: guilty of murder in the first degree. Kinney seemed unaffected by the decision, confident that an appeal would exonerate him. Twenty-four hours later, he stood once again before Judge Spencer, who handed down the mandatory sentence of death, to be carried out during the week of July 25. Kinney had just five weeks to live.

Spencer also granted the DA's request that any money found on the killer after the crime be turned over to the estate of Adolphus Bouvia.

Kinney remained in the packed courtroom, greeting many familiar faces and assuring well-wishers that an appeal would win him a new trial. But shortly after the court session ended, reality began to set in: Kinney was immediately sent on his way to Dannemora for a cell on Death Row. He would arrive just in time to take the place of an Albany murderer, whose execution was scheduled for the following morning.

Following Kinney's departure from the courthouse, a brief and somewhat odd occurrence was related in local newspapers the next day:

> Shortly after John Kinney had started for prison, his mother appeared at the courthouse and requested to see her son. When she was informed that he had started for Dannemora, she stood for a few moments as if stunned. Then with the simple word, "Well!" she turned and left the building.

The filing of an appeal led to delays in Kinney's execution, and eleven months later, during which time three of his fellow Death Row inmates were sent to the chair, the court began reviewing his case.

In mid-June 1911 came the long-awaited news: the judgment against him had been reversed, and Kinney would get a new trial. A year and a day after he was sent to Death Row, John Kinney gladly returned to the Clinton County jail.

In reversing the earlier decision, the high court addressed several issues. Typical among them was the chain of possession regarding keys that were found in the courthouse bathroom the morning after Kinney had used the facility. One of the keys fit the padlock on Bouvia's house.

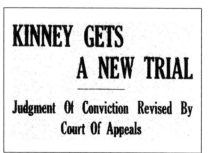

The appeals court noted that the keys could conceivably have been left there a few days earlier. Allowing them to be presented in court as evidence was misleading, and might have been powerful enough to sway the verdict.

The ruling also suggested that the defense should have been

granted greater leeway in attempting to prove its assertion that Kinney's confession was induced by fear. But the justices were careful to cite their colleague, Judge Spencer, for doing a good job overall in the face of extreme personal hardship. Their deference to his lapses stemmed from Spencer's ongoing battle against severe illness, which had since resulted in his death.

> In his anxiety conscientiously to fulfill his duties, he undertook, in the trial of this case, burdens which it was beyond his strength to carry. ... And in charging the jury, he did inadvertently and unintentionally do several things that would best be corrected by allowing a new trial, however strong the people's case may be regarded.

A local reporter assessed Kinney's appearance after returning to the county lockup:

> One year ago yesterday, John Kinney was taken to Dannemora by Nash ... and has been in the Death Row section since then. Kinney shows plainly the effects of this close confinement. He is pale and weak and almost staggers when walking. He is in the best of spirits, and is overjoyed at being given another fight for his life.
>
> He speaks in the highest terms of the treatment he received at the hands of the prison officials, but says the suspense one undergoes while awaiting the time for the carrying out of the death sentence is something terrible.
>
> He will be confined in jail here until he is again placed on trial in Supreme Court next winter.

In December, six months after his return and almost exactly two years after Bouvia was killed, Kinney learned his new trial would begin in February. Attorneys Tierney and Agnew began meeting frequently with Judge Henry Kellogg in hopes of avoiding a second trial.

In late January, when jury selection was to begin, Tierney outline in court the terms of a plea deal that Kellogg had grudgingly agreed to. In urging the court's acceptance of Kinney's change of plea, he presented several arguments. In most juries, said Tierney, at least some individuals opposed capital punishment; both Governor Dix and the superintendent of prisons had taken a stance against the death penalty; several bills were before the state in hopes of abolishing the practice; and the county would avoid the expense of a second trial. He added that, at age thirty-eight, Kinney probably would not outlive his sentence. For those reasons, all parties should accept John Kinney's plea of guilty to second-degree murder.

Judge Kellogg granted Tierney's request, but noted for the record that he was "loathe to accept such a plea," believing Kinney deserved the full legal punishment for his crime.

Sentence was pronounced as life, with a minimum of twenty years.

For Kinney, it was a new beginning of sorts after narrowly escaping the chair. Upon returning to Dannemora, he addressed a lifetime of illiteracy (which was not uncommon in those days) by learning to read and write. He was also said to have been a model prisoner, although no evidence was provided to support that claim.

In late August 1919, seven years after he returned to Dannemora, John Kinney was found hanging in his cell. Prison officials declared his death a suicide, though the circumstances were somewhat suspect in that the news wasn't released until at least a week after his body was found. Perhaps the delay was to allow the completion of an internal investigation. Whatever the case, details of his death were not provided to the public, and that, too, was not uncommon.

19

Burying the Hatchet

But in the eyes of the law, William Jackson was just doing his job. No matter how the scene had played out, what could justify planting a hatchet in a man's chest?

As a haven for wild game, the Adirondacks have been forever victimized by poachers. Enforcement has never been easy, particularly in the early days when individual officers were sometimes required to cover vast areas, and many woodsmen and their families lived off the land.

Around the year 1900, the Schroon Lake region, sparsely populated and featuring expansive tracts of wilderness, was typical of those times. With little fear of getting caught, hunters and fishermen frequently treated themselves to year-round seasons. Other common violations were fishermen ignoring daily limits, and hunters using dogs to hunt deer. Game protectors didn't look kindly on such behavior, doing their best to bring offenders to justice, often at great peril to themselves.

Among the many suspected scofflaws in the Schroon area was the Lagoy clan. Several of Frank Lagoy's sons were believed to have routinely ignored game laws and operated pretty much as they pleased. In 1897, with strong evidence that Frank Lagoy Jr. had taken a deer during the summer months, his arrest was ordered.

Issuing a warrant was one thing, but executing it was something else entirely. Experienced woodsmen were quite adept at making themselves scarce for extended periods.

Lawmen, however, could be just as persistent as their elusive quarry. After several months of frustration at the county level, a Schroon Lake man, William Jackson, was deputized by Essex County Game Protector Fletcher Beede and charged with executing the warrant on Lagoy. William, 23, the son of a Mineville miner, was strong and tough, like many of the other young men in the neighborhood, including some members of the Jenks and Lagoy families.

Jackson took the job seriously and he knew the territory, but the Lagoys could be a hard bunch to pin down. Locals knew of his quest, and finally, on the evening of Friday, September 17, he received a tip. Three of the Lagoys—Frank, 41, George, 28, and William, 20—were seen on the outskirts of the village. Jackson, anxious to take advantage of the opportunity, prevailed upon neighbor Michael Jenks to use his rig and bring William to the site.

A minute or two outside the village, they encountered the three Lagoy brothers walking along the road. Frank, for whatever reason (perhaps from working in the woods), was carrying a large hatchet. According to Jenks, he pulled the rig to a halt and Jackson stepped to the ground, telling Frank that he had been looking for him long enough. (Since he had been dodging the law for some time, Lagoy was aware he was wanted on charges of game-law violations.)

What happened next remains a point of controversy. The only account considered at all trustworthy was reported by Michael Jenks, but specifics of the story changed as he became confused during questioning. Although some of the details were cloudy, the outcome was not.

Approaching the three men, Jackson informed Frank that he was executing an arrest warrant, and that Lagoy should accompany him to the village. Lagoy's reply was to bury the hatchet in Jackson's upper chest.

Knowing that the Lagoys might be dangerous to deal with, Jackson had come armed. Though badly injured, he fired one shot from his pistol and then fled. The gunfire spooked Jenks' horse, which broke for the village. The last sight witnessed by Jenks was Jackson running down the road, with Frank Lagoy in pursuit. When he managed to gain control of his horse, Jenks returned to the site and called out to Jackson, but there was no reply.

Driving to Schroon Lake village, he sounded the alarm. A number of residents accompanied Jenks to the scene, where they found blood in the road, but no sign of either Jackson or the Lagoys. A quick search turned up nothing, and the prevailing assumption was that they had killed Jackson and disposed of his body in the lake. When no evidence was found near the shore, some of the men returned to search along the road.

About three hours later, Jackson's body was found. It had taken remarkable physical strength to flee the Lagoys, considering the damage inflicted by Frank's first blow with the hatchet. The blade had cut through Jackson's collarbone, severed two and a half ribs, and exposed a lung.

That alone should have been enough to kill him on the spot, but

Jackson tried to escape, making it more than a hundred yards before collapsing, either from impending death or further blows. There was also a large slice in his back and several other cuts to the back of the head and shoulders, indicating he had been struck repeatedly while on the run. The nature of the cuts, long and deep, supported that theory and made it highly unlikely he had been struck while lying face down on the ground.

Coroner Emery Dunn of Schroon Lake was summoned, and after quickly empaneling a jury to determine that death had come by means of foul play, he issued a county-wide alert:

> Wanted—Frank LaGoy, aged about 40 years, about 5 feet 11 inches, heavy build, black mustache, round shouldered; George LaGoy, aged 28 years, slight build, smooth face, about 5 feet 8 inches; William LaGoy, aged about 18 years, about 5 feet 4 inches, medium build. They are brothers and may travel together or separately. They are of mixed Indian and French descent with straight black hair, but not very dark complexion. They fish and hunt often. Arrest them and communicate with the Sheriff or other Essex County officers.
>
> E. J. Dunn, Coroner, Schroon Lake, N.Y.

A posse was formed from a number of men who were enlisted as special deputies. In the immediate area of Paradox Lake, about six miles north of Schroon Lake village, teams of searchers scoured the woods. On Saturday afternoon, the men sighted a dog belonging to Lagoy's father, Frank Sr. Someone had the idea of scaring the dog so it would return to its master, and the plan worked. A shot was fired, the dog ran off as expected, and within minutes, Frank Lagoy Sr. was in custody. Although he claimed to be hunting for bees to gather honey, Lagoy was held under guard while others continued the pursuit of his sons.

MURDER AT SCHROON LAKE

AN OFFICER KILLED WHILE SERVING A WARRANT.

Finally, just after dark, their efforts paid off when the youngest of the three, Will Lagoy, was taken in. On Sunday, though, the other two remained at large. The county sheriff ordered men posted along the fifty miles of Lake Champlain shoreline from Port Henry to Whitehall, cutting off the escape route east to Vermont. Then, to divide the regular stomping grounds of the Lagoys, he enlisted citizens to man the road spanning twenty-five miles from Lake Champlain to Schroon Lake.

At daybreak Monday, two and a half days after the manhunt began, George Lagoy was captured. He was carrying supplies (including two loaves of bread tucked beneath his arms) presumably for Frank, but if he knew where his older brother was, he wasn't talking.

More men were enlisted to help as a cold drizzle enveloped the area, making life miserable for everyone in the woods. Fortunately, that included their quarry. Frank Lagoy was cold, hungry, and tired, and the woods were crawling with armed searchers who had hunted him relentlessly for nearly three full days. He eventually managed to sneak into his father's Paradox Lake house, undetected.

At one point during the day, a Lagoy daughter rode on horseback to the lake, ostensibly to check for the presence of a boat. Whether it was, in fact, a scouting trip was not known, but that was the suspicion. The posse leaders questioned her about Frank's possible presence in the house. She denied he was there and was allowed to return home.

About an hour later, she returned, confirming that Frank was at the house and was prepared to surrender. She admitted that he had a pair of guns, and his earlier vow to not be taken alive cast doubt on her story of his willingness to surrender. Wary of a trap, the men moved through the woods carefully, surrounding the house.

At their request, she delivered both of Frank's rifles, convincing them that this was no ploy. The men then entered the house, and at about 5:00 PM, Lagoy gave himself up, just hours after the funeral and burial of his victim, William Jackson, had taken place.

Lagoy was removed to Schroon Lake, where an angry mob of about five hundred greeted him with threats of lynching. While Frank's crime was no doubt vile, it was the law's duty to protect him until a trial was held. Sheriff Nye ordered the armed guards to prevent the crowd from taking the law into their own hands.

Historically speaking, it was a remarkable situation. Lynching, one of great evils in America's past, is most often linked to an angry mob of white citizens acting against a black criminal suspect. But in this case, the outcry of the white citizenry for a lynching was to serve justice for the death of a black man. It was indeed the rarest of circumstances. William Jackson, described in newspapers of the day as "colored" or "mulatto," was the son of William Jackson, a black miner who had married a white woman. (The elder Jackson died earlier in a mining accident at Mineville.)

The next morning, all three Lagoys appeared in court before Justice Robert Taylor. Frank entered a plea of not guilty to murder, while his two brothers pleaded not guilty to accessory to murder. All four were then moved to the county jail in Elizabethtown. It was reported in the media that William Lagoy blamed Frank for the killing, adding that after slaying Jackson, his brother washed the hatchet and went home to change out of his bloodstained clothing. If William, the youngest at twenty, had made those statements, it was doubtful he would dare take that position in court.

In early October, investigators located a hatchet, presumed to be the murder weapon, hidden on the Lagoy property. It was a nice addition to the evidence already compiled for presentation to the grand jury in February, which was still nearly four months away.

But if it was left up to Frank Lagoy, he wouldn't be around that long. On the night of November 27, he and a cellmate, notorious burglar Harry Harris, pulled up a section of the stone floor, dug under the wall, and escaped from the county jail. With a killer on the loose, Sheriff John Nye contacted the district attorney and received approval to offer a $200 reward ($5000 in 2012) for Lagoy's capture. Nabbing Harris was valued separately at $100.

Men in the Schroon Lake area took to the woods in the vicinity of the Lagoy home, confident that Frank would return to the family homestead at some point. Sheriff's deputies were dispatched to Keene, Lewis, and Westport to search barns and other outbuildings where he might be hiding.

Frank Lagoy

A crew in North Hudson staked out a promising location, and soon enough, along came Lagoy. Anticipating an easy capture and a hefty reward, they ordered him to raise his hands and surrender. Frank immediately broke for cover, at which point the men opened fire. Several shots were sent his way, including two shotgun blasts and three rifle slugs, but Lagoy managed to escape into the woods.

After hiding out during the night, he headed south, making excellent time. By Sunday night, he was nearing Paradox Lake, but he never made it. Two armed men managed to capture him, and within twenty-four hours, Lagoy was back in the

Essex County jail, where he was chained in his cell to ensure there would be no more escapes.

No escapes for Frank, that is. On February 10, 1898, William Lagoy absconded and followed much the same path that Frank had taken in trying to reach Paradox Lake. But Will's escape was much less spectacular: he had been a jail trustee and was allowed to work outside. On the night in question, he simply walked away.

Eighteen days later, with searchers approaching a barn, Will buried himself and his rifle beneath a layer of hay, but to no avail. He was discovered, recaptured, and taken back to Elizabethtown without incident.

The two escapes diverted attention from the principal issue of why the Lagoys were incarcerated, but that was remedied when the grand jury met in May, indicting Frank on a charge of murder and his brothers for accessory to murder.

By the time the trial began on November 21, fourteen months had passed since the crime was committed. District Attorney Perry led the prosecution team, while Jude Whitman represented Frank Lagoy. Whitman's strategy for defending Frank was to admit the killing of Jackson, claiming it was done in self-defense. Former DA Robert Dornburgh acted on behalf of George and William.

Twenty-eight witnesses, ranging from coroners and lawmen to local woodsmen, appeared on the stand for the prosecution. The testimony of Michael Jenks, who accompanied Jackson to the scene on that fateful night, should have been pivotal, but under intense examination, he varied in the details. Had he actually witnessed the confrontation? Did Jackson fire the gun after being struck with the hatchet, or did Lagoy strike him after the gun was discharged? With Jenks as the only eyewitness, it had to be considered: had he fled the scene when the confrontation turned violent, or was the horse actually spooked by the gunshot?

The defense presented fifteen witnesses, including all three of the accused. At one point, Frank may have injured his own cause, denying that the hatchet displayed by the DA was the murder weapon, but later reversing himself. His dishonesty on the witness stand may have cast doubt on the testimony provided by several friendly witnesses, including a half-dozen members of the Lagoy family. All of them swore that in the past, Jackson had threatened to kill Frank Lagoy, and that bad blood had existed between them for three years, erupting at least once in violence when Jackson, athletic and strong, bested Lagoy in a fistfight.

Offsetting testimony for the prosecution came from two witnesses who verified that when teased about losing the fight, Frank had said, "I'd sooner kill Jackson as kill a snake."

For their part, all three brothers swore that during the fatal confrontation, Jackson fired his gun and Frank reacted in self-defense. As proof offered while on the stand, Lagoy displayed a scar on his left hand, where he said a bullet had penetrated his palm.

There had no doubt been ongoing issues between the two men, and in retrospect, handing one of the parties a warrant to arrest the other seemed a rather poor idea. But in the eyes of the law, William Jackson was just doing his job. No matter how the scene had played out, what could justify planting a hatchet in a man's chest?

And the Lagoys, widely perceived in Essex County as of dubious reputation, were less than ideal as witnesses. The defense cased hinged on reasonable doubt, which was a distinct possibility. After all, only the three Lagoys had witnessed the entire confrontation, and Michael Jenks had perhaps seen only the first few moments.

The trial lasted four days, and after several hours of discussion, the jury found Frank Lagoy guilty of second-degree murder. He was given the standard sentence, twenty years to life at Dannemora. It was a victory of sorts for the defense, having created enough doubt to avoid a finding of first-degree murder, which mandated the death penalty. Both George and Will were released after being found not guilty.

> **LAGOY SENTENCED FOR LIFE.**
>
> **The Schroon Lake Murderer Found Guilty in the Second Degree.**

In early April 1918, after nearly eighteen years in prison, Frank Lagoy Jr. was granted parole. In 1920, at the age of sixty-four, he was married for the first time, to Etta May Fish, thirty-one. They had three children together, of which two survived. The last child was born when Lagoy was sixty-nine years old.

He also managed to get into more legal trouble after his release from prison, showing no signs of having mellowed. In 1921, his brother George lived on land belonging to Orlin Smith, and had been cutting wood there without the owner's permission. When George refused to stop, Smith brought charges, seeking financial damages. The court agreed, but after a period of time during which nothing was paid, Smith successfully sought a "body execution," which imposed a jail sentence on violators who failed to comply with court-ordered solutions.

With his brother in jail, Frank, now sixty-five years old, took over the feud. Paying Smith a visit, he pulled out a revolver and threatened to shoot Smith's horse if he attempted to haul any of the cut timber away.

Smith pressed charges and Frank was arrested, but detention in jail was the least of his problems. As a convicted felon on parole, he faced the likelihood of returning to Dannemora if convicted.

George, who was still in jail, paid Frank's bail, and after some legal wrangling, a solution was found that satisfied all parties. Several of Frank's friends had petitioned the court for an outcome that would allow Lagoy to remain free. To appease all parties, George would be allowed to move in with his elderly mother and care for her, on condition that he complete his jail term first. Frank was given a suspended sentence, saving him from a return to prison, and was required to report once a week to the county parole officer. Both Lagoys consented to cause no further trouble for Smith.

Frank had more problems in 1926 when he was charged with carrying a concealed weapon. At the time, Clinton Prison was enduring overcrowded conditions that had been widely publicized. The problem was attributed to new laws imposing strict sentencing requirements on judges, thus reducing the use of court discretion. When Lagoy's case was heard, Dannemora's prison population had ballooned to nearly four hundred above capacity, requiring inmates to sleep in bunk beds in the cell corridors.

Fortunately for Frank, those conditions, along with the ages of his young children and his own status as a senior citizen, were factors in keeping him out of prison.

Lagoy died in 1938 at the age of eighty-two.

20

Scissors to the Sinus

The condition of Joseph's body, still lying on the floor, was frightful... bruises and abrasions to the face, and excessive bleeding from the nose, which had been nearly severed.

After being out and about the village of Tupper Lake on the morning of Sunday, November 6, 1921, young August Mercier, 21, returned home to join his father for dinner. Joseph, 56, who emigrated from France in 1893, was a blacksmith, currently employed on road construction projects. August was his apprentice and assistant. It was good, hard work, which helped distract them from problems at home. The two men were struggling to maintain the household in the absence of Mrs. Mercier, who had suffered mental problems serious enough to require confinement in the St. Lawrence State Hospital in Ogdensburg.

When August arrived at home that day, the house was empty, which was unusual, but not particularly so. Joseph had been with friends on Saturday night, and perhaps after several drinks, he had decided to wait for the light of day to return home. By mid-afternoon, though, his father's absence caused growing concern.

Meanwhile, at the home of young August's godfather, Auguste Barrois, a crisis was playing out. Michael Lahaye, a friend who had spent the night in Barrois' home, staggered through the village streets to the residence of Dr. Peter Monakey. Bleeding badly and obviously drunk, Lahaye urged the doctor to visit Barrois' home, where Joseph Mercier was severely injured. [Official records contain a variety of spellings for the Lahaye and Barrois surnames. Michael Lahaye was about forty-eight years old, and August Barrois about fifty.]

Monakey immediately contacted Police Chief Edward Clohosey, who took three men with him and carefully approached the Barrois house, uncertain what dangers might lurk within. They eventually gained entry by smashing through the locked kitchen door, revealing a jolting sight.

Before them on the floor was Joseph Mercier, sprawled in a pool of blood.

A search of the house led to the discovery of August Barrois, who was in a deep sleep on the second floor. After awakening with some difficulty, he expressed shock upon learning that Mercier was apparently dead in the kitchen, and that Lahaye was badly bloodied, but still alive.

HOME WHISKEY CAUSED FIGHT IN MOUNTAINS

Repeated questioning elicited few answers from Barrois: he had gone to bed about five hours earlier, leaving Mercier on the ground floor with Lahaye. All three men had been drinking heavily, he said, and even with hours of sleep, Barrois himself was still far from sober.

After confirming that the victim was deceased, Monakey resumed intense questioning of the two immediate suspects. Judging by his appearance, it seemed certain that Lahaye could shed some light on what had happened. His face was badly cut and bruised, and his sweater and other clothes were covered with blood.

Lahaye admitted that the men were moonshiners and had made a gallon of whiskey, which they drank the night previous, but he professed no knowledge of Mercier's demise, and was unable (or unwilling) to explain his own injuries. Like Barrois, he was still at least partially intoxicated.

Communicating with the suspects was further hindered by a language barrier. Both men spoke versions of the thick, French dialects common to Quebec, Canada. Until an adequate translator could be found, they were unable to accurately decipher the police chief's questions. Likewise, he was having difficulty understanding their answers.

Despite the issue of limited communication between officers and suspects, a dead body on the floor and a bloodied, beaten associate were deemed sufficient grounds for holding both men in custody.

At that point, three facts had been established: a man had died; three friends had been drinking heavily most of the night; and there was an illegal still in the house for producing moonshine alcohol. After Chief Clohosey made some calls, state police, sheriff's deputies, and a Prohibition agent were dispatched to conduct the investigation.

In a shed they found the alcohol still, which proved to be small, obviously intended to produce booze for personal consumption, and not for resale. Corn and raisins were used to make this particular version of homemade hooch. All the materials, including a barrel of mash and finished bottles of whiskey, were confiscated by the federal Prohibition agent.

Surrounding the crime scene were pieces of evidence and possible murder weapons: shards of glass, an axe, a pair of shears, and a butcher knife. Furniture was upset, blood was widely splattered, and at least one window was broken.

The condition of Joseph's body, still lying on the floor, was stomach-turning: a stab wound to the hip and to one wrist; several cuts to the hands and forehead; bruises and abrasions to the face, likely from blows struck with a piece of wood, which lay nearby; and excessive bleeding from the nose, which had been nearly severed. Only the general mayhem associated with a fierce brawl could account for such a mess, but neither Barrois nor Lahaye could, or would, explain what had happened.

Joseph's son told investigators that his father had approximately $100 on him when he left home on Saturday, but a search of the body fell well short of that total, making robbery a possible motive. It was found that both Barrois and Lahaye had paper money in their pockets, and it appeared to be soiled with blood.

Initial reports on Mercier's death appeared in city newspapers across New York, featuring sensationally graphic headlines, and embellishments bordering on outright fabrication. Butchery by mountain moonshiners was the theme, with lurid descriptions of a booze-crazed, axe-wielding backwoodsman chopping a body into pieces.

Joseph Mercier, Blacksmith, Found by Son Lying in Pool of Blood.

TWO UNDER ARREST

Owner of Cabin, Found Sleeping, and Partner in Still Held.

Those articles were well off the mark, containing only snippets of accuracy. But going to such extravagant extremes to entice readers was hardly necessary, especially in cases like Mercier's, where the suspected cause of death was sufficient to make even the most hardened among men shudder. The coroner had reached the conclusion that a pair of scissors had been shoved up one of Mercier's nostrils, penetrating his brain. The ensuing hemorrhage killed him.

After a hearing conducted by District Attorney Ellsworth Lawrence before Justice John Chalmers, and lasting until 3:00 AM, the suspects were arrested on suspicion of murder and held without bail in the Franklin County jail at Malone. Two days after the crime, a funeral was held, after which August Mercier laid his father to rest.

In late November, nearly thirty witnesses testified for two days before the grand jury, which indicted both men on charges of first-degree manslaughter. The lesser crime automatically transferred the case from the Supreme Court to the county court level. Pleas of not guilty were entered by attorney Andrew Cooney, and bail was set at $10,000 each ($125,000 in 2012).

The trial began in late January 1922, and the key moments arrived when both defendants took the witness stand, aided by an interpreter. In addressing the issue of Mercier's missing money (about $85) and the money found in the suspects' pockets, Barrois said Joseph had given him twenty dollars to repair a window that had been broken. The discoloration of the bill, he said, and similar stains on his pants, had both come from the whiskey mash, not from blood. Barrois reiterated having been asleep during the apparent fight that ended in Mercier's death, adding that he was Joseph's close friend and godfather to his son.

Lahaye testified that Mercier (whom he referred to as "my pal") had given him ten dollars for the broken window. When he offered to return it, Mercier told him to keep it as payment for the whiskey. The cut on Lahaye's head had occurred when he was working on the still, and the blood on the money was his own, deposited there when he reached into his pocket for a handkerchief to wipe his forehead. Plausible, of course, but Michael Lahaye's story was sometimes less than consistent.

Where he had once denied to police that there had even been a fight, Lahaye subsequently claimed he was alone in the shed when the fight occurred. Only later did he finally admit to two arguments that day with Joseph, one of which led to a tremendous battle.

Lahaye, who was of slight build and weighed only 135 pounds, described

> **GRUESOME MURDER AT TUPPER LAKE**
>
> Two Men in Custody as a Result of Drunken Debauch that Ended in Murder

a fierce life-and-death struggle, which was initiated by his comment that Mercier's wife was in the insane asylum because of Joseph, and that he alone was to blame. Lahaye's testimony about the fight was featured in reports on the trial's progress:

> Mercier yelled, "Damn you, you're going to die," and punched Lahaye, knocking him down. He got up and hit Mercier, who fell into a door, which had glass in the upper part. Mercier got up and came at him with an axe. There was a struggle. Mercier fell into a chair and Lahaye twitched the axe from him and put it away.
>
> Mercier got up and struck Lahaye in the forehead, and he (Lahaye) fell against a pail of water. Mercier tried to pick up the axe again, but Lahaye jumped on him to keep him from getting the axe. Then Lahaye struck him on the forehead while intending to hit him on the arm, grabbed the axe, and threw it into the hall.
>
> Mercier went into a fit and Lahaye threw the bucket of water on him to cool him off. Then Lahaye was sick, went to a toilet, and there fell asleep. Lahaye swore that the axe cut Mercier when he fell in the chair, that he did not strike Mercier with the knife, and did not see or have the shears in evidence. He declared that he had no intention of injuring Mercier, but was merely defending himself.

During summations, the defense conceded that cuts suffered by Mercier might have been inflicted by the knife or axe during the fight, but the fatal wound to the brain remained unaccounted for, perhaps the result of accidental contact with a narrow piece of broken glass. The prosecution dismissed that claim, asserting that the preponderance of evidence supported their argument that scissors had been used.

After four hours, the jury absolved August Barrois of all blame in Mercier's death and found Michael Lahaye guilty of a lesser crime, second-degree manslaughter. He was sentenced to Dannemora for a term ranging from six years and seven months to a maximum of fifteen years.

21

Pieces of Louise

Closer inspection revealed the torso to be intact, but there was no head, and only one limb was attached. The remains were nude, with one exception: the lone limb, a leg, bore a yellow bobby sock.

There are good days and bad days on just about any job, and on the evening of January 14, 1946, Saratoga Springs Assistance District Attorney John Doyle was having what most of us would consider a bad day. Had he won the lottery that morning, it could not have overshadowed in his memory the work he would do that night.

In a way, it sounded innocent enough: he was driving to different locations, retrieving evidence critical to an ongoing case. That would make it a routine job, but it was the nature of the evidence—a severed head, two severed arms, and a severed leg—that stood a pretty good chance of making a lasting impression on Doyle's mind.

The story had begun just five days earlier as a missing person's case when twenty-year-old Louise DeChants failed to return home after leaving her parents house early in the morning. Police were called, but they had little to go on. The sole clue was that a woman named Sonja had driven to the DeChants home and Louise had left with her.

Police Chief Patrick Rox began investigating, with men working in two principal directions. Several of Louise's friends said she was very pretty and had many boyfriends, which opened up several possibilities. Others followed up on the woman last seen with Louise. The fact that Sonja was an unusual name at least narrowed the possibilities in a city of about fifteen thousand residents.

In a few days, strong suspicions were directed towards a local nurse, fifty-six-year-old Sonja Leggett. It was determined that Louise was "in trouble," which for girls once had a single meaning: pregnant. Among the few women in town named Sonja, Leggett was one who could have "helped" Louise solve her problem. Other clues also pointed towards Leggett, resulting in a search warrant allowing access to the cottage she shared on nearby Lake Lonely with her husband, Clarence.

On Sunday morning, January 13, investigators scoured the property. For Detective Walter Ahrens and Patrolman Dominick Isolde, it was either their lucky day or their unlucky day (depending again on perspective). But like Doyle's experience, it was one guaranteed to be unforgettable.

On the Leggett property was a chicken coop, and near the back of the coop, protruding from beneath loose dirt and manure, was a body—or at least *part* of a body. Closer inspection revealed the torso to be intact, but there was no head, and only one limb was attached. The remains were nude, with one exception: the lone limb, a leg, bore a yellow bobby sock.

The find was only seven miles from the DeChants home, and it was believed to be Louise's corpse. Family members were notified, and Joseph, the twenty-three-year-old brother of Louise, made an attempt to identify the remains. He was understandably unable to do so, but when told that one foot was covered with a yellow sock, Joseph somehow recalled that she left home that morning wearing yellow socks.

While preparations were made for an autopsy, police began interrogating the Leggetts about the horrible discovery made on their property. Authorities otherwise remained tight-lipped, making no arrests, but questioning potential witnesses (including the Leggett's neighbors) while awaiting the autopsy results. It was uncertain how helpful those results might be, considering that a good percentage of the body was still missing. It was believed that a sharp knife had been used to cut off the arms and leg, and perhaps a hacksaw was employed for removing the head.

Even without the head and limbs, the torso did reveal one very important fact: the person who died was three months pregnant. Armed with that information, detectives pressed Leggett, who finally broke down and confessed to the events of the past five days, a gruesome story that was carried in newspapers around the world. The front page of the *Courier-Mail* of Brisbane, Australia, noted that it was America's second corpse-dismemberment murder in nine days (the other was in Chicago).

Leggett revealed that Louise had hired her to perform an abortion, paying the nurse $50 in advance (about $600 in 2012). On the morning of January 9, she picked up DeChants at her home and drove her to the Leggett cottage. Once inside, the two discussed the procedure, and an argument erupted over the girl's failure to follow Leggett's instructions.

Pieces of Louise

Find Headless Body of Woman Near Saratoga

The confrontation turned physical, and Sonja punched Louise, who fell backward, striking her head on a dresser.

According to Leggett (the only witness), the girl appeared to be merely unconscious, but an examination revealed no pulse, and she soon realized that the sharp blow to the head had killed Louise. Sonja placed the body on a couch, uncertain what to do next.

A decision was made overnight, and on the following afternoon, she dragged the corpse outside and proceeded to dismember it with a carving knife. The severed parts were placed in a box and discarded somewhere near the Saratoga Raceway, according to Leggett, and the torso was buried near the rear of the chicken coop. Her husband, said Sonja, was completely unaware of the situation.

At the arraignment, where a mandatory plea of not guilty was entered, Sonja was accompanied by the two officers who had discovered the torso. She wept during the hearing and nearly collapsed, clutching Officer Ahren's arm for support. Her husband Clarence did not appear in court.

Later that same day, Sheriff Frank Hathon notified the district attorney's office about a tip concerning the missing body parts, which still hadn't been located. Although Leggett said they were at the Saratoga Raceway, new information placed them at Ballston Spa. The source of the tip, if known, was not revealed.

Sonja was brought in immediately for further questioning, finally agreeing to lead police to the severed body parts. On Tuesday, newspapers everywhere detailed the grisly tour:

> The severed head was found about 10:00 PM yesterday in a pine grove, near a place known as Bishop's Tavern, on Greenfield Avenue in the town of Milton. The head, unwrapped, was lying in a thick clump of pines just

off the road. About a quarter mile away, on Middlebrook Avenue in the village of Ballston Spa, the investigators discovered a cardboard box which had apparently been hurled down a forty-foot embankment from the road. This contained the missing arms and the right leg.

All the parts of the body were returned to Saratoga Springs, where they will be used for completion of the autopsy begun Sunday night. They were turned over to county pathologist Dr. Joseph Lebowich.

After the autopsy was completed, a funeral was held for Louise DeChants. It was later found that the results of the examination contradicted Sonja's version of events. No injuries to the head had been found, and the coroner's conclusion was that Louise died from heavy blood loss.

Sonja had originally lied about the location of the missing body parts, casting doubt on the truthfulness of the rest of her confession. A battle ensued over the autopsy findings, with the defense maintaining that Leggett had since provided an honest account. With the two sides at an impasse, an exhumation order was issued just days after the funeral.

Two days later, and a week after the missing body parts were found, the coroner's original determination was revised. The cause of death was still officially listed as heavy blood loss, but a small fracture had been located near the base of Louise's skull.

The new findings supported Sonja's claim that the victim had suffered a serious head injury, but it also suggested a ghastly possibility. The coroner maintained that the cause of death was excessive blood loss, which could only have occurred if the dismemberment was performed while DeChants was still alive.

That very question was posed to the district attorney, who responded with information provided by the autopsy physicians: the small fracture had caused Louise to become comatose, a condition that might last for an unspecified amount of time.

Pressed for more, Doyle addressed the live-dismemberment issue:

> All we can do is compare what we found in the body with what Mrs. Leggett said. But yes, it is possible.

A few days after the new findings were released, Sonja Leggett pleaded not guilty to one count of abortion and two counts of first-degree murder

Might Have Dissected Girl Alive

(one for murder with premeditation and deliberation, and one for murder while committing a felony). The trial was set for February 8, exactly a month from the day of the crime.

In mid-February, at a routine hearing to address a defense motion, observers were stunned to hear Mrs. Leggett offer to plea to a lesser charge. District Attorney John Doyle gave his consent, and Sonja pleaded guilty to a single count of second-degree murder.

Appealing for leniency in sentencing, defense attorney James McNaughton noted that Mrs. Leggett was a native of Hamburg, Germany, who had come to the United States in 1922. Since 1930, she had worked as a nurse in the Saratoga area and became a naturalized citizen.

The details of her past failed to impress Supreme Court Justice Daniel Imrie, who sentenced her to twenty years to life at Bedford Hills, the state's only maximum security facility for women.

Twenty years later, following her release from prison, Sonja Leggett died in 1966 at the age of seventy-seven.

22

Murder in the Mucklands

She had been dealt a truly horrible, vicious beating. Her right arm was broken, likely while attempting to fend off repeated blows from the hammer.

In central New York State, between Canastota and the southern shores of Oneida Lake, a narrow strip of land known as "The Mucklands," covering perhaps thirty square miles, was once among the top vegetable-producing sites in the state. While potatoes, celery, and other vegetables did well in the rich black soil, the Mucklands' most famous crop earned Canastota the nickname, "Onion Capital of the World."

The Mucklands' heyday was the first five decades of the twentieth century, and its success was driven largely by immigrant Italian farmers, many of whom first worked the land as sharecroppers before assuming ownership. As the Roaring Twenties came to a close, the Mucklands was among the nation's top suppliers of high-grade onions. There was no doubting the crop's potency. During the dog days of summer, the growing fields sometimes smelled so strongly of onion, it made the eyes burn.

On December 5, 1942, Canastota resident Philip Lombardi was completing some chores, dumping brush into Cowessalon Creek, which slices through the Mucklands. The creek's path is paralleled by Ditch Bank Road, which runs northwest from Canastota village.

Something unusual caught his eye, perhaps a deer carcass down the bank, but closer inspection raised the hackles on his neck. It was the dead body of a female, and as Lombardi later told police, "I got scared and ran for help." With the aid of a nearby farmer, the coroner was contacted. In short order, the site was awash with lawmen.

The Mucklands was now a crime scene, with a victim whose skull was badly battered. The woman's corpse, frozen solid, was fully clad in a green dress and a winter coat, casting doubt on the probability of sexual assault. She still wore a watch, a pin, and three rings, including at least

25 Diabolical Adirondack Murders

The Mucklands

one with a diamond, ruling out the likelihood of robbery as a motive. A pair of eyeglasses lay nearby. Other than a wedding ring indicating she was married, there were no items of identification on or near the victim.

But police weren't entirely clueless. One ring was engraved with the initials R. O. C., and the pin was distinctive, confirmed by instructors at the Marinello chain of beauty schools as the institution's graduation gift.

As the days passed, pieces of the puzzle gradually accumulated, but the key that brought it all together—the number 6493-74WG—confirmed the victim's identity a week after the body was found. Those eight digits were the manufacturer's number on the eyeglasses found at the crime scene. After plenty of sleuthing, the trail led two hundred miles northeast to Plattsburgh in Clinton County, to the office of Dr. Charles Holt. Those glass frames, according to his records, had been sold five years earlier to Rose O'Connell of Ausable Forks. The engraved ring, of course, reflected her initials—R. O. C. But who was Rose O'Connell? Why was she halfway across the state, and who would want her dead?

Background work revealed that she was the thirty-eight-year-old daughter of James and Mary O'Connell of Keene, New York, in the Adirondacks. Both of her parents were deceased, and in 1937, Rose moved to Ausable Forks, having found employment at the firm of J & J Rogers. An uncle there, John Willis, confirmed that Rose had visited as recently as

Labor Day, 1942, and that to keep in touch with local goings-on, she still subscribed to an area newspaper. Investigators now had a name and an address, which was in Watervliet, across the Hudson River from Troy. They would soon learn much more.

In recent years, Rose's life had undergone many changes. She was now Rose Patane, wife of Joseph Patane, whom she married in 1939. The two had met while living in the same boarding house in Schenectady when Rose was attending the Marinello Beauty School. They now had a two-year-old daughter, Patricia.

The immediate concern of investigators suddenly focused on Patricia. If the mother had been killed, what had become of the daughter? Their fears increased exponentially when it was learned that Joseph Patane's parents (his mother and stepfather) were living in Canastota.

While relatives performed the difficult task of identifying Rose's remains, police were relieved to locate Patricia Patane at the home of Mr. and Mrs. Anthony Mascari, Joseph's parents. The Mascaris said their son had visited about two weeks earlier and left his daughter with them, but hadn't returned for her yet. Ominously, it was the coroner's estimate that Rose had died two weeks ago.

The Mascaris also told police that this was the first time they had seen their granddaughter, and they had never met Rose, who was their son's second wife. More and more, the trail of suspicious events pointed towards one person: Joseph Patane.

The next day, police questioned him at his workplace, a Menands produce business where he drove a delivery truck. He answered their questions, but as the process was repeated, Patane's replies vacillated. Rose, he said, was somewhere in Troy, but he later claimed to have left her on the road near Canastota and didn't know where she was at the moment.

Joseph was taken to the police station, where the questioning continued for about twelve hours, at which point police had enough information to reconstruct the events surrounding Rose's death. The admissions elicited from Patane during the interview gradually blossomed into a full-blown confession. Other details accumulated as investigators delved deeper into issues mentioned in Patane's replies.

The results so far weren't pretty, but no charges were filed against him. That would come only after a bizarre series of events in which Patane and his supposed accomplice readily participated. The conspirator in question was Anna Lenway of Troy, his lover and/or wife (their marital status was still under investigation).

Patane and Lenway accompanied authorities, including Police Sergeant Charles Manning of the BCI unit (Bureau of Criminal Investigation), on a trip to central New York. Near Canastota, they guided the team to the exact place where the murder of Rose O'Connell was committed. So specific were they in the details that Lenway, for the sake of accuracy, told police to move the car about ten feet from where it had first been placed.

The two of them willingly demonstrated their roles in the crime, Lenway playing the part of Rose in order to show both Joseph's position and the victim's behind the car as he struck the killing blows. During the actual murder, Lenway was seated in the rear of the car, watching the slaying through the back window. Also seated in the car was two-year-old Patricia Patane. Reporters observing the reenactment later wrote that Anna could be seen laughing at times as she re-created the fatal assault.

When police were satisfied they had the full story, Patane and Lenway were arraigned at Chittenango on first-degree murder charges, to which they pled not guilty. The information sworn to in court by Sergeant Manning was hardly nebulous, reporting that the murder was committed with a hammer wielded by Joseph Mascari in accordance with a plan concocted by Mascari and Lenway. Anna Gelina Lenway, said Manning, "did aid and abet and act in concert with him."

Following the hearing, they were held in the Madison County jail at Wampsville, two miles east of Canastota.

During the next several days, the remainder of Mascari's twisted marital history was deciphered. As Joseph Mascari, he had wed Mary Licciardello of Canastota a decade earlier, a union that produced a son and a daughter. The couple experienced problems, and they were officially divorced in late 1941. However, two years prior to his divorce, Joseph Patane had married Rose O'Connell in Essex County. They had one child, daughter Patricia.

After killing Rose in the Canastota Mucklands on December 5, 1942, Joseph left Patricia with his parents, and with his partner, Anna, returned to the Troy area. A few days later, they journeyed east to Vermont, where they claimed to have married on December 9. Mascari was either twice a bigamist or possessed a dreadful sense of timing.

One question continued to dog investigators: How had he managed to get both his wife and lover to travel with him 120 miles, confined in the close quarters of an automobile?

Joseph Mascari and his lover/accomplice Anna Lenway re-enact Mascari's murder of his wife in the Mucklands near Canastota, New York

Joseph Mascari and Anna Lenway enjoy a meal before the trip to Chittenango, where they were arraigned on charges of first-degree murder

Interviews with neighbors, relatives, and friends of Joseph, Rose, and Anna began providing the answers to that question, and clued investigators in on another stunning discovery: Joseph Mascari had been leading a double life, and at locations just a few miles apart.

Mrs. Miles Landry of Schenectady, a cousin of Rose and the person who identified her remains, said that O'Connell had confided in her a deep unhappiness

> **PATANE, WOMAN ARE HELD ON A MURDER CHARGE**
>
> Accused in Hammer-Slaying of Former Rose O'Connell of Ausable Forks

related to marital suspicions. Joseph Patane, she said, routinely came home from work each day between 9:00 and 10:00 PM, even though his daily shift ended hours earlier at 6:00 PM. Furthermore, he spent most weekends in New York City on business.

Mrs. Alice Pangburn, who lived in the Watervliet apartment across the hall from Joseph and Rose, was confused when police showed her the photograph of Joseph Mascari, for she knew him only as Joseph Patane. Rose had visited Alice's apartment on December 5 to show off the new green dress she bought for the trip to Canastota, and had commented, "It's my first visit to Joe's, and I want to make a good impression." She was wearing the same green dress when Joe killed her.

Acquaintances of Anna Lenway proved every bit as helpful. Anna lived just two miles from the Patanes, boarding in the home of George and Alice Whinnery, where she worked as nursemaid and housekeeper. Upon viewing the photographs of Joseph Patane, the Whinnerys identified him as Joseph Mascari, the man who visited Anna on almost a nightly basis (instead of going home after work to Rose), and who spent most weekends with her (during the "trips to New York," he was actually just two miles away with his lover). Mrs. Whinnery recalled that on December 5, Mascari had stopped by early in the morning, reminding Anna to be ready for the upcoming trip that afternoon to Canastota.

Joseph's cover story, concocted to later explain his wife's disappearance, was simple: Rose was taking a trip to visit relatives in Chicago. He would drive her as far as Canastota, where his parents could meet their daughter-in-law and new granddaughter for the first time. Rose would then continue to Chicago, and Joseph would return home. Anna, a nursemaid by profession, would accompany them and look after Patricia's needs.

The four of them set off late in the afternoon on December 5, and everything went as planned. But when Joseph and Anna arrived back in Troy and Watervliet, there were questions to be answered. The Patanes' neighbor, Alice Pangburn, saw Joseph packing and moving the apartment contents. When she asked about Rose, Patane explained that she was visiting her mother in Chicago, and that he had purchased a home outside the city so that Patricia could be raised in pleasant, fresh-air surroundings.

A couple of miles away at the Whinnery home, where Anna lived, Joseph told a different story, claiming trouble with his landlady and asking if he could stay with Anna for a few days. The Whinnerys consented, and two weeks later, Joe and Anna announced that they had been married.

In two homes, separated by only two miles, and with two women, he had been leading two lives—as Joseph Patane of Watervliet and Joseph Mascari of Troy. No one would ever question whether the man had cojones.

Those facts alone were titillating enough, but the story unraveling around Patane was about to get worse. In mid-February 1943, a grand jury indicted him for first-degree murder, but returned no indictment against Anna. She was instead ordered confined under $25,000 bail ($315,000 in 2012) as a material witness. Lenway had turned state's evidence!

Despite the statement in court by Sergeant Manning—that Joseph had bludgeoned Rose to death as the culmination of a plan assembled by Joseph and Anna—the district attorney was willing to set her free in exchange for testimony against Patane. The case against Joseph was already strong, but Lenway's testimony would provide the highest probability of success. Although they were newlyweds of barely two months duration, Anna was ready and willing to send her husband to the electric chair in order to save her own skin.

Two attorneys, Stanley Bliss and A. G. (Antonio) Waldo, had been assigned to defend Mascari, but after two weeks on the job, they were at wit's end. Joseph, they said, was uncooperative, and at times had acted

Joseph Mascari/Patane

irrationally. He refused to share any information with the attorneys, and claimed to be on a hunger strike, although it seems he failed to grasp the concept once popularized by Ghandi.

After a so-called hunger strike of one day, Joseph feasted on a spaghetti supper. Fully sated, he announced a renewed hunger strike. And after going without food the next day, he again feasted on spaghetti. But according to Joseph's brother, his actions were misrepresented in the media. During the times when he wasn't eating, Mascari said he feared someone was tinkering with his food. His attorneys remained baffled by it all.

With the possibility of an insanity defense looming, the judge granted their request for a psychiatric evaluation. A sanity commission at Marcy State Hospital in Utica performed the examinations, and in a nutshell, they found that Joseph Mascari was "mentally deficient, but is not insane."

The trial was held at Wampsville, just east of Canastota. Mascari was prosecuted by District Attorney Clarence Conley, with support from Assistant DA Nelson Neidhardt. From the beginning, it was a contentious battle. Defense attorney Bliss resented the damage to his arguments caused by the DA's offer of immunity to Anna Lenway, who had earlier admitted helping plan the murder. There were frequent interruptions for objections, many of which were sustained by Justice William Coon.

Two of his rulings were decidedly unusual: preventing a prosecution witness from referring to Rose Patane as "the victim," and forbidding use of the word "blood" in describing a man's suit introduced as evidence (said to be the suit Joseph wore when he battered Rose's head with the hammer).

Madison County Coroner Dr. John Boyd testified to the extent of Rose's injuries, reporting several head lacerations and six skull fractures, the latter of which killed her. She had been dealt a truly horrible, vicious beating. Her legs were bruised and scraped, and her right arm was broken, likely while attempting to fend off repeated blows from the hammer.

Among the physical evidence presented was nothing of great impact. Rose's dress, rings, watch, pin, and glasses were poignant, for sure, but the jury already knew she had been beaten to death. The real issue boiled down to one question: who did it, and where was the proof?

One other exhibit—the blue suit, with large reddish stains on the knees and lower legs—had excellent potential for the prosecution. Railroad workers had found it wrapped inside a copy of the *Troy Record*, discarded along the tracks about five miles from Albany. As a piece of men's clothing soiled with blood, it strongly suggested that Joseph, and not Anna, was the person who actually killed Rose.

But when Judge Coon honored Bliss' objection to using the word "blood" when referring to the suit, he was legally correct. It wasn't clear what had caused the stains, and no forensic experts could state with certainty they were of blood, let alone the blood of Rose O'Connell. Mrs. Whinnery came closest to identifying the suit, saying it was similar to the one Mascari wore when he had left on December 5 with Anna Lenway.

For the prosecution, the greatest damage to Patane was inflicted by Lenway. To mitigate the effect of Joseph's claim that they had planned the murder together, Anna testified simply that, "I didn't believe him." In describing the scene in the Mucklands, she said:

> … I heard Rose scream and yell. I looked out, and Joe's hands were going up and down, and Rose was on her knees.

But she also admitted that when the attack began, Anna did nothing to stop it, and denied that any confrontation had occurred in the car between her and Rose. She also denied helping Joseph to hide the murder weapon, said to be a "crate hammer," which hadn't been found, and said it was untrue that she and Joseph had later married in Vermont.

At that point, another bitter battle erupted between Bliss and DA Conley over the granting of immunity to a witness who had admitted complicity in a murder. The heated exchange directly addressed the issue:

> DA CONLEY: Tell the court what I said about immunity.
> ANNA LENWAY: As long as I told the truth, I have nothing to worry about.
> DEFENSE ATTORNEY BLISS: Yet as far as you know, you will be discharged from jail and go home a free woman, won't you?
> ANNA LENWAY: Yes.
> ATTORNEY BLISS: Has the district attorney told you about any charges against you?
> ANNA LENWAY: Not in this county.

In all, thirty witnesses took the stand for the prosecution. For the defense, Mascari himself was the only one to testify. A review of Joseph's marital history included claims that his union with Rose was dissolving,

> **TROY GIRL DENIES SHE AIDED PATANE IN KILLING WIFE**
>
> Anna Lenway Says She Didn't Believe Watervliet Man Would Really Slay His Spouse.

> **Patane Charges On Stand Anna Lenway Was Actual Killer**
>
> Says He Gave Another Version of Crime Because He Loved Woman He Now Accuses.

and that Lenway had said the same about her marriage. (Lenway and her husband had been separated for some time when she took up with Mascari.) From that discussion about unhappy marriages grew the plan to murder Rose and start a new life together.

When asked about the killing, Joseph said that on the trip from Troy to Canastota, Rose and Patricia were seated in front with him, and Anna was in the back seat alone. In describing the events leading up to his wife's death, Mascari's version was much different from the story told earlier by Anna Lenway:

> We were going through Canastota and Rose was arguing constantly. She was picking at me about where I had been the night before. Suddenly, she turned around, pointed at Anna, and said, "You were out with that."
>
> Rose hit me on the head with her bag. Then Anna hit Rose. I heard Rose cry. I pulled to the curb and shook her, but she didn't answer. I asked Anna what I should do, and she said, "Isn't there some place we can throw her off?" As I opened the door, Rose fell out on the road. As I tried to lift her, I slipped, and she fell down the embankment. Anna wrapped up the hammer and tossed it away. ... Anna asked me not to tell the real truth. I had to cover her up because I loved her and I still love her.

Whether or not Mascari's story rang true, the final trump card was played by the prosecution. Despite vigorous objection by the defense that Joseph Mascari's initial confession had been made under great duress,

Judge Coon allowed it to be read into the record. Excerpts from the twenty-page document were devastating.

> On our way to Canastota from Watervliet, my wife, Rose O'Connell, called me a dirty skunk after she accused me of being out with someone else the night before. Rose continued to argue when we arrived in Canastota. I stopped the car and punched her. When she got out of the car, I went to her, and we argued again and she called me names. ... I punched her, and she fell and hit her head on the bumper of the car. I picked her up and punched her again. ... I don't remember whether she screamed or not. ... I didn't push her off the road into the ditch. ... I noticed blood on my trousers when I returned to my car and told Anna that I was scared. I drove to my father's house and left Patricia with them. I told them that my wife was sick.

Mascari described the return to Troy and the subsequent drive to Vermont, where he paid seven dollars to get married. But during cross-examination, Joseph caused perhaps as much damage to his own defense as Lenway's testimony had done earlier. To a series of questions—What did you do with the hammer? How many times did Rose hit Anna? What side of Rose's head did Anna hit? Where did you dispose of the body? Did you tell the troopers that Anna had struck your wife with a hammer?—his answer was either "I don't know" or "I don't remember."

To others—In which town did you marry Anna? Which road did you take to Vermont? Who was the minister? Where is the marriage certificate?—it was more of the same.

With thirty witnesses and fifty exhibits against him, and a death sentence staring him in the face, all that Mascari could muster in his own defense, perhaps to literally save his life, was, "I don't remember."

Although the odds were heavily stacked against him, Stanley Bliss delivered a passionate final summation on Joseph's behalf, pleading with the jury to consider Anna Lenway's role:

> The simple truth is that Joe never got out of that front seat until Rose was dead. The state has failed to produce even one rebuttal witness to contradict Joe's story here. He valiantly protected the woman he loved, but

in return was "thrown in" by her at compound interest. Joe told police investigators everything but the part that implicated Anna. He would confer with Anna, and she would instruct him. Then she came into this courtroom and repaid him. Little Anna has committed no wrong, oh no, but a door will open for her.

The last reference was Bliss' parting shot at the district attorney's decision to absolve Anna of all responsibility for a murder that she helped plan so that she and Joseph could be together, unfettered.

DA Conley left nothing to chance, reviewing the evidence and emphasizing even lesser points, like the low ceiling of Mascari's car, which precluded the delivery of a killing blow from the back seat. Rose, he said, was not struck in the car, but was killed behind it by her husband, who delivered numerous impacts to her skull, any one of which could have been enough to kill her. And all the while, their two-year-old daughter sat just a few feet away. The callousness of such an act was difficult to comprehend.

After absorbing two weeks of testimony, it took eight hours of deliberation for the jury to arrive at a verdict: guilty of first-degree murder. Mascari and the defense attorneys waited anxiously for further comments, but none were forthcoming. The jury had the option of including a recommendation for clemency (mercy), but had chosen not to exercise it.

Without the benefit of such a recommendation, the judge had no leeway in sentencing: New York State

Mascari Found Guilty Murder In First Degree

Death Penalty Mandatory; Jury Returns Verdict On Charge Of Slaying Wife, Former Ausable Resident

law mandated the death penalty.

When Anna Lenway, still incarcerated, was advised of the verdict, she said, "He did it and he ought to be punished." When told that Mascari had taken the witness stand and tried to lay the crime on her head, Anna called him "a rat."

Two old idioms, "The pot calling the kettle black" and "two peas in a pod" come to mind, but for two people so much alike, they could not have been dealt more disparate fates. Anna was destined to be free, and Joseph faced the electric chair.

In early April, sentenced was passed, ordering Mascari held at Sing Sing Prison for electrocution during the week of May 16. An appeal was filed, bringing two principle defense claims before the state Court of Appeals: that Mascari's confession had been forced during fifty-five hours of interrogation, and that a reversible error had been committed by the district attorney's office in failing to charge Anna, based on her own admission of culpability.

But the high court was unmoved, issuing an order in December that Mascari be electrocuted on January 6, 1944. The only remaining hope for a reprieve was executive clemency.

Bliss took the argument to Governor Thomas Dewey, who listened to his claims that Joseph Mascari was truly insane, as suggested by his crimes and his extreme anti-social behavior. A week before the scheduled execution, Governor Dewey received an assessment of Mascari's condition as judged by a sanity commission: "He is sane at present, and was at the time of the crime."

On January 6, Joseph ate heartily, but did not avail himself of the "last meal" option for any special requests. His head was shaved and he was transferred to the pre-execution cell. Most of his last day on earth was spent in silence.

Some men resist, some cry, and some remain stoic when faced with execution. Observers reported that Mascari walked unaided to the electric chair, smiling slightly prior to sitting down for the last time. A few minutes later, he was gone.

23

A Blade for His Brother

When told Thomas was in a dangerous condition, his reply was as hard-hearted as they come: if it looked like recovery was possible, he would put a bullet in his brother's head to end it.

Many men of the Adirondacks have earned reputations as tough, rugged individuals, and deservedly so. Others shared the same traits but set the bar much lower, focusing on lawlessness, and often to excess. The worst of them seemed to have no conscience, accompanied by a complete disregard for societal rules. Those men frequently found themselves in reformatories, jails, and prisons.

Among their number was James Patterson of Moriah, both a blacksmith and lumberjack, and a man not to be messed with. There were those who did, and they paid a price. He was known to some as "Redhead Jim," a guy who would fight at the drop of a hat when sober, but when drinking, as he did frequently and heavily, no provocation was needed for him to start a ruckus. James was in and out of jail so often, it was hard to believe he had time to commit so many offenses. A knack for evading charges was his forté, but the "minor" transgressions landing him in court included burglary, robbery, destroying schoolhouse property, public intoxication (several times), assault (varying degrees), and illegally discharging a firearm.

He once did time for shooting a man (not fatally), but Patterson's preferred weapon was the knife. He used it often for intimidation, and it was no idle threat. At least two men who had been stabbed by him could attest to that fact.

Even in the lumber camps that he frequented, where plenty of dangerous characters found work, James was given a wide berth. He once felled a tree that struck and killed a man, an act that couldn't be proven as intentional. He worked at odd jobs, but Patterson was primarily a blacksmith, a trade he learned—where else?—in prison.

And his threatening persona wasn't just for strangers and folks who irritated him. The Patterson family shared in it as well. The most serious incident occurred when James, then 40, and his brother, Thomas, 43, lived with their parents, John, 80, and Mary, 73. Tom was regarded by friends as non-confrontational, and was nothing like his notorious brother.

Arriving at home one night in a drunken rage, James attacked his elderly parents. He might have killed them if not for physical intervention by Thomas, who gave him a good-old-fashioned ass-kicking and threw him out. Even as he was evicted, James threatened to kill his brother.

After the violent incident, Patterson lived in boarding houses and wasn't seen around his parents' home for a long time. But holding a grudge was one of his strengths, and there was little doubt he would someday return with vengeance on his mind.

Within the next two years, pneumonia took a toll on the family, and Thomas inherited the property, which did nothing to diminish James' resentment towards him. That may well have been what prompted Jim to return to his former haunts, but that can't be known for certain.

In January 1913, fully three years after Tom had thrown him out for the attack on their parents, the two brothers found themselves at an all-night party in Moriah. For several hours, there was no trouble between them, but with lots of booze flowing, something was bound to happen.

Emboldened by the alcohol, Jim Patterson began the persistent hassling of his older brother, and shortly before 4:00 AM, a fight broke out. As was his wont, Jim pulled out his knife and went after Thomas. Of two eyewitnesses to the attack, one feared Jim and didn't dare intervene. The other tried to separate them, but was unsuccessful.

During the fight, Thomas was cut badly on the arm. Then, when the opportunity presented itself, Jim slammed the knife into the left side of his brother's chest. The damage, unseen at the time, was frightening. The blade sliced off one rib and partway through another, entering the heart. Thomas dropped to the floor, and James left the building. No one was foolish enough to stand in his way.

Within two hours, Jim returned, carrying a rifle, and inquired of his brother's condition. When told Thomas was in a dangerous condition, his reply was as hard-hearted as they come: if it looked like recovery was possible, he would put a bullet in his brother's head to end it.

In the uncertainty of the situation, Jim sat by the stove, still holding his rifle. He was no one to trifle with, and everyone kept their distance. Soon, the noise of a rig outside caused a commotion within as Jim, suspecting it was the law, prepared to defend himself. The visitor, however, was a doctor, and Jim was surprised to learn that no one had summoned the sheriff or state police. After grabbing a quick nap, he learned of the doctor's assessment: Thomas had little chance for survival. Swearing he wouldn't be taken alive, Patterson departed the premises and began trekking in the direction of North Hudson, some ten miles or more distant.

Hiding out in the woods, he took meals at the home of a cousin, William Greenough. The day after the stabbing, news of Thomas' death reached Greenough, who counseled James to return home and give himself up. Surprisingly, he got through to Patterson, who began the long walk back to Moriah. On the way, he encountered one of the search parties that had been pursuing him. Much to their relief, he gave himself up without a fight.

Once in custody, though, James had a change of heart. Within a short time, having relaxed his captors with an uncharacteristically amiable, passive demeanor, he seized the first opportunity to escape. Word spread quickly that a murdering desperado was again on the loose. Posses took to the woods, and the call was made for a team of regionally famous bloodhounds from Plattsburgh, about fifty miles north.

Patterson immediately headed south to familiar territory, the woods of North Hudson near Greenough's home. A group of searchers, led by Deputy Sheriff Richard Spring, paid a visit to the property. Jim hadn't returned, but Greenough took Spring and the others outside into the pitch-black of night and pointed towards a glow on one of the small mountains nearby. Evidently, to keep warm in the cold winter air, Patterson had built a large fire.

Approaching a man like James, known for his prowess in the woods, was best done on their terms, not his. It was decided to postpone the pursuit until morning and spend the night

> **MURDERED HIS OWN BROTHER**
>
> Moriah Man Drives Knife Through Brother's Heart
>
> BLOODHOUND TO BE USED TO TRAIL MURDERER

at Greenough's. But Patterson lived up to his reputation. Although the posse left early the next morning, Spring's men arrived to find the campsite abandoned.

A reward of $100 had been offered for capturing James, which added to the number of men hunting for him in the forest from Moriah to North Hudson. Through the maze of searchers, Patterson somehow made it back to Moriah undetected. About a mile from the crime scene, he took refuge in an abandoned farmhouse. After preparing a roaring fire, he lay back in a chair, smoking his beloved corncob pipe until sleep overtook him.

When the door suddenly flew open, Patterson sprang instantly to his feet, but only from surprise. Before him, two lawmen with guns at the ready soon learned that he was following Greenough's advice a second time and giving himself up. All he had ever known was the vast woods of Essex County, and there was simply nowhere else to run. Besides, Patterson knew that there was always a chance he would once again wriggle off the hook legally, as he had done many times in the past.

He was arraigned at Port Henry and transferred to the county jail at Elizabethtown. Representing him was former district attorney Patrick Finn, a man who knew his way around a courtroom, and his partner, Harry Owen. Arguing for the People was District Attorney Fred LaDuke. The case was brought before Justice Henry Borst in mid-July 1913.

The defense team had much to overcome: two eyewitnesses; their client's widely known, abominable reputation; and the dead body of the defendant's own brother. But there existed one potential weakness in the prosecution's case—the medical treatment applied to the victim, who died later the same day of the stabbing. The wounds Thomas endured were serious, but had the services of a hospital been available close at hand, perhaps he could have survived. Although it wasn't an argument for exoneration, it might open a path for the jury to consider a lesser charge, one that would save Patterson from the electric chair. From all appearances, that's where he was headed.

Dr. Arthur Reed, who treated Thomas at the crime scene, bore the brunt of the defense attorneys' assault, which was intentionally rapid-fire. The purpose was to rattle him on the witness stand, a tactic that was effective at times, making the doctor appeared confused. But until a verdict was announced, it was unclear just how much the jury's perception had been impacted.

It was risky, of course, but it was the only real option in a case where fifteen people took the stand for the prosecution, but not a single defense witness was called. Patterson's fate relied entirely on the cross-examination skills of his attorneys. Finn and Owen considered having the defendant tell his story in court, but were dissuaded by the prospects of a withering counter-attack by the district attorney, which was a virtual certainty.

When the jury returned in less than two hours, the death penalty was expected. Patterson's terrible past might have played on their collective subconscious, and such a short deliberation suggested quick agreement on a guilty charge.

That much was correct, but observers were surprised to learn that the jury had opted for second-degree murder. They arrived at that decision after five ballots, the first of which found three jurists in favor of first-degree murder, five for second-degree murder, and four for manslaughter.

There were only two potentially mitigating factors that could have influenced the outcome: the drunken state of Patterson when he killed his brother, and the suggestion that medical treatment of the victim had been less than optimal.

Whatever the case, tough guy James Patterson, 43, was visibly relieved that he was going to live, although the quality of his life was about to diminish sharply. Judge Borst imposed a minimum sentence of twenty years in Clinton Prison at Dannemora, with a maximum term of life.

24

Dalliance, Deceit, Death, Double-Cross

Poulin knew he was in a precarious situation. The woman he loved, and who had expressed the same sentiment, had completely abandoned him during the trial.

In August 1911, Rensselaer County newspapers reported on a shooting just minutes outside of Albany. Thirty-year-old Charles Leonard was killed, and the man who allegedly shot him, Frederick Poulin, was in the Troy Hospital, undergoing treatment for wounds suffered during a suicide attempt. Mrs. Anna Leonard, mother of two and Charles' wife of four years, but now widowed, was held in custody as a witness in a case that appeared to have complexities.

But Frederick Poulin soon removed much of the mystery surrounding the shooting by offering a full confession. Anna, he said, was his lover. He had become acquainted with the Leonards in Schenectady and established a friendship. When Charles and Anna moved to Brookview, just south of Albany, Poulin, an unemployed bartender, boarded with them. His affection for Mrs. Leonard soon became apparent, and Charles evicted him from the home.

Out of anger, Poulin, armed with a revolver, returned to the Leonard home about two weeks later and lay in wait, planning to kill Charles. When Leonard exited his bedroom early in the morning and went downstairs, Frederick seized the opportunity and opened fire. Charles immediately broke for the stairs, and despite being hit by two of the four shots sent his way, made it into the bedroom, closing the door behind him.

Poulin pursued him, and although Leonard resisted, the bedroom door was forced open. Confronted by his assailant, who obviously planned to finish the job, Charles wrestled with him for control of the weapon. Weakened from the bullet wounds and losing the fight, he took the only option available and leapt headfirst from the second-floor window.

Although his torso cleared the sill, the window came down heavily on his ankles. Bleeding profusely from the bullet wounds, he dangled helplessly against the side of the house. It was believed that Charles died there and then either fell, or was released from the window. Despite the fall from nearly twenty feet, the cause of death was later attributed to the effects of the bullets, which had penetrated his lungs and liver.

At that point, distraught over the situation, Poulin had taken a small knife from his pocket and slashed his own throat. Whether he bungled the attempt or made only a halfhearted effort wasn't known for certain, but doctors were confident that Poulin would survive. With a signed confession already in hand, it appeared the murder was solved, and that prosecutors would be pursuing the familiar scenario of a love triangle ending in disaster.

But when the trial was held four months later, revelations made in court suggested that the district attorney might have acted hastily in accepting the grieving widow, once loved by two men, as a prosecution witness. Or maybe it was decided to go after the shooter, and that only the testimony of his possible conspirator could yield victory. Whatever the reason, by trial's end, there was the distinct possibility that Anna had played a much bigger role in her husband's death than first believed.

Early testimony revealed that intimacy between Poulin and Mrs. Leonard had caused many fights between Charles and Anna over the course of a few months. On one occasion, after warning Poulin to stay away from her, Charles returned home to find him once again pursuing Anna. Hours later, Frederick Poulin was in an Albany hospital, courtesy of a beating with a metal pipe.

But Charles' marital miseries continued, and in late July, he kicked his wife out of the house. Schenectady residents confirmed in court that during the time of separation, Anna and Frederick lived together in a boarding house in that city for about two weeks before she finally returned home to Charles in early August. The shooting occurred the next morning.

On the witness stand, Anna admitted that it was true—she

> **POULIN UP ON MURDER CHARGE**
> On Trial at Troy for Death of Charles Leonard
> BEFORE JUDGE COCHRANE
> Leonard Had Objected to Attentions to His Wife Paid by the Accused

had stayed with Poulin in Schenectady. Although *she* wasn't on trial, acknowledging an ongoing affair with her husband's killer suggested that there might be more to the story than had been published in the media. Perhaps this wasn't so transparent a case after all.

As Anna told it, she did return home to Charles, but during that first night, unbeknownst to her, Poulin had quietly slipped into the house through a cellar window. When Charles went downstairs the next morning, he was ambushed by Poulin. Her husband fled to the bedroom, where Anna helped him hold the door shut against his attacker. Their combined efforts to keep him out were unsuccessful, and after a struggle, Charles jumped from the window but was caught at the ankles. She grabbed his legs and tried to pull him back to safety, but was unable to do so.

During cross-examination, defense counsel George Sands attacked Anna's story and accused her of complicity in the murder of Charles. She denied any involvement, but it was an argument he pursued vigorously, prompting a scolding from Supreme Court Justice Aaron Cochran for browbeating the witness.

The courtroom can be a grim place, especially when dealing with as dark a subject as murder, but one witness perhaps unintentionally provided a bit of levity for a packed house of courtroom observers. When Emma Scouton was subjected to the aggressive cross-examination methods of Sands, she came away less than impressed, according to a reporter for the *Schenectady Gazette*:

> The witness for the prosecution ... told Attorney Sands it was none of his business how her cousin, with whom she lived, was related to her father. At another time, she informed the attorney for the defense that he made her tired and that he could not scare her.

The final piece of prosecution evidence, Poulin's original confession, was read aloud in court by District Attorney Abbott Jones. It was a tough act to follow, and George Sands knew it. He admitted to having difficulty procuring witnesses, and considering the weight of evidence already presented against his client, there appeared no other option than to put the defendant on the stand. Acknowledging Sands' request, the court granted him a one-hour recess before presenting the defense case.

Poulin knew he was in a precarious situation. The woman he loved, and who months earlier had expressed the same sentiment for him, had completely abandoned him during the trial. He was on his own, with a future almost certain to end in the electric chair. Only a last-ditch effort to create reasonable doubt in the minds of one juror stood between him and a death sentence.

When Frederick took the stand, he recited a quite different chain of events from those described by Mrs. Leonard. Elements of Anna's story were true, he said, but much of it was modified to suit her own purposes and save her own hide. When they departed the Schenectady boarding house, Mrs. Leonard had indeed returned to her husband, but only after instructing Poulin to come that night to the Leonard home, where he would gain access through an unlocked back door. The defense dismissed the assertion that he had entered through a basement window, claiming that Frederick would not be able to fit through such a small opening.

Once inside, he went to sleep in the room that formerly served as his living quarters, only to be awakened in startling fashion by a burning pain in his throat. Opening his eyes, Poulin saw Charles Leonard standing over him, holding a razor. According to the court reporter's notes, Frederick immediately fought back:

> I jumped up and we struggled for the razor, but I fell to the floor. As I lay there, I heard a shot, and Leonard cried out, "My God, Ann, don't shoot me."

Charles then summoned the strength to run up the stairs and tried to escape through the window. Anna became hysterical, wondering what to do, but Frederick had the answer. Bleeding from a slashed throat, he believed death was imminent. As a last, chivalrous act, he told Anna:

> Put the gun in my pocket. Save yourself and put the blame on me.

During cross-examination, the district attorney attacked the story and questioned why Frederick had initially confessed to the murder, but now accused Anna of killing her husband. Poulin attributed his change of heart to two things: the confession came when he believed he was going to die from the neck wound, and because of the lies Anna had told about him in court (claiming he killed Charles by sneaking into their home, an idea that was his and his alone, she said).

Although some of the details were shaky, it wouldn't have been the

POULIN'S STORY OF THE MURDER

Says That Woman Killed Her Husband.

first time lovers joined forces to rid themselves of an unwanted spouse so they could be together. And in many such cases, the woman proved to be the mastermind behind the plot to kill. Despite having very little to work with, George Sands may have created the smidgeon of doubt necessary to keep his client alive.

Final summations were scheduled to begin first thing in the morning, but the court allowed a few minutes for the prosecution to rebut certain claims made during Poulin's testimony. The defense had dismissed the notion of Frederick entering the home through a basement window, citing his body size as too large to fit. If that were true, it added plausibility to the claim that Mrs. Leonard had left the door unlocked for him. By doing so, she might have been found complicit in the murder.

After Poulin's testimony, two men, one of them a doctor, had put the defense theory to the test during a visit to the Leonard home. They both testified that the second man—visibly larger than Poulin, fully dressed, and wearing a sweater beneath his coat—was able to crawl through the basement window. It was an additional, unexpected blow to an already shaky defense.

As George Sands presented his two-and-a-half-hour final summation—Poulin's last, best hope—Frederick's parents and sisters sat near him, at times weeping. Following another ninety minutes for the prosecution's synopsis, the judge charged the jury and deliberations began.

Less than five hours later, Frederick was found guilty of first-degree murder. He appeared shaken by the words, perhaps more so due to the loud wailing of his relatives, for even without pronouncement of sentence, they already knew his fate.

Three days later, at the official sentencing, Poulin stood before the court and presented a letter, disclosing that he had rejected a plea deal guaranteed to keep him alive. He went on to defend George Sands for doing an excellent job on his behalf, contrary to some reports in the media.

> I told Mr. Sands when the offer was made to me, I would prefer to be sent to the electric chair than plead guilty to Mr. Leonard's murder, for I am innocent of that crime. I also say that I am entirely satisfied with Mr.

> Sands. I believe he is defending me as well as any man charged with murder ever has been defended, and I am deeply gratified for all that he has done for me.

Appreciative of Poulin's statement and fully aware that the jury had left him no discretion in passing sentence, Justice Cochrane offered a civil response to the letter's contents:

> I have no desire to utter a single word at this time which may unnecessarily wound your feelings or add to your mental distress. The law will be more tender towards you than you were toward Mr. Leonard, because it will give you time for thought and reflection.

Poulin was sentenced to die in Dannemora's electric chair on the week of December 18, but the customary appeal prolonged his life for an additional two months. The Court of Appeals finally upheld the verdict, and Frederick was sentenced to die the week of February 10, when three other prisoners were destined to meet the same fate. His was the only execution scheduled for Dannemora.

Sands made a plea to Governor William Sulzer for executive clemency, but it was rejected. Instead of a last-minute ruling, Sulzer made his decision nine days before the date of execution, allowing plenty of time for Frederick to prepare … or to sweat.

Poulin was electrocuted on the morning of February 12, 1913.

25

Confession Conned from a Convict

> The coroner added that Yale Morris had suffered "compound fractures of all bones of the head and face," and that his skull was collapsed to the extent that it appeared pointed at the top.

In the 1920s, one of the best-known, most notorious bootleggers in the North Country was Charles "Muskrat" Robare. Although his principal base of operations was Clinton County, Robare helped supply speakeasies in many cities, including New York and Philadelphia. He was high on the federal list of targets, but continued as a very successful booze smuggler, even while serving prison time in Montreal, Atlanta, and places in between.

And Muskrat wasn't just a bootlegger. When his anonymity was lost in the wake of several arrests, making it especially difficult for him to work along the border, Robare took to bribing customs officials and highjacking the shipments of other bootleggers.

As a criminal, Charles was as diversified as he was prolific. Smuggling illegal aliens and a variety of products across the border in either direction proved lucrative. He was involved in one of the largest car-theft operations on the East Coast. The automobiles were channeled north after being stolen in urban locations, with New York City as the top supplier.

Although he wasn't averse to petty crime, he always seemed to have something big in the works. When Prohibition ended, dedicated bootleggers like Robare reversed the system, making their own whiskey and selling it at great profit, illegally, in Canada. One of his North Country stills had a capacity of five thousand gallons.

When lawmen finally put him out of the moonshine and bootleg businesses, Muskrat worked as a farmer, but with the usual Robare twist. Taking a cue from the Old West, he generated profits by cattle rustling, which he did successfully from Plattsburgh to Lake Placid until a high-profile arrest landed him in Dannemora Prison. For that violation, he was sentenced to two terms of two and a half to five years each, with release scheduled for late September 1944.

ROBARE GIVEN TWO-FIVE YRS IN DANNEMORA

But because of time already served in jail, and a reduction of sentence for good behavior (ironically, his "good behavior" happened only while he was in prison), Muskrat was released at the end of May 1941. A year later, he moved to Peru and operated a farm owned by Michael O'Connell. Muskrat's wife lived with him on the farm, even though they had previously been separated for several years.

But working a legitimate job to survive had never been on his radar. Robare was accustomed to making money through criminal behavior, and running a farm just wasn't cutting it for him. His high-profile reputation as a former bootlegger, moonshiner, and cattle thief ensured that locals were wary of dealing with him, which limited his prospects. Few, if any, respected him, but many feared him. And a lifetime criminal like Muskrat Robare, disdainful of the law, could be one dangerous man.

On June 2, 1942, a year after Robare's release from prison, Plattsburgh's chief of police, Clifford Fleming, received a missing person report. The subject's name was Yale Morris, well known locally as a butcher and cattle dealer. He had been missing overnight, which the family said was very unusual. From the chief's perspective, there was reason for concern, but at the age of fifty-five, Morris was more than capable of taking care of himself. He was often out and about in pursuit of cattle deals, leading to the initial assumption that Yale was been delayed somehow on business.

But Fleming knew that in a case like this, the habits of the individual were best known by the family. If they were concerned, then he was too. Even more worrisome: it was common knowledge that, as a cattle buyer, Morris routinely carried considerable cash with him.

Concern mounted when another day passed with no sign of Yale. While police investigated, residents of Bridge Street in Plattsburgh noticed something out of the ordinary. Near the intersection with Peru Street, a pickup truck, with the keys in the ignition, had been parked in their neighborhood for a full day. It was a vehicle none of them recognized, causing tongues to wag over who the owner might be.

Police were notified, and it was soon confirmed through family members, including his nephew and his brother Max that it was Yale's truck. The Morris family provided another critical piece of information.

Among the stops Yale planned to make that day was the O'Connell farm in Peru, where he hoped to close a deal on the purchase of several cattle for butchering. The meat was intended for the store in Plattsburgh operated by Yale, Max, and other Morris family members.

The investigation now focused on the Peru area, where a gas station operator recalled seeing Yale's truck on the day of his disappearance, as did a farmer, who added that the vehicle headed down a dirt road near his property. Pieces of the puzzle were gradually coming together.

While contemplating the many possibilities, Police Chief Fleming perused property maps covering the area near Peru, where the best leads were being pursued. An important part of police work involves tracking the whereabouts of inmates recently released after serving time, particularly those who are best described as habitual criminals. Fleming noticed that the truck sightings in Peru were near the Mike O'Connell farm, which had been operated for the past year by Charles Robare.

It was all circumstantial, but convincing enough, based on the tenant's lengthy criminal record. The decision was made to bring Robare and his hired man in for questioning, while at the same time obtaining a search warrant allowing inspection of the O'Connell property. Officers tasked with delivering the suspects to the police station approached the assignment cautiously, but completed it without incident.

The interrogation of Muskrat Robare became the subject of legend among local lawmen, principally because it was the focus of an article by Lionel White in the magazine *Startling Detective*. White was a noted crime novelist whose books were frequently made into movies. Although he employed poetic license in the story, embellishing and revising some facts, the basic reporting was correct. (Story "enhancements" were a common feature in magazines of that genre, where sensationalism was a priority.)

The marathon questioning lasted for twelve hours, the first eleven of which featured several lawmen using a tag-team format, only to be stonewalled by Robare. But the focus of White's story was on the final sixty minutes, during which the suspect was alone in a room with a pair of opponents, Chief of Police Clifford Fleming and—a telephone.

With the lawmen at wit's end, Fleming executed a plan, instructing the men to call him on the phone every fifteen minutes. They were to stay on the line while he talked, listened, and asked questions, but it mattered not if they replied or said anything at all: it was all a sham.

As White told it in the magazine, Robare remained stoic from the start—that is, until the phone rang. The chief listened, and in the pretend conversation, said:

> I understand. Well, if it's not there, it's not there. Now do this. Have a bunch of men start digging under the barn. Yes, the barn. Then take another group and start in the basement of the house. I want a third group to go out to those woods back of the place. Get a couple of bloodhounds and see what happens.

All the while, Fleming was subtly observing Robare's behavior, which seemed to change at the mention of bloodhounds and the woods behind the farm buildings. But had it really affected him? It was hard to tell. As he hung up the phone, Fleming, looking for some sort of response, turned towards Muskrat, who apparently still had no interest in talking.

Fifteen minutes later, the phone rang again. The chief listened for a few minutes, adding brief grunts and comments, and finally ending the conversation with further instructions:

> Okay, I understand. Must be covered up or buried. Send them out a couple of shovels and start right where the dogs began to circle.

Good interrogators are especially sensitive to minute changes in their subjects, and this time Fleming felt strongly that Robare's subtle changes in behavior were a dead giveaway. Muskrat seemed deeply worried, so much so that the chief decided to go for broke when the next phone call rang in.

Acting for all he was worth, Fleming listened intently, revealing in his grim demeanor that something dark was being reported. Ratcheting up the pressure, he began to speak:

> Well, that was fortunate. No, he hasn't said a thing yet. But he will now. I want to bring him out before you do anything with it. That's right, let it lay right there until we get out. In the meantime, get hold of the medical examiner so he can look it over before it's moved. That's right. Yes, as soon as I can make it. And this rat will be right with me, you can bet. I don't care now if he never talks!

According to White, the ruse worked perfectly. Bob Newhart himself

Confession Conned from a Convict

would have been impressed with Fleming's fake-phone-call skills. From the side of the conversation Robare had heard, he knew the jig was up. He was hungry, tired, and believed his crime had been discovered.

The results were even more than the relieved lawmen could have hoped for—a twenty-one page confession, signed in the presence of Chief Fleming, an assistant district attorney, two state troopers, other officials, and with the police stenographer recording it all.

When Robare finished at around 4:00 AM, the entire group, accompanied by newsmen and photographers, formed a motorcade. Still under cover of darkness, they drove to the O'Connell farm, where flashlights were used to locate the body of Yale Morris, lying in a hollow, covered with branches and other forest debris.

Robare was then placed under arrest and charged with "willful and premeditated murder." As a parole violator, he was already ensured of returning to Clinton Prison at Dannemora. The only question was whether he would remain an inmate or occupy one of the cells for doomed prisoners. Attorney Jay Davern was entrusted with the defendant's life, burdened with the task of somehow avoiding the death penalty for his client.

It wasn't going to be easy. District Attorney John Cummins immediately went public, revealing that Robare had willingly offered a twenty-one-page admission of guilt:

> The statement was taken yesterday forenoon during a two-hour question-and-answer period. Robare gave us a clear case of premeditated, cold-blooded murder.

There appeared no need to try the case in the media, but Cummins added a morbid, tantalizing snippet from Muskrat's confession:

> ... I stepped back and hit him on the side of the head with the axe. He fell down and his feet were still kicking, so I hit him again over the forehead.

Within a few hours of Robare's arraignment, a chapel service at the Beth Israel synagogue bade a sad farewell to Yale Morris. Plattsburgh Barracks provided an honorary escort for the World War One veteran, and "Taps" was played before he was lowered into his grave. Morris was just fifty-five when he died. There stood a good chance his killer, thirty-nine, wouldn't see forty.

Muskrat's confession was only the starting point for developing the prosecution's case. Investigators set about confirming or disproving every element of Robare's extensive statement, and in doing so, established a solid chain of evidence.

It was confirmed that Charles had actually visited Morris' home two days before the murder, and was quoted by witnesses as saying, "Come up early Monday morning and they'll be ready for you," in reference to some beef cattle. Neighbors had seen Yale leave his home early that Monday morning, and others saw him in the Peru area.

> **'MUSKRAT' ROBARE ADMITS USING AX TO SLAY MORRIS; BODY IS LOCATED IN WOODS**

The axe, which Robare admitted to washing after the crime, was recovered. A quantity of money was also found, well hidden in the barn. Some of it was Robare's own, he claimed, but $290 of it ($4000 in 2012) was money he had stolen from the victim's pockets. A portion had already been used to pay Robare's bills.

Several local motorists came forward, clearing the confusion surrounding Morris' truck and how it arrived at the Plattsburgh location where it was found. After the murder, Robare had driven the truck to Plattsburgh, parked it on Bridge Street, and hitchhiked home. Even though multiple rides were involved, he was back on the farm within three hours of the killing.

At a preliminary hearing in mid-June, several lawmen swore that Robare had given three different versions of the crime. Added to testimony from Dr. Leonard Schiff, it was enough to send the case to the grand jury:

> … death was caused by a laceration of the brain, due to a compound fracture of the skull, the result of the force of a blow.

Five months later, in November 1942, the grand jury indicted Robare on a charge of first-degree murder, to which Davern entered the mandatory plea of not guilty on behalf of his client. Three weeks later, the trial began. Much of the testimony recounted events that had already been reported extensively in the press.

The coroner added that Yale Morris had suffered "compound fractures of all bones of the head and face," and that his skull was collapsed to the extent that it appeared pointed at the top.

Trooper James Smith of the BCI contributed one of the more memorable sound bites, quoting Robare's comment that when he hit Morris with the axe, "… he went down like a beef."

Mike O'Connell, the eighty-year-old owner of the farm where Morris died, recalled a moment of cruel irony that occurred on that fateful morning. He had driven to the farm and noticed a pickup truck in the yard. As the old man stood in the milkhouse doorway, Robare came walking by alone, carrying an axe on his shoulder. O'Connell testified that he jokingly asked, "What did you do with your partner, kill him?" Which was exactly what Robare had just done.

> **ROBARE TO GO ON TRIAL HERE TODAY IN AX-SLAYING OF YALE MORRIS; FACES DEATH SENTENCE**

Mrs. Robare, Muskrat's ex-wife, also took the stand, confirming the encounter between Charles and Mr. O'Connell, including the facetious comment and the presence of both the truck and the axe. She testified that soon after, both the truck and her ex-husband were absent.

The prosecution's description of the murder was as devastating as any testimony. Based on the confession and a subsequent reconstruction of the crime, Robare had lured Morris to the farm, they said, based on the false premise that he would butcher some cattle and sell him the meat. Thus, there was no suspicion on the part of Morris when Muskrat carried an axe, a butchering weapon, as they went to view the cows.

When an opportunity presented itself, Robare slammed the flat side of the double-bit axe against Yale's head. Morris went down, but he was still alive, so Robare delivered several more blows to finish the job. After stealing the money, Muskrat got rid of the truck and returned home. A day later, using a canvas and some rope that he had taken from Yale's truck, he wrapped the body, tied it securely, and dragged it seventy-five feet to a small hollow, where he covered it with leaves and branches.

With an abundance of testimony to support the prosecution's scenario, the defense case appeared bleak indeed. There was little doubt that Robare would have to take the stand. He had no other witnesses.

The day of reckoning was Friday, December 11, 1942. Muskrat Robare, notorious North Country criminal for the past two decades, and murderer of Yale Morris, was scheduled to testify in an effort to save himself from a near certain death sentence.

Court reconvened at 9:30 AM, and with the jury box filled, Defense

Attorney Jay Davern called the first witness—Sheriff Elmer Caron. His testimony began with one line that shocked the courtroom:

> The defendant, Charles W. Robare, was found dead in his cell this morning.

The jury was visibly stunned, having been shielded from the news. Caron explained that Robare's behavior had given no indication he was a suicide risk. Nonetheless, his cell was monitored every fifteen minutes. The 5:45 AM check found the defendant getting dressed for breakfast, but at 6:00, he was dead. Working within a small time-frame and limited space, Robare had worked hard to end his life. By linking a towel and his belt, he created a makeshift noose and tied it to the grating above the cot. Allowing himself to fall forward resulted in steady pressure against his neck. It was determined that several minutes of slow strangulation had preceded death.

In describing Robare's commitment to the process, jail personnel noted that at all times, his feet were within easy reach of the floor and his hands could reach the cot. Robare had apparently kept his legs drawn up beneath his body until death overtook him. He was found slumped forward, with one hand and both feet touching the floor.

Coroner Dr. George Gonyea followed Sheriff Caron on the witness stand, confirming that death was a result of suicide by strangulation. Justice Ellsworth Lawrence then thanked the jurors for their service and dismissed them, bringing to a close the saga of Charles "Muskrat" Robare.